PENGUIN REFERENCE

The State of the World Atlas

sixth edition

Dan Smith is Director of the International Peace Research Institute (PRIO) in Oslo, Norway.

He is the author of the third edition of *The State of War and Peace Atlas* and co-author, with Michael Kidron, of both previous editions of the atlas. His many other books include *Pressure: How America Runs NATO; The Economics of Militarism* (co-authored with Ron Smith); and Protest and Survive and *Prospectus for a Habitable Planet*, both co-edited with E.P. Thompson

Dan Smith is also the author of three crime novels.

Also in this series:

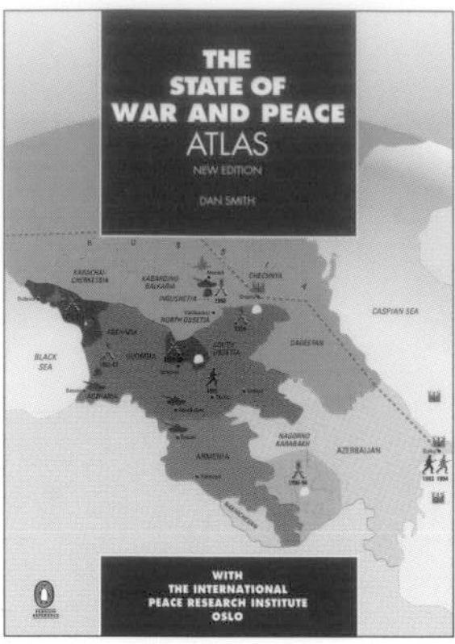
THE
STATE OF
WAR AND PEACE
ATLAS
NEW EDITION
DAN SMITH
WITH
THE INTERNATIONAL
PEACE RESEARCH INSTITUTE
OSLO

The State of War and Peace Atlas
second edition
by Dan Smith

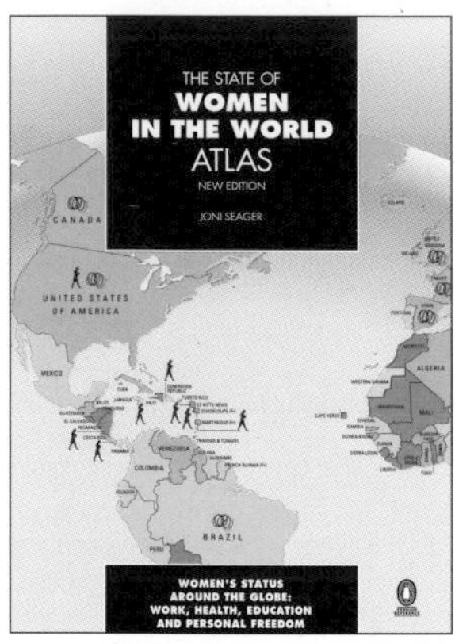
THE STATE OF
WOMEN
IN THE WORLD
ATLAS
NEW EDITION
JONI SEAGER
WOMEN'S STATUS
AROUND THE GLOBE:
WORK, HEALTH, EDUCATION
AND PERSONAL FREEDOM

The State of
Women in The World Atlas
second edition
by Joni Seager

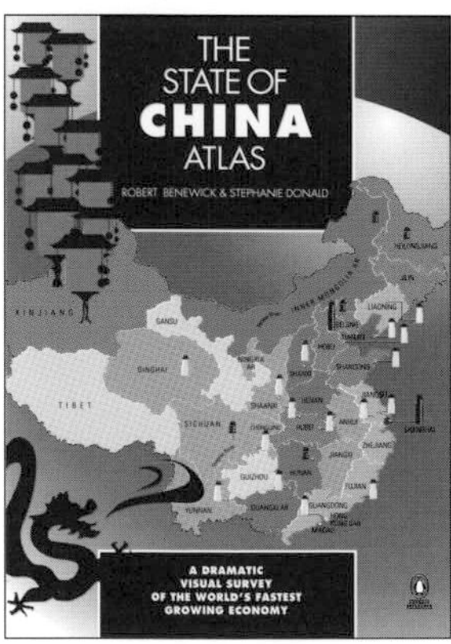
THE
STATE OF
CHINA
ATLAS
ROBERT BENEWICK & STEPHANIE DONALD
A DRAMATIC
VISUAL SURVEY
OF THE WORLD'S FASTEST
GROWING ECONOMY

The State of China Atlas
by Robert Benewick and Stephanie Donald

The State of the World Atlas

new revised sixth edition

Dan Smith

PENGUIN
REFERENCE

PENGUIN REFERENCE

Published by the Penguin Group
Penguin Books Limited, 27 Wrights Lane,
London W8 5TZ, England
Penguin Putnam Inc., 375 Hudson Street,
New York, New York 10014, USA
Penguin Books Australia Limited,
Ringwood, Victoria, Australia
Penguin Books Canada Limited, 10 Alcorn Avenue,
Toronto, Ontario, Canada M4V
Penguin Books (NZ) Limited, 182-190 Wairau Road,
Auckland 10, New Zealand

Penguin Books Limited, Registered Offices:
Harmondsworth, Middlesex, England

This sixth edition published in Penguin Reference 1999
Reprinted 2001
10 9 8 7 6 5 4 3 2

Penguin Reference paperback 0 14 05.1446 5

Produced for the Penguin Group by
Myriad Editions Limited
www.MyriadEditions.com

Edited and co-ordinated for Myriad Editions
by Anne Benewick and Candida Lacey
with Jannet King and Mary McKeown

Design and graphics by Corinne Pearlman
Front cover image by Minoru Tomoda/The Image Bank
Maps created by Angela Wilson
with Suzanne Epps for All Terrain Mapping

Printed and bound in Hong Kong
Produced by Phoenix Offset Limited
under the supervision of The Hanway Press, London

Contents

Introduction

For over three hundred years, the world of politics and power has been defined by the strengths, the capacities and the existence of states.There have never been more states than there are at the turn of the millennium, and state power is more able now than ever to know about and to shape the lives of individuals. In the past half century, the rate at which new states have been formed has been historically unprecedented. In the 1990s, with the break-up of the Soviet Union and of the old Yugoslavia, there was still a considerable increase in the world's total number of states.

And yet the state has also arrived at a period of fragility and possibly of change. The sovereignty of states – their capacity and right to the monopoly of power within their territory – is in question. There are multiple sources of pressure on states, producing multiple actual and potential cracks in the edifice.

Some states cannot maintain internal order. In extreme situations, such as in Yugoslavia in 1991 and 1992, the state breaks up. Or its authority collapses entirely, as in Somalia, Liberia and Sierra Leone for periods in the 1990s, and in Albania briefly in 1997. Less drastically, the authority of states can dwindle in one part of their territory, as did Russia's authority over the separatist republic of Chechnya, Colombia's in the northern part of the country, and Sri Lanka's in the Tamil areas. Some states maintain order only by giving private companies the contract for law enforcement and by hiring mercenary soldiers.

In a separate development, made especially salient by the spread of internal chaos, international laws on human rights and humanitarian standards are becoming more important and more intrusive. International treaties and actions of the United Nations' Security Council combine to deny states the sovereign right to massacre and torture their citizens. International legal precedent has been set for bringing dictators to account. In Europe, the European Court of Human Rights, whose decisions can and do over-rule those of national courts, regularly settles issues of rights.

In another sphere of activity, many states are ready to give authority over important trade and economic decisions to inter-state bodies. The World Trade Organisation has extensive powers over governments' decisions on imports. And the establishment of a single currency by eleven member governments in the European Union means they have handed over a core state function to a supra-state body. In handling issues such as ocean-fishing, whaling, global warming and industrial pollution, it is widely argued that environmental regulation cannot be achieved without extensive and intrusive international controls.

Not the least of current impingements on state sovereignty is the trend in the 1990s towards forcible intervention in conflict-prone regions and countries. If the state is classically defined as the entity that has the monopoly of the legitimate means of force within a given territory, intervention both breaks the monopoly and rejects its legitimacy.

These developments do not have one source, and they do not amount to one process. Some of the changes are the result of deliberate state decisions, some are pushed by the forces of economic change and globalization, some are consequences of faster global communications, and some are produced by internal injustice and weakness. Yet, for different reasons, in different ways, in different spheres, many things move in the same direction: the authority of individual states is being steadily eroded.

This is not the end of the world of states. As states weaken in one field, they strengthen in another. As some states get weaker overall, others get stronger. Forcible intervention is an attack on state sovereignty, yet it is carried out by other states, themselves claiming sovereignty. This is a period of contradictory pressures, of politico-economic changes, of a re-ordering of the world system based on economic globalization, ease of travel, speed of communication, and a degree of cultural inter-change that is unprecedented at a global level. It is a period in which all sorts of human freedoms are severely threatened, yet in which many systems of power have opened up for more participation. Equality between the genders is still a long way off, but is a little closer than two or three decades ago. Racism is powerful, but in most places there are powerful pressures against it, and in some it is on the retreat.

Many of the maps and cartograms in this atlas show these contradictory pressures at work. It is still hard to make out the contours of the world towards which these changes are taking us, and this is a period that is hard to define. We tend to define it by what it is not – a post-modern world, the post-Cold War era, states whose political system is neither one thing nor another but transitional.

Power remains a reality. The degree of access to power by ordinary people defines the degree of democracy and equality. One way to understand this period of change is to keep your eye on power, to see who benefits and who loses. Some of the power issues are fought out between contrary global and local pressures. Both the local and the global have become more important and the state is caught between the scissor blades. Most states are too small and have too short a reach to be able to handle the big questions, the global issues. And most are also too big and too clumsy to be able satisfactorily to handle the small questions, the local issues, the quality of lives as we live them day to day.

Two things matter as this evolution continues. The big blind global developments are dangerous if they are allowed to flatten the local differences and particularities that give our lives texture and richness. At the same time, there is a danger that the initiative and creativity that gains its strength from local particularities, when frustrated by the larger forces, is perverted into chauvinistic fear and hatred of whatever and whoever is different. It seems likely that the only protections against this double peril lie in emphasising the full panoply of human rights, in understanding the world's diversity and its problems, and in active participation in democracy.

This is the sixth edition of *The State of the World Atlas*. Michael Kidron and Ronald Segal prepared the first five editions. To them goes the credit reserved for pioneers. I am following in their footsteps, albeit in my own shoe-size. Theirs is the basic theme and shape of the atlas; mine are some variations of form and perspective, particularly the greater use of text alongside the visual presentations.

Anne Benewick was involved from the beginning as the atlases' creative editor and coordinator. She died in December 1998 when preparation of this edition was well advanced. This is one of the last two of many atlases to carry her imprint. I hope it is worthy of her.

Starting from the first edition of *The State of the World* in 1981, Anne nurtured a whole range of "State of..." atlases. Together they add up to an extraordinary stockpile of easily understood information. I have drawn on them liberally, particularly *The State of Health* by Judith Mackay (1993), *The State of Religion* by Joanne O'Brien and Martin Palmer (1993), *The State of Women in the World* by Joni Seager (1997, 2nd edition), and *Atlas of the Future*, edited by Ian Pearson (1998).

The following people and organizations supplied data that helped Myriad prepare particular maps:

on **Population** and on **Age**, Kevin Kinsella of the US Bureau of the Census, Washington D.C.;

on **Working Abroad**, Sophia Lawrence of the International Labour Office, Geneva and Ann Nilsson of Eurostat, Brussels;

on **Political Systems**, Michael Kidron;

on **Peacekeeping**, Pavel Baev, PRIO;

on **Human Rights**, Dominique Muller of Amnesty International, London;

on **Communications**, Dalia Mendiluce of the International Telecommunication Union, Geneva and Ian Pearson;

on **Religion**, Joanne O'Brien of the International Consultancy on Religion, Education and Culture (ICOREC), Manchester;

on **Sexual Freedom**, Dr Zoe-Jane Playdon of the South Thames Department of Postgraduate Medical and Dental Education, University of London;

on **Reproductive Rights**, Nada Chaya of Population Action International, Washington D.C.;

on **Smoking**, Neil Collinshawn and Dr Judith Mackay of the World Health Organization;

on **Health Risks**, Jill Lewis of the Nordic Institute for Women's Studies and Gender Research, Oslo;

and on the **World Table**, Christian Ottke of World Resources, Washington D.C.

I am grateful to all for their help, and also to my assistant Olav Høgberg who surfed the net assiduously for me.

Even more, my thanks go to the editorial and creative design team of Candida Lacey and Corinne Pearlman at Myriad. Candida coordinated the project, and kept my efforts on track and boosted my energy when it flagged. She is in every way a pleasure to work with.

Dan Smith
Oslo, June 1999

Part One People

RICH WORLD, POOR WORLD

A child born in the industrial world adds more to consumption and pollution over his or her lifetime than do 30-50 children born in developing countries.

Source: UNDP, 1998

In 1999 there were nearly 6 billion people in the world. Another 80 million are added each year. During the 1990s, population growth slowed down considerably to an annual rate of 1.4 percent.

World population doubled between the late-1950s and the late-1990s. It is projected to reach 9.4 billion by 2050.

The fastest rates of population growth are concentrated in Africa, together with some parts of the Middle East, and a few countries in Central and South America, and Southeast Asia.

Growth has slowed significantly in the two most heavily-populated countries: China and India. In the richest countries of the world, population growth has almost stopped. In a few countries, the number of people has begun to decline.

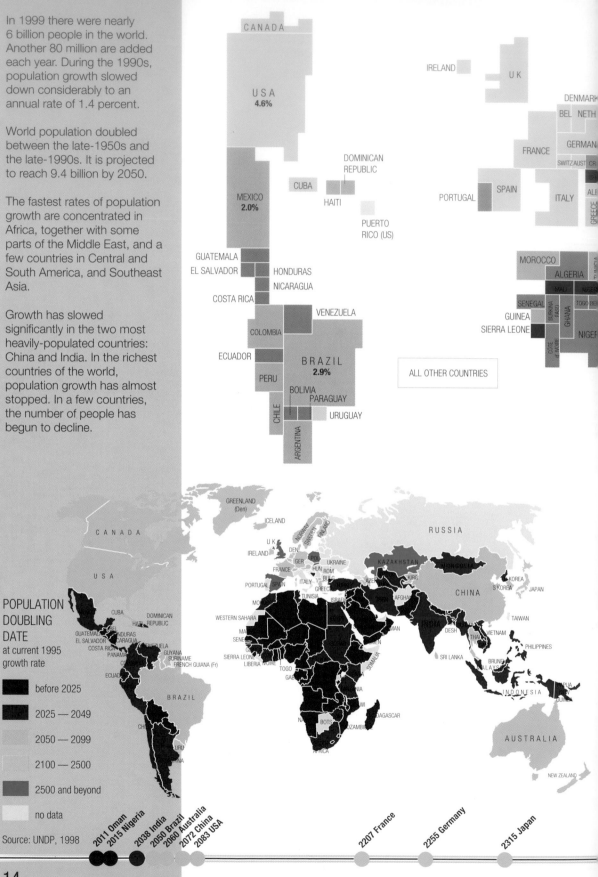

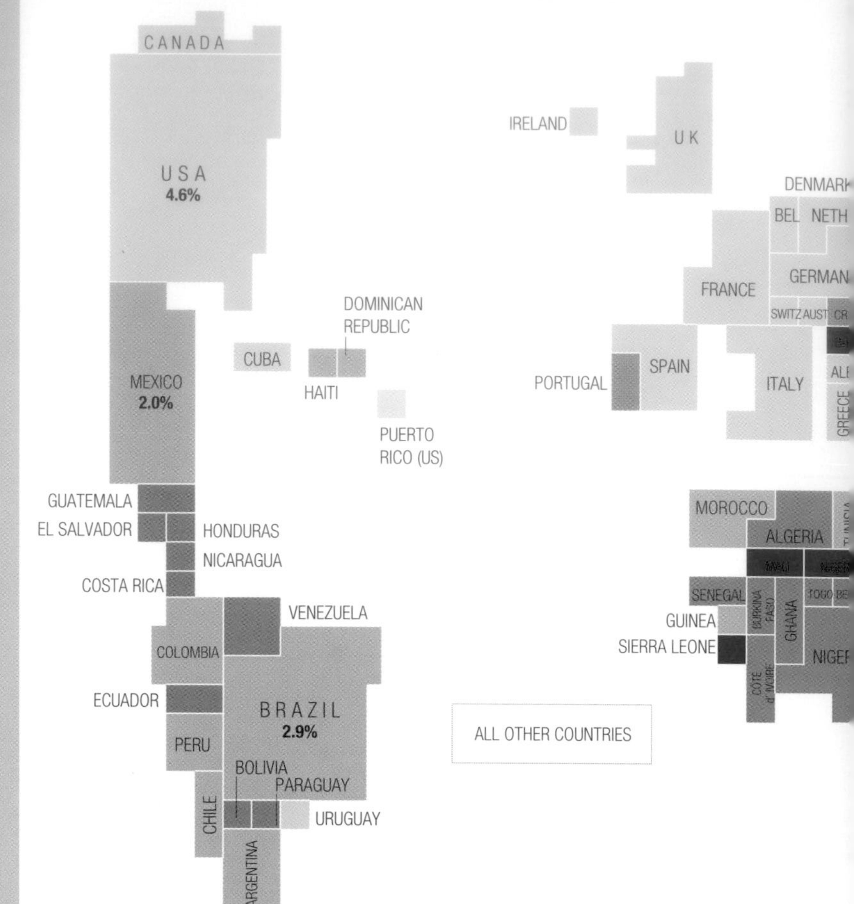
CANADA
USA
4.6%
MEXICO
2.0%
GUATEMALA
EL SALVADOR
HONDURAS
NICARAGUA
COSTA RICA
CUBA
HAITI
DOMINICAN REPUBLIC
PUERTO RICO (US)
VENEZUELA
COLOMBIA
ECUADOR
PERU
BRAZIL
2.9%
BOLIVIA
PARAGUAY
URUGUAY
CHILE
ARGENTINA
IRELAND
UK
DENMARK
BEL
NETH
FRANCE
GERMAN
SWITZ
AUST
PORTUGAL
SPAIN
ITALY
GREECE
MOROCCO
ALGERIA
SENEGAL
GUINEA
SIERRA LEONE
BURKINA FASO
GHANA
CÔTE d'IVOIRE
TOGO
NIGER
ALL OTHER COUNTRIES

POPULATION DOUBLING DATE
at current 1995 growth rate

- before 2025
- 2025 — 2049
- 2050 — 2099
- 2100 — 2500
- 2500 and beyond
- no data

Source: UNDP, 1998

2011 Oman
2015 Nigeria
2038 India
2050 Brazil
2060 Australia
2072 China
2083 USA
2207 France
2255 Germany
2315 Japan

Population

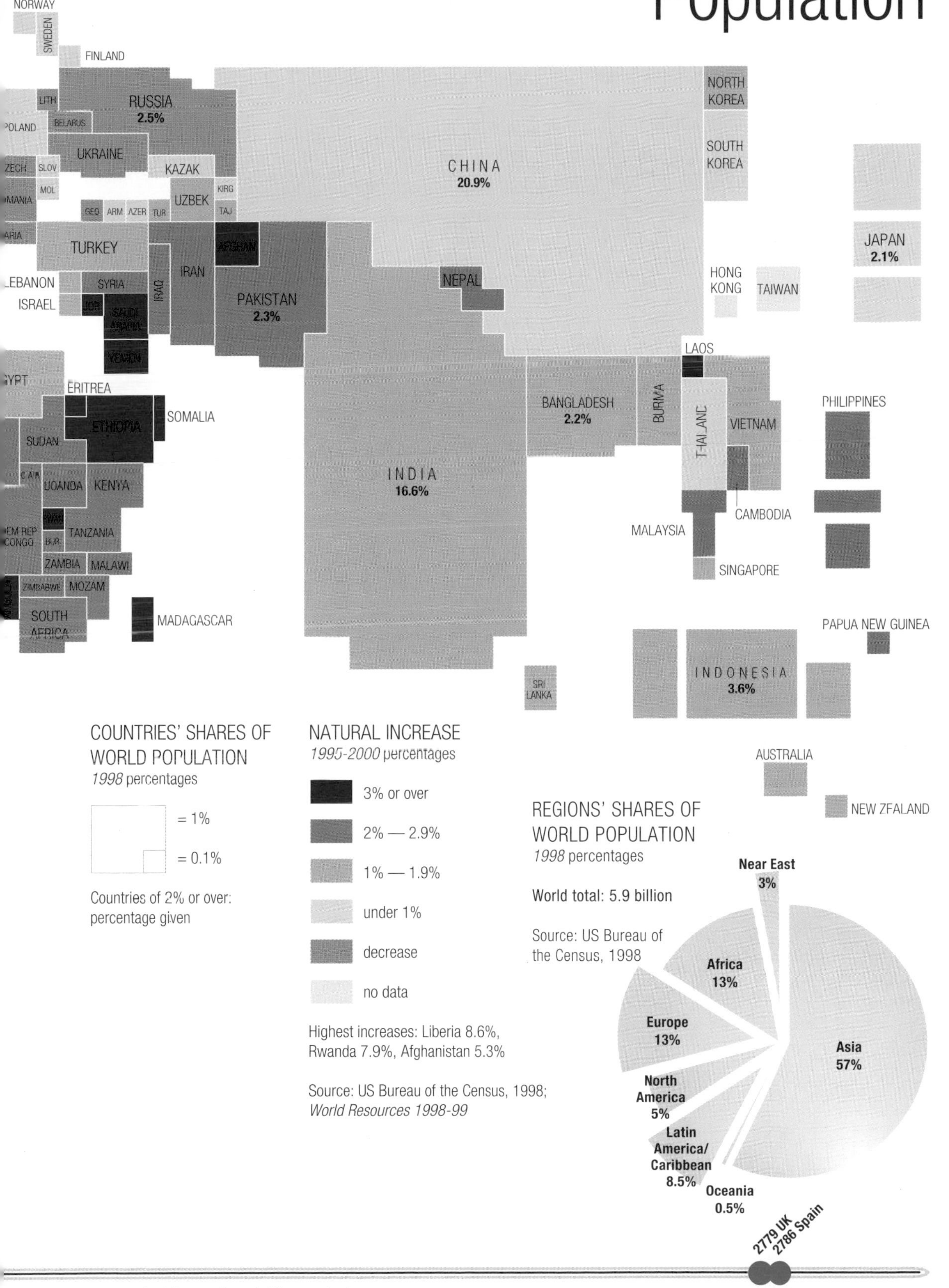
NORWAY
SWEDEN
FINLAND
RUSSIA
2.5%
LITH
BELARUS
POLAND
UKRAINE
KAZAK
SLOV
MOL
KIRG
UZBEK
TAJ
GEO
ARM
AZER
TUR
TURKEY
IRAN
AFGHAN
PAKISTAN
2.3%
LEBANON
SYRIA
ISRAEL
JOR
SAUDI ARABIA
IRAQ
YEMEN
ERITREA
SOMALIA
ETHIOPIA
SUDAN
UGANDA
KENYA
TANZANIA
BUR
ZAMBIA
MALAWI
ZIMBABWE
MOZAM
SOUTH AFRICA
MADAGASCAR
CHINA
20.9%
NEPAL
INDIA
16.6%
SRI LANKA
BANGLADESH
2.2%
BURMA
LAOS
THAILAND
VIETNAM
CAMBODIA
MALAYSIA
SINGAPORE
NORTH KOREA
SOUTH KOREA
HONG KONG
TAIWAN
JAPAN
2.1%
PHILIPPINES
PAPUA NEW GUINEA
INDONESIA
3.6%
AUSTRALIA
NEW ZEALAND
COUNTRIES' SHARES OF WORLD POPULATION
1998 percentages
= 1%
= 0.1%
Countries of 2% or over: percentage given
NATURAL INCREASE
1995-2000 percentages
3% or over
2% — 2.9%
1% — 1.9%
under 1%
decrease
no data
Highest increases: Liberia 8.6%, Rwanda 7.9%, Afghanistan 5.3%
Source: US Bureau of the Census, 1998; World Resources 1998-99
REGIONS' SHARES OF WORLD POPULATION
1998 percentages
World total: 5.9 billion
Source: US Bureau of the Census, 1998
Near East 3%
Africa 13%
Europe 13%
North America 5%
Latin America/ Caribbean 8.5%
Oceania 0.5%
Asia 57%
2779 UK
2786 Spain

Average life expectancy continues to increase, though slowly and unevenly.

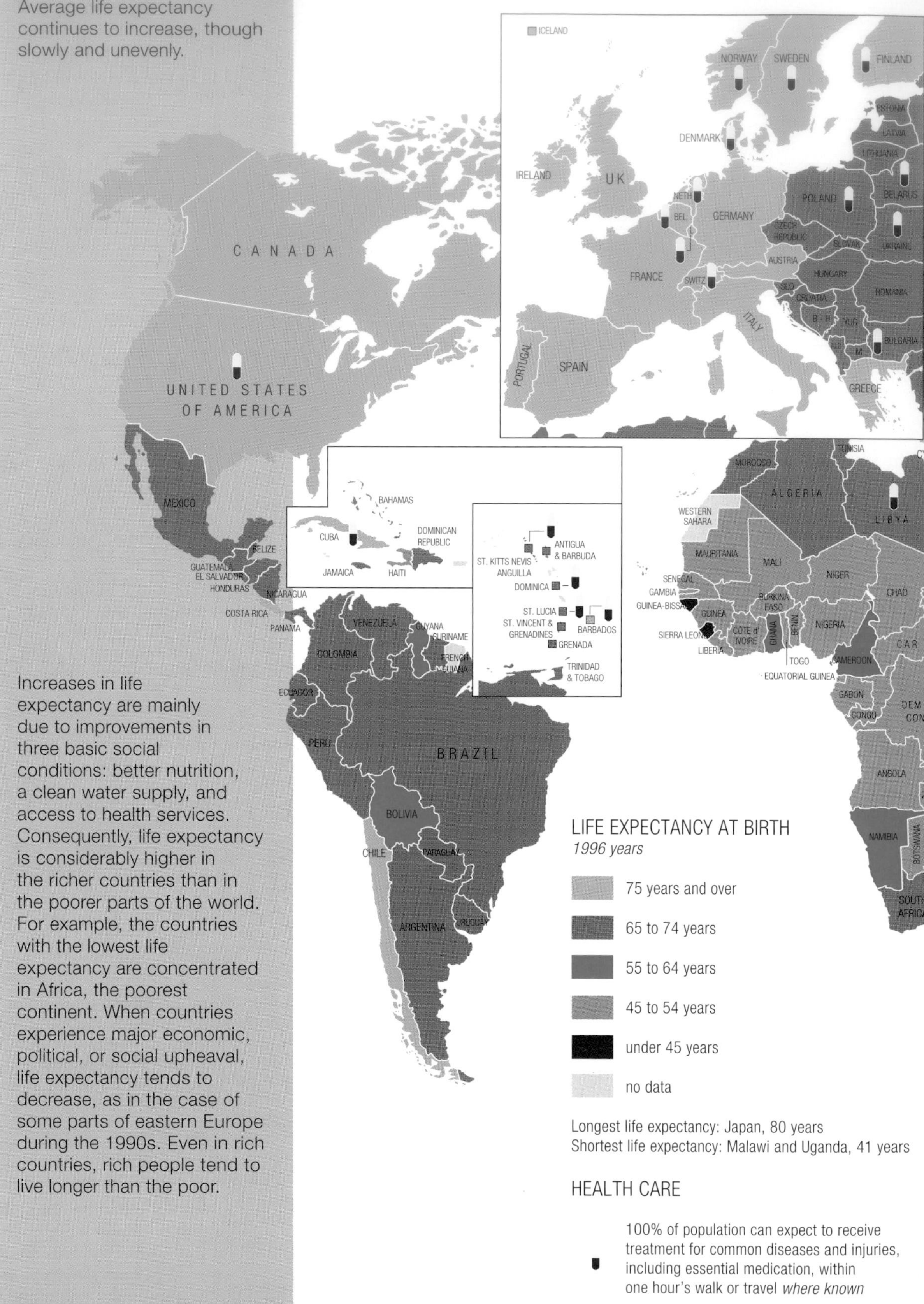

ICELAND
NORWAY
SWEDEN
FINLAND
ESTONIA
LATVIA
LITHUANIA
DENMARK
IRELAND
UK
NETH
BEL
GERMANY
POLAND
BELARUS
CZECH REPUBLIC
SLOVAK
UKRAINE
AUSTRIA
HUNGARY
FRANCE
SWITZ
SLO
CROATIA
ROMANIA
B - H
YUG
ITALY
BULGARIA
ALB
M
PORTUGAL
SPAIN
GREECE
CANADA
UNITED STATES OF AMERICA
MEXICO
BELIZE
GUATEMALA
EL SALVADOR
HONDURAS
NICARAGUA
COSTA RICA
PANAMA
BAHAMAS
CUBA
DOMINICAN REPUBLIC
JAMAICA
HAITI
ANTIGUA & BARBUDA
ST. KITTS NEVIS
ANGUILLA
DOMINICA
ST. LUCIA
ST. VINCENT & GRENADINES
BARBADOS
GRENADA
TRINIDAD & TOBAGO
VENEZUELA
GUYANA
SURINAME
FRENCH GUIANA
COLOMBIA
ECUADOR
PERU
BRAZIL
BOLIVIA
CHILE
PARAGUAY
ARGENTINA
URUGUAY
TUNISIA
MOROCCO
ALGERIA
LIBYA
WESTERN SAHARA
MAURITANIA
MALI
NIGER
CHAD
SENEGAL
GAMBIA
GUINEA-BISSAU
GUINEA
SIERRA LEONE
LIBERIA
BURKINA FASO
CÔTE d' IVOIRE
GHANA
BENIN
TOGO
NIGERIA
CAMEROON
EQUATORIAL GUINEA
CAR
GABON
CONGO
DEM RE CONGO
ANGOLA
ZAM
NAMIBIA
BOTSWANA
SOUTH AFRICA
LIFE EXPECTANCY AT BIRTH
1996 years
75 years and over
65 to 74 years
55 to 64 years
45 to 54 years
under 45 years
no data
Longest life expectancy: Japan, 80 years
Shortest life expectancy: Malawi and Uganda, 41 years
HEALTH CARE
100% of population can expect to receive treatment for common diseases and injuries, including essential medication, within one hour's walk or travel where known
Source: UNICEF, The State of the World's Children, 1998; World Bank Atlas 1998

Increases in life expectancy are mainly due to improvements in three basic social conditions: better nutrition, a clean water supply, and access to health services. Consequently, life expectancy is considerably higher in the richer countries than in the poorer parts of the world. For example, the countries with the lowest life expectancy are concentrated in Africa, the poorest continent. When countries experience major economic, political, or social upheaval, life expectancy tends to decrease, as in the case of some parts of eastern Europe during the 1990s. Even in rich countries, rich people tend to live longer than the poor.

Life Expectancy

RUSSIA
KAZAKHSTAN
MONGOLIA
N KOREA
S KOREA
JAPAN
UZBEKISTAN
KIRGISTAN
TURKMEN
GEO
AZER
CHINA
IRAQ
IRAN
ISRAEL
KUWAIT
BAHRAIN
QATAR
UAE
SAUDI ARABIA
OMAN
YEMEN
ERITREA
DJIBOUTI
ETHIOPIA
SOMALIA
KENYA
PAKISTAN
NEPAL
BHUTAN
B DESH
INDIA
BURMA
LAOS
VIETNAM
THAILAND
CAM
TAIWAN
HONG KONG
PHILIPPINES
KIRIBATI
BELAU
MALDIVES
SRI LANKA
BRUNEI
MALAYSIA
SINGAPORE
SEYCHELLES
INDONESIA
PAPUA NEW GUINEA
SOLOMON ISLANDS
COMOROS
MAURITIUS
MADAGASCAR
VANUATU
AUSTRALIA
WESTERN SAMOA
FIJI
TONGA
NEW ZEALAND
WATER
Share of population with access to safe drinking water
1990-96 percentages
100%
66% – 99%
33% – 65%
under 33%
no data
Lowest: Afghanistan, 12%
Source: UNICEF, *The State of the World's Children*, 1998

Worldwide 1.3 billion people live in absolute poverty. Nearly half of them suffer from chronic malnutrition.

Each year 40 million people die from hunger-related diseases. This is the equivalent of 300 airplane crashes every day. There are no survivors. Half the passengers are children.

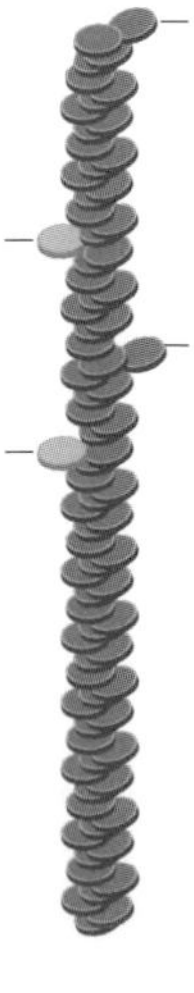

PIES IN THE SKY
Annual and estimated expenditures

$17 billion amount spent on pet foods in Europe and the USA

$13 billion amount needed to provide basic health and nutrition for all

$11 billion amount spent on ice cream in Europe

$9 billion amount needed to provide water and sanitation for all

Source: UNDP,1998

GREENLAND
ICELAND
NORWAY
SWEDEN
CANADA
DENMARK
IRELAND
UK
NETH
BEL
L
GERMANY
POLAND
CZECH
AUS
S
C
FRANCE
S
ITALY
PORTUGAL
SPAIN
UNITED STATES OF AMERICA
TUNISIA
MOROCCO
ALGERIA
MEXICO
WESTERN SAHARA
CUBA
DOMINICAN REPUBLIC
JAMAICA
BELIZE
HAITI
HONDURAS
27%
GUATEMALA
EL SALVADOR
28%
NICARAGUA
23% MAURITANIA
27% MALI
36% NIGER
22% SENEGAL
GAMBIA
30% BURKINA FASO
23% GUINEA-BISSAU
COSTA RICA
PANAMA
VENEZUELA
TRINIDAD & TOBAGO
GUYANA
SURINAME
FRENCH GUIANA (Fr)
COLOMBIA
26% GUINEA
29% SIERRA LEONE
LIBERIA
CÔTE d' IVOIRE 24%
GHANA 27%
TOGO
BENIN
NIGERIA 36%
CAMEROON
EQUATORIAL GUINEA
GABON
CONGO 24%
ECUADOR
BRAZIL
PERU
BOLIVIA
PARAGUAY
CHILE
URUGUAY
ARGENTINA
26% NAMIBIA

Nutrition

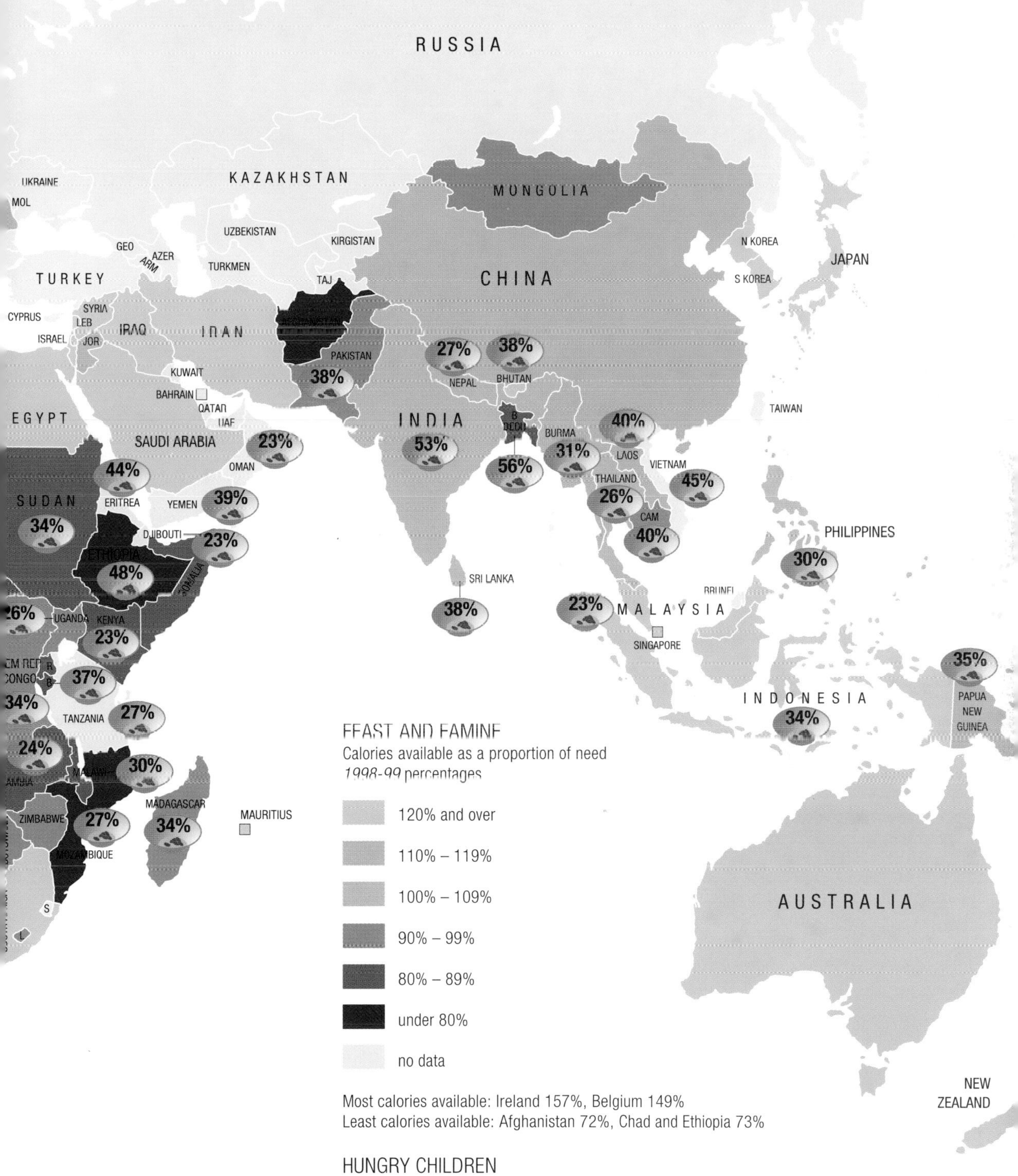

FEAST AND FAMINE

Calories available as a proportion of need

1998-99 percentages

- 120% and over
- 110% – 119%
- 100% – 109%
- 90% – 99%
- 80% – 89%
- under 80%
- no data

Most calories available: Ireland 157%, Belgium 149%
Least calories available: Afghanistan 72%, Chad and Ethiopia 73%

HUNGRY CHILDREN

1990-97

percentage of underweight under-5-year-olds
where percentage exceeds 20%

Sources: UNDP, *Human Development Report 1998; World Resources 1998-99*

To the extent that it is possible to measure the quality of life, richer countries offer better quality.

CANADA
MEXICO
BAHAMAS
CUBA
DOMINICAN REPUBLIC
ANTIGUA & BARBUDA
JAMAICA
HAITI
BELIZE
HONDURAS
GUATEMALA
EL SALVADOR
ST. KITTS NEVIS
DOMINICA
ST. VINCENT & GRENANDINES
GRENADA
BARBADOS
TRINIDAD & TOBAGO
NICARAGUA
COSTA RICA
PANAMA
VENEZUELA
GUYANA
SURINAME
FRENCH GUIANA (Fr)
COLOMBIA
ECUADOR
PERU
BRAZIL
BOLIVIA
PARAGUAY
CHILE
ARGENTINA
IRELAND
UK
DENMARK
NORWAY
SWEDEN
FINLAND
ESTONIA
LATVIA
LITHUANIA
BELARUS
POLAND
NETH
BEL
GERMANY
CZECH REPUBLIC
SLOVAK
UKRAINE
FRANCE
SWITZ
AUSTRIA
HUNGARY
ROMANIA
SLO
CROATIA
B - H
YUG
BULGARIA
ITALY
ALB
M
PORTUGAL
SPAIN
GREECE
MOROCCO
TUNISIA
ALGERIA
LIBYA
WESTERN SAHARA
MAURITANIA
MALI
NIGER
CAPE VERDE
SENEGAL
GAM
GUINEA-BISSAU
GUINEA
BURKINA FASO
CHAD
SIERRA LEONE
CÔTE d' IVOIRE
GHANA
BENIN
NIGERIA
LIBERIA
TOGO
CAMEROON
CAR
EQUATORIAL GUINEA
GABON
SAO TOME & PRINICIPE
CONGO
DEM REP CONGO
ANGOLA
ZAMBIA
NAMIBIA
BOTSWANA
SOUTH AFRICA

Whether they do as much as they can is a matter of the choices they make about allocating the nation's resources.

Some elements of the quality of life are intangible but nonetheless real. Happiness is as hard to measure as the misery that drives people to suicide. Both are partly the result of individual personalities, partly of general social conditions.

RESOURCES

Public expenditure on education exceeds six percent of GNP

1993-95

Source: UNDP, 1998

over 9%
Botswana
Namibia
Uzbekistan

8%-8.9%
Denmark
Norway
Swaziland
Sweden
Tajikistan

7%-7.9%
Canada
Finland
Kenya
Ukraine
Yemen

6%-7%
Czech Republic
Estonia
Hungary
Ireland
Israel
Jordan
Kirgistan
Latvia
Lithuania
Moldova
New Zealand
South Africa
Tunisia

The Quality of Life

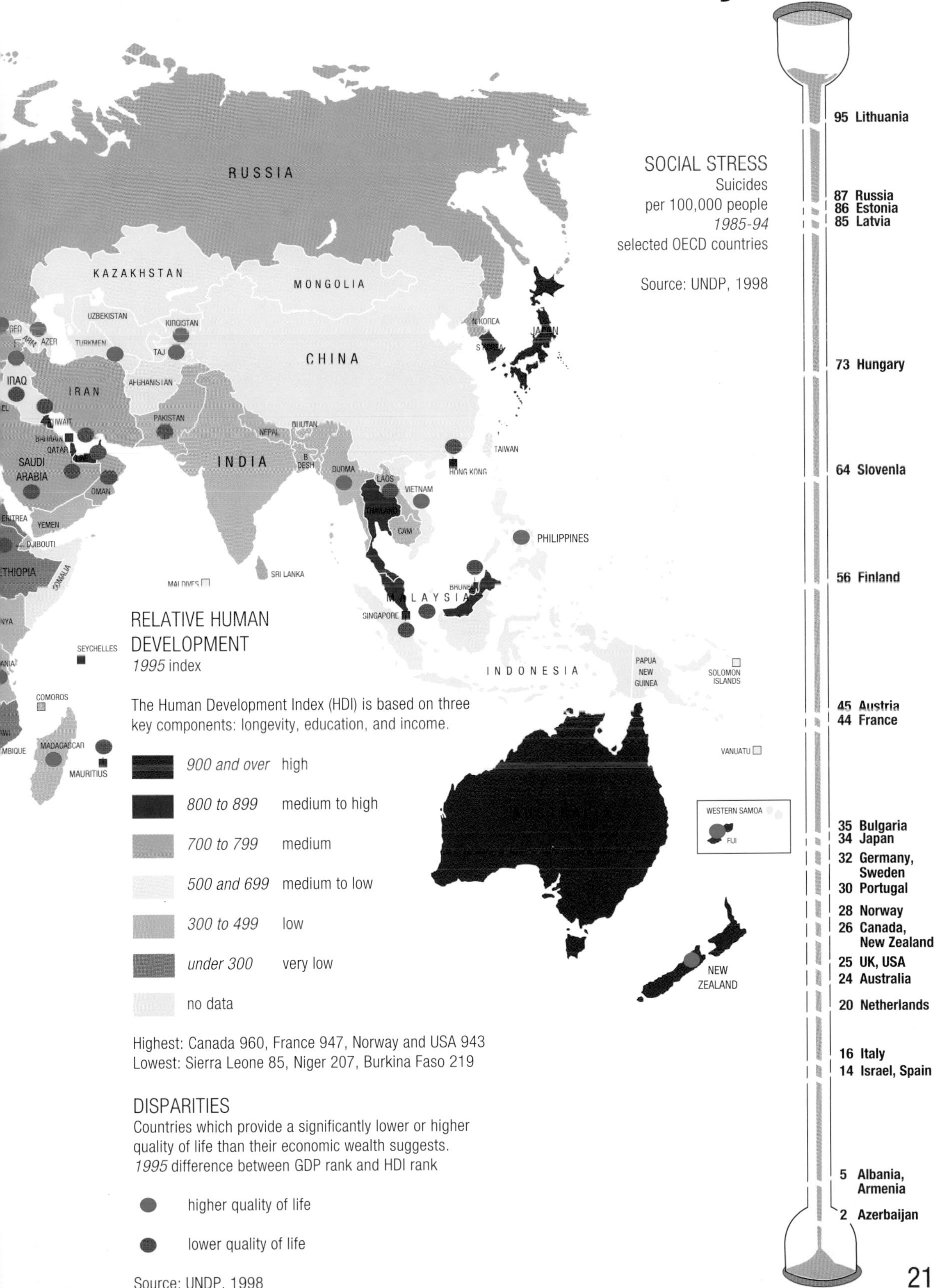

RUSSIA
KAZAKHSTAN
MONGOLIA
UZBEKISTAN
KIRGISTAN
TURKMEN
TAJ
AZER
ARM
CHINA
N KOREA
JAPAN
IRAQ
IRAN
AFGHANISTAN
KUWAIT
BAHRAIN
QATAR
UAE
SAUDI ARABIA
OMAN
YEMEN
ERITREA
DJIBOUTI
ETHIOPIA
SOMALIA
PAKISTAN
NEPAL
BHUTAN
INDIA
B DESH
BURMA
LAOS
THAILAND
VIETNAM
CAM
HONG KONG
TAIWAN
PHILIPPINES
SRI LANKA
MALDIVES
MALAYSIA
BRUNEI
SINGAPORE
INDONESIA
PAPUA NEW GUINEA
SOLOMON ISLANDS
VANUATU
WESTERN SAMOA
FIJI
AUSTRALIA
NEW ZEALAND
SEYCHELLES
COMOROS
MADAGASCAR
MAURITIUS
SOCIAL STRESS
Suicides
per 100,000 people
1985-94
selected OECD countries
Source: UNDP, 1998
95 Lithuania
87 Russia
86 Estonia
85 Latvia
73 Hungary
64 Slovenia
56 Finland
45 Austria
44 France
35 Bulgaria
34 Japan
32 Germany, Sweden
30 Portugal
28 Norway
26 Canada, New Zealand
25 UK, USA
24 Australia
20 Netherlands
16 Italy
14 Israel, Spain
5 Albania, Armenia
2 Azerbaijan
RELATIVE HUMAN DEVELOPMENT
1995 index
The Human Development Index (HDI) is based on three key components: longevity, education, and income.
900 and over high
800 to 899 medium to high
700 to 799 medium
500 and 699 medium to low
300 to 499 low
under 300 very low
no data
Highest: Canada 960, France 947, Norway and USA 943
Lowest: Sierra Leone 85, Niger 207, Burkina Faso 219
DISPARITIES
Countries which provide a significantly lower or higher quality of life than their economic wealth suggests.
1995 difference between GDP rank and HDI rank
higher quality of life
lower quality of life
Source: UNDP, 1998

The combined wealth of the world's 225 richest people is the same as the annual income of the poorer half of the world population.

The 20 percent of the world's population that live in the richest countries consume 16 times as much per person as the 20 percent living in the poorest countries.

The inequalities are lowest in terms of food. The richest populations consume 7 times as much fish and 11 times as much meat as the poorest. The richest also consume 17 times as much energy per person and almost 80 times as much paper. Measured in terms of cars, the consumption levels of the rich are 145 times higher than those of the poor.

Disparities of wealth are as great within countries as between them. In most of the rich countries more than 10 percent of the population live in poverty. Norway and Sweden are the exceptions.

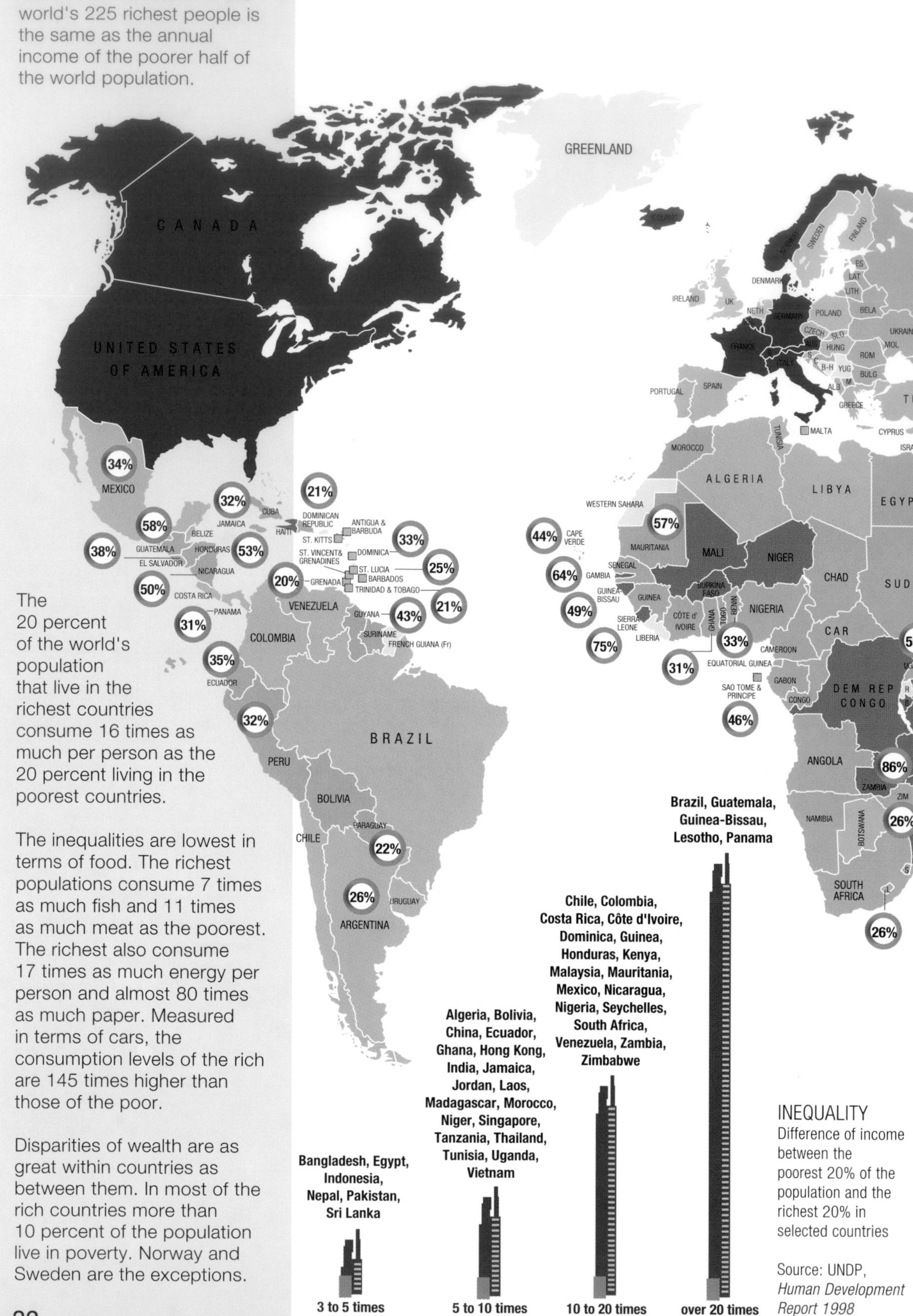

GREENLAND
CANADA
UNITED STATES OF AMERICA
34%
MEXICO
32%
JAMAICA
CUBA
21%
DOMINICAN REPUBLIC
HAITI
58%
BELIZE
38%
GUATEMALA
HONDURAS
53%
EL SALVADOR
NICARAGUA
50%
COSTA RICA
PANAMA
31%
ANTIGUA & BARBUDA
ST. KITTS
33%
ST. VINCENT & GRENADINES
DOMINICA
ST. LUCIA
25%
BARBADOS
20%
GRENADA
TRINIDAD & TOBAGO
21%
VENEZUELA
GUYANA
43%
SURINAME
FRENCH GUIANA (Fr)
COLOMBIA
35%
ECUADOR
32%
PERU
BRAZIL
BOLIVIA
PARAGUAY
22%
CHILE
26%
URUGUAY
ARGENTINA
ICELAND
NORWAY
SWEDEN
FINLAND
ES
LAT
LITH
DENMARK
IRELAND
UK
NETH
GERMANY
POLAND
BELA
CZECH
SLO
UKRAINE
AUS
HUNG
MOL
FRANCE
S
C
B-H
YUG
ROM
ITALY
BULG
M
ALB
PORTUGAL
SPAIN
GREECE
TURK
TUNISIA
MALTA
CYPRUS
ISRAEL
MOROCCO
ALGERIA
LIBYA
EGYPT
WESTERN SAHARA
44%
CAPE VERDE
57%
MAURITANIA
MALI
NIGER
SENEGAL
64%
GAMBIA
CHAD
SUDAN
GUINEA-BISSAU
49%
GUINEA
BURKINA FASO
SIERRA LEONE
CÔTE d' IVOIRE
GHANA
TOGO
BENIN
NIGERIA
LIBERIA
75%
33%
CAR
55%
CAMEROON
31%
EQUATORIAL GUINEA
UGANDA
SAO TOME & PRINCIPE
GABON
CONGO
DEM REP CONGO
R
B
TANZANIA
46%
50%
ANGOLA
86%
ZAMBIA
ZIM
NAMIBIA
BOTSWANA
26%
MOZAM
S
SOUTH AFRICA
L
26%
Brazil, Guatemala, Guinea-Bissau, Lesotho, Panama
Chile, Colombia, Costa Rica, Côte d'Ivoire, Dominica, Guinea, Honduras, Kenya, Malaysia, Mauritania, Mexico, Nicaragua, Nigeria, Seychelles, South Africa, Venezuela, Zambia, Zimbabwe
Algeria, Bolivia, China, Ecuador, Ghana, Hong Kong, India, Jamaica, Jordan, Laos, Madagascar, Morocco, Niger, Singapore, Tanzania, Thailand, Tunisia, Uganda, Vietnam
Bangladesh, Egypt, Indonesia, Nepal, Pakistan, Sri Lanka
3 to 5 times
5 to 10 times
10 to 20 times
over 20 times
INEQUALITY
Difference of income between the poorest 20% of the population and the richest 20% in selected countries
Source: UNDP, *Human Development Report 1998*

Inequality

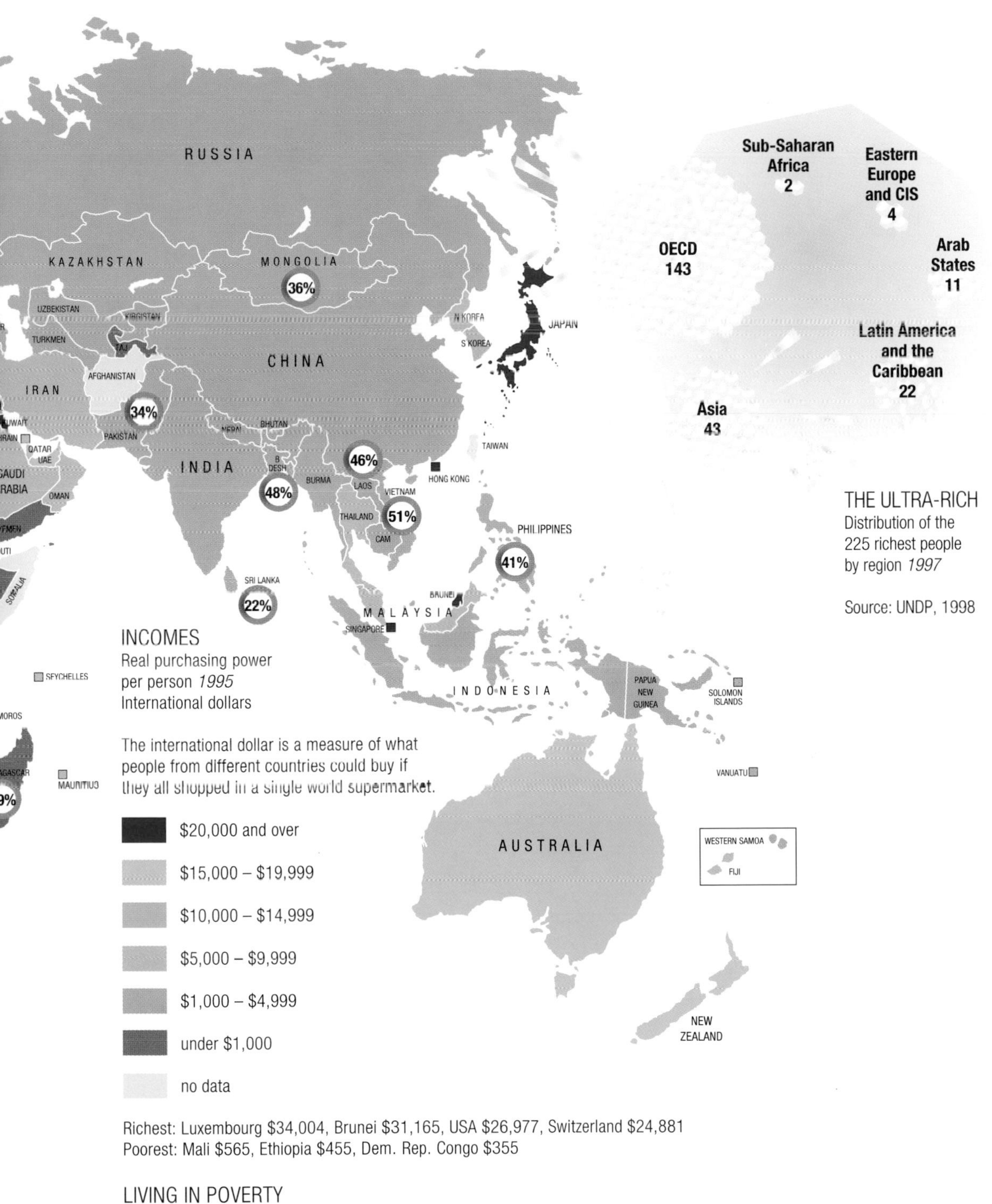
RUSSIA
KAZAKHSTAN
MONGOLIA
36%
UZBEKISTAN
KIRGISTAN
TURKMEN
TAJ
AFGHANISTAN
IRAN
CHINA
N KOREA
S KOREA
JAPAN
34%
KUWAIT
BAHRAIN
QATAR
UAE
PAKISTAN
NEPAL
BHUTAN
SAUDI ARABIA
INDIA
B DESH
48%
46%
HONG KONG
TAIWAN
OMAN
YEMEN
BURMA
LAOS
VIETNAM
THAILAND
51%
CAM
PHILIPPINES
41%
SOMALIA
SRI LANKA
22%
BRUNEI
MALAYSIA
SINGAPORE
SEYCHELLES
INDONESIA
PAPUA NEW GUINEA
SOLOMON ISLANDS
COMOROS
MADAGASCAR
MAURITIUS
VANUATU
AUSTRALIA
WESTERN SAMOA
FIJI
NEW ZEALAND
Sub-Saharan Africa 2
Eastern Europe and CIS 4
OECD 143
Arab States 11
Latin America and the Caribbean 22
Asia 43
THE ULTRA-RICH
Distribution of the 225 richest people by region *1997*
Source: UNDP, 1998
INCOMES
Real purchasing power per person *1995*
International dollars
The international dollar is a measure of what people from different countries could buy if they all shopped in a single world supermarket.
$20,000 and over
$15,000 – $19,999
$10,000 – $14,999
$5,000 – $9,999
$1,000 – $4,999
under $1,000
no data

Richest: Luxembourg $34,004, Brunei $31,165, USA $26,977, Switzerland $24,881
Poorest: Mali $565, Ethiopia $455, Dem. Rep. Congo $355

LIVING IN POVERTY
1989-94

percentage living below the national poverty line
where percentage exceeds 20%

Source: UNDP, *Human Development Report 1998*

Where average life expectancies increase and family sizes decline, the proportion of older people in a population increases.

One result is that the economically-active part of the population must support not only itself but an increasing proportion of people who are effectively dependent.

In the richer countries, where better living conditions mean longer lives and less population growth, a welfare crisis is looming for older people. In poorer countries with lower average life expectancy, people tend to remain economically active for more of their lifetimes. In many countries, older people do work that does not appear in economic statistics.

Age is a different issue between rich and poor countries, and between rich and poor people within a country. Whether retirement from active employment for up to a third of one's adult life is a relief or a burden depends to a large extent on whether it has been possible to enjoy a personally rewarding working life.

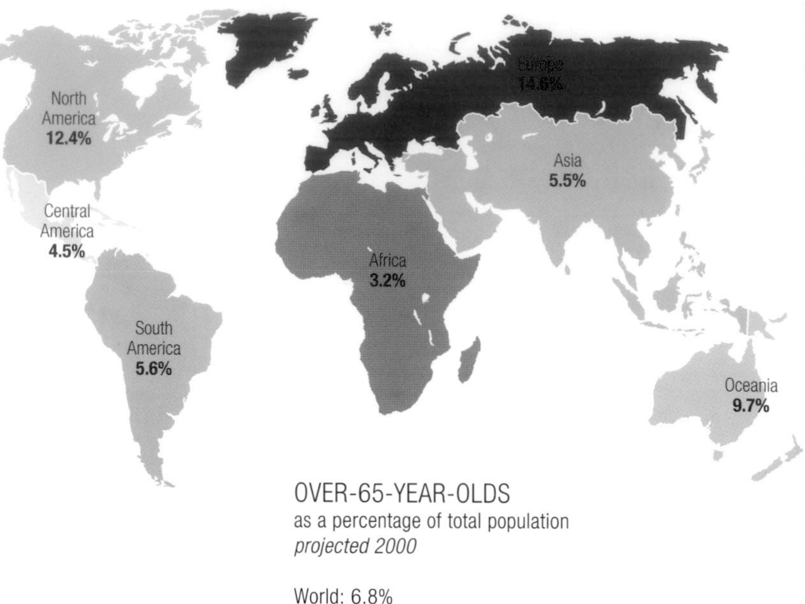
North America
12.4%
Europe
14.6%
Asia
5.5%
Central America
4.5%
Africa
3.2%
South America
5.6%
Oceania
9.7%

OVER-65-YEAR-OLDS
as a percentage of total population
projected 2000

World: 6.8%
Developing countries: 5.0%
Developed countries: 14.2%

Source: *World Resources 1998-99*

OVER-75-YEAR-OLDS
Regions' shares of world population aged 75 and over
1996 percentages

Source: US Bureau of the Census, 1996

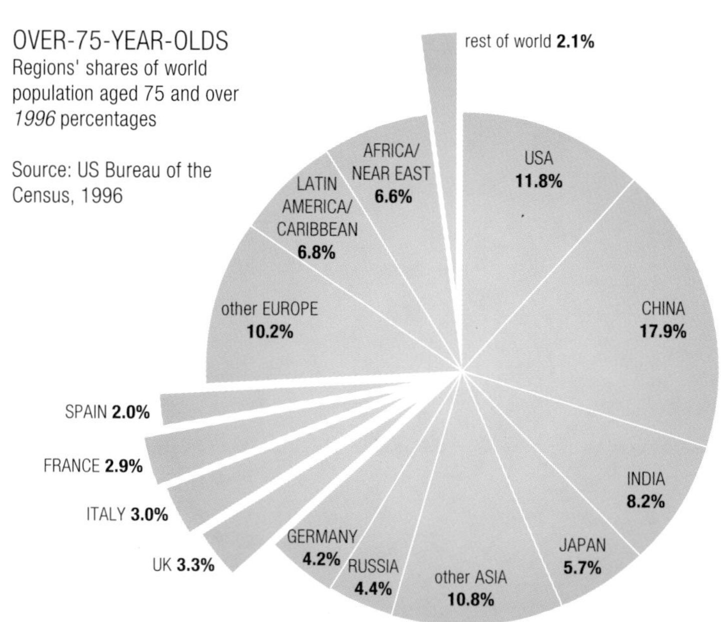
rest of world **2.1%**
USA
11.8%
CHINA
17.9%
INDIA
8.2%
JAPAN
5.7%
other ASIA
10.8%
RUSSIA
4.4%
GERMANY
4.2%
UK **3.3%**
ITALY **3.0%**
FRANCE **2.9%**
SPAIN **2.0%**
other EUROPE
10.2%
LATIN AMERICA/ CARIBBEAN
6.8%
AFRICA/ NEAR EAST
6.6%

Age

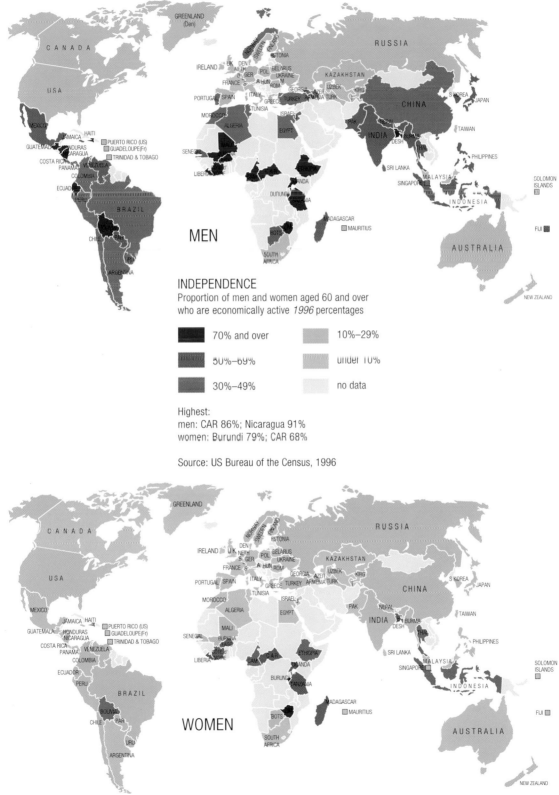

MEN

INDEPENDENCE

Proportion of men and women aged 60 and over who are economically active *1996* percentages

70% and over	10%–29%
50%–69%	under 10%
30%–49%	no data

Highest:
men: CAR 86%; Nicaragua 91%
women: Burundi 79%; CAR 68%

Source: US Bureau of the Census, 1996

GREENLAND
CANADA
USA
RUSSIA
KAZAKHSTAN
CHINA
INDIA
BRAZIL
AUSTRALIA
INDONESIA
MALAYSIA
MEXICO
ARGENTINA
PERU
CHILE
BOLIVIA
ALGERIA
EGYPT
MALI
ETHIOPIA
MADAGASCAR
SOUTH AFRICA
NEW ZEALAND
WOMEN

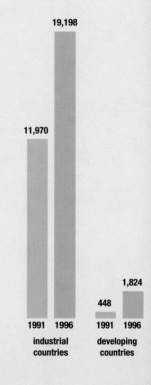

19,198
11,970
1,824
448
1991
1996
1991
1996
industrial countries
developing countries

Part Two The Global Economy

HAVE A NICE DAY
Growth of McDonald's restaurants
numbers by region 1991–96

Source: UNDP, 1998

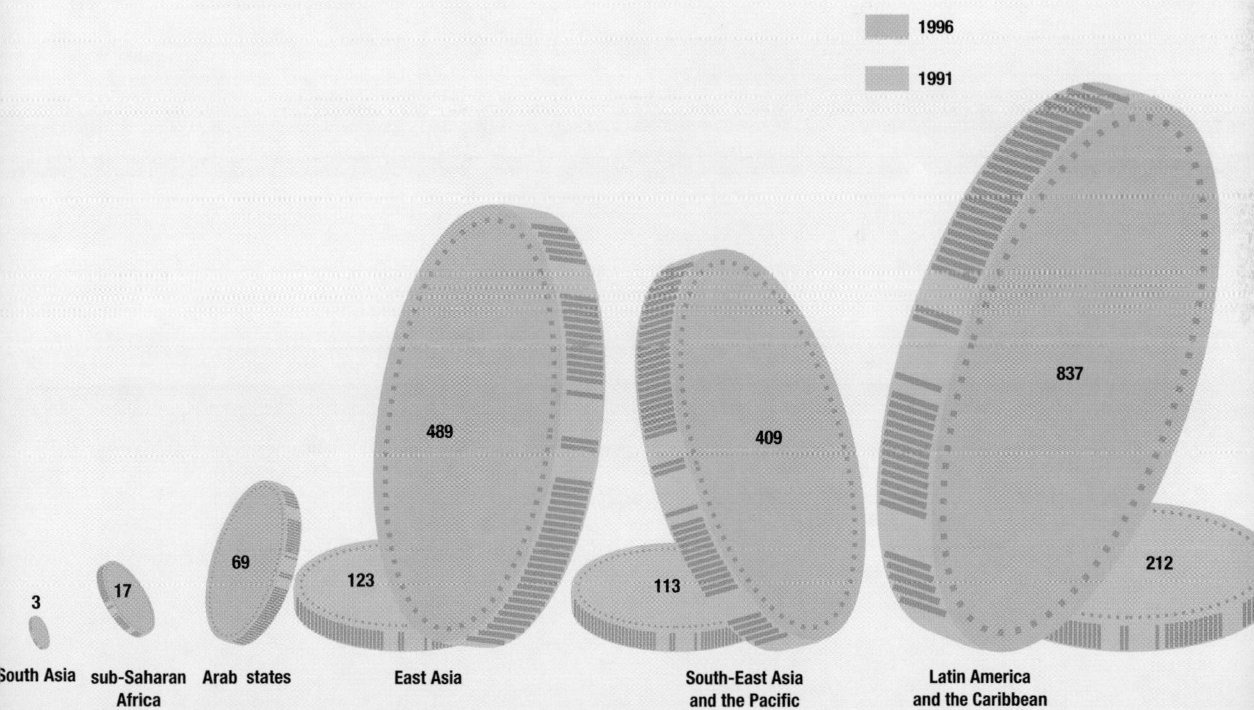

1996
1991
3
17
69
123
489
113
409
837
212
South Asia
sub-Saharan Africa
Arab states
East Asia
South-East Asia and the Pacific
Latin America and the Caribbean

The world economy is shaped by repetitive cycles of growth, slump and renewed growth.

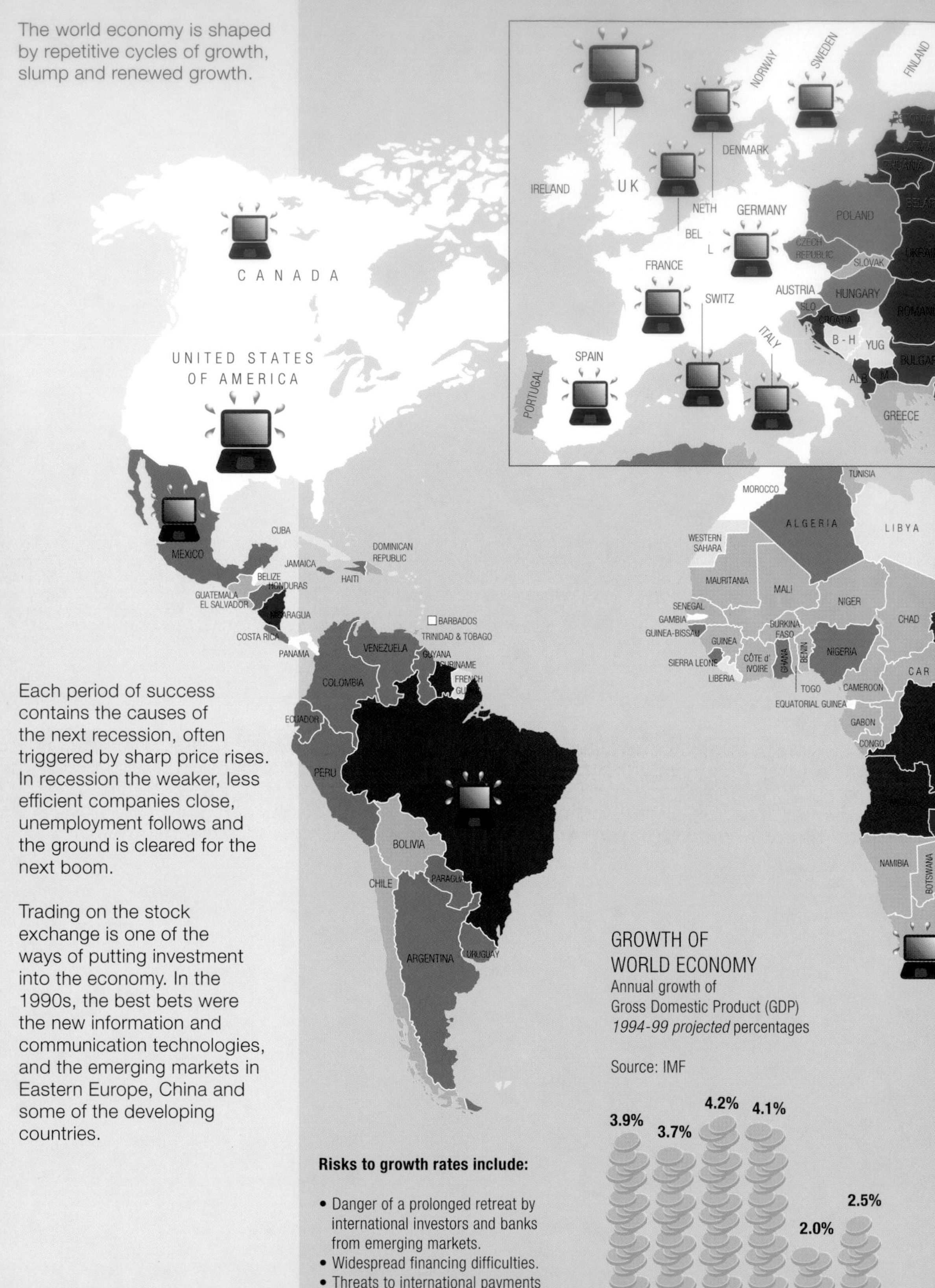
IRELAND
UK
NORWAY
SWEDEN
FINLAND
DENMARK
NETH
GERMANY
POLAND
BEL
L
CZECH REPUBLIC
SLOVAK
UKRAINE
FRANCE
SWITZ
AUSTRIA
HUNGARY
SLO
CROATIA
ROMANIA
B - H
YUG
ITALY
SPAIN
PORTUGAL
BULGARIA
ALB
M
GREECE
CANADA
UNITED STATES OF AMERICA
MEXICO
CUBA
DOMINICAN REPUBLIC
JAMAICA
HAITI
BELIZE
HONDURAS
GUATEMALA
EL SALVADOR
NICARAGUA
BARBADOS
TRINIDAD & TOBAGO
COSTA RICA
PANAMA
VENEZUELA
GUYANA
SURINAME
COLOMBIA
ECUADOR
PERU
BOLIVIA
CHILE
PARAGUAY
ARGENTINA
URUGUAY
TUNISIA
MOROCCO
ALGERIA
LIBYA
WESTERN SAHARA
MAURITANIA
MALI
NIGER
SENEGAL
GAMBIA
GUINEA-BISSAU
GUINEA
BURKINA FASO
CHAD
SIERRA LEONE
CÔTE d' IVOIRE
GHANA
BENIN
NIGERIA
LIBERIA
TOGO
CAMEROON
CAR
EQUATORIAL GUINEA
GABON
CONGO
NAMIBIA
BOTSWANA

Each period of success contains the causes of the next recession, often triggered by sharp price rises. In recession the weaker, less efficient companies close, unemployment follows and the ground is cleared for the next boom.

Trading on the stock exchange is one of the ways of putting investment into the economy. In the 1990s, the best bets were the new information and communication technologies, and the emerging markets in Eastern Europe, China and some of the developing countries.

GROWTH OF WORLD ECONOMY
Annual growth of Gross Domestic Product (GDP)
1994-99 projected percentages

Source: IMF

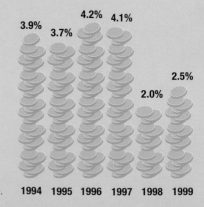

1994	1995	1996	1997	1998	1999
3.9%	3.7%	4.2%	4.1%	2.0%	2.5%

Risks to growth rates include:

- Danger of a prolonged retreat by international investors and banks from emerging markets.
- Widespread financing difficulties.
- Threats to international payments and associated disruptions to trade.
- Further decline in stock markets and other asset prices, with losses of financial wealth and contraction of consumption and investment worldwide.

World Markets

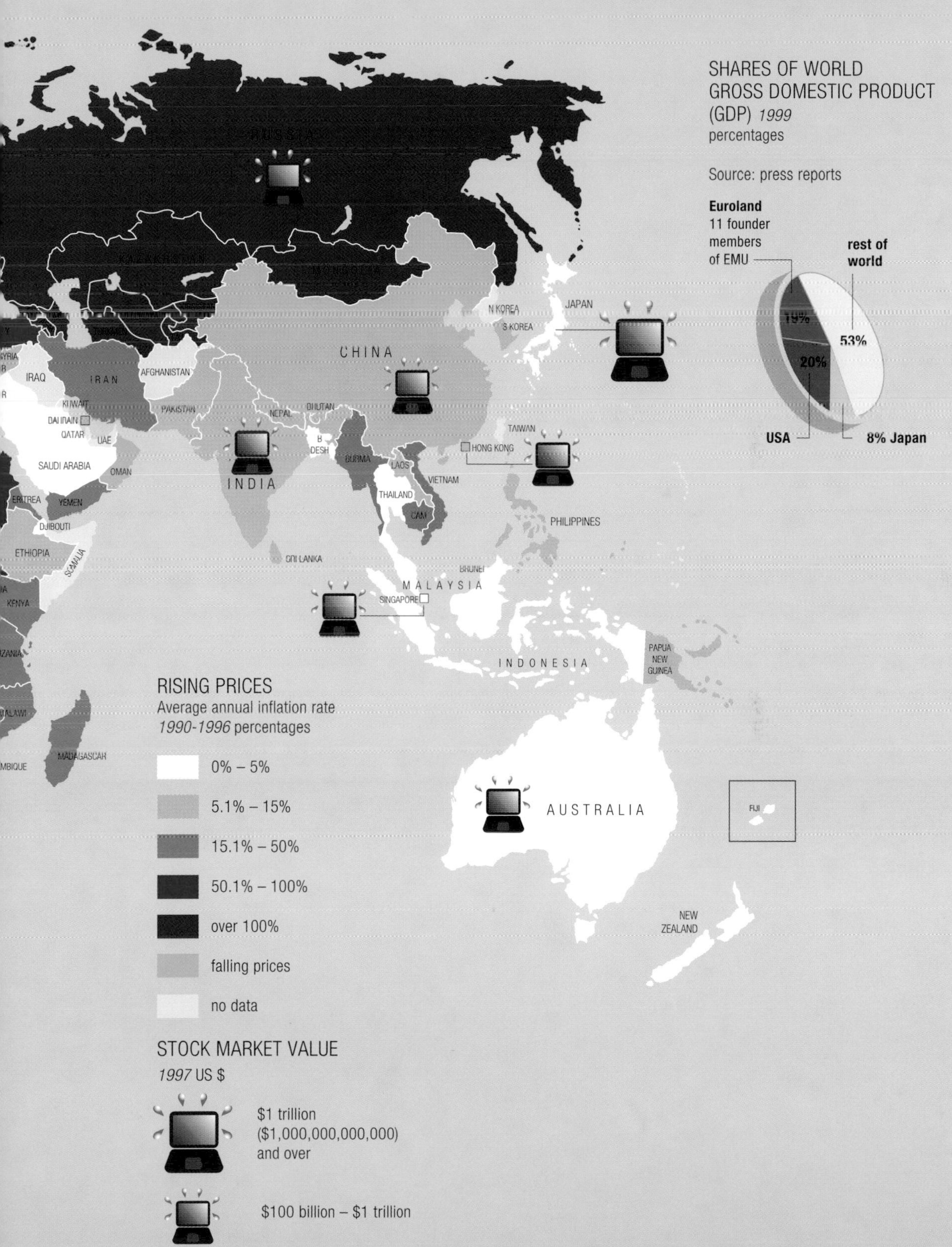
SHARES OF WORLD GROSS DOMESTIC PRODUCT (GDP) 1999
percentages
Source: press reports
Euroland
11 founder members of EMU
rest of world
19%
53%
20%
USA
8% Japan
RUSSIA
KAZAKHSTAN
MONGOLIA
N KOREA
S KOREA
JAPAN
CHINA
SYRIA
IRAQ
IRAN
AFGHANISTAN
KUWAIT
BAHRAIN
QATAR
UAE
PAKISTAN
NEPAL
BHUTAN
SAUDI ARABIA
OMAN
INDIA
B DESH
BURMA
LAOS
TAIWAN
HONG KONG
VIETNAM
THAILAND
CAM
PHILIPPINES
ERITREA
YEMEN
DJIBOUTI
ETHIOPIA
SOMALIA
KENYA
SRI LANKA
BRUNEI
MALAYSIA
SINGAPORE
INDONESIA
PAPUA NEW GUINEA
MALAWI
MADAGASCAR
AUSTRALIA
FIJI
NEW ZEALAND
RISING PRICES
Average annual inflation rate
1990-1996 percentages
0% – 5%
5.1% – 15%
15.1% – 50%
50.1% – 100%
over 100%
falling prices
no data
STOCK MARKET VALUE
1997 US $
$1 trillion ($1,000,000,000,000) and over
$100 billion – $1 trillion

Source: *World Bank Atlas 1998*

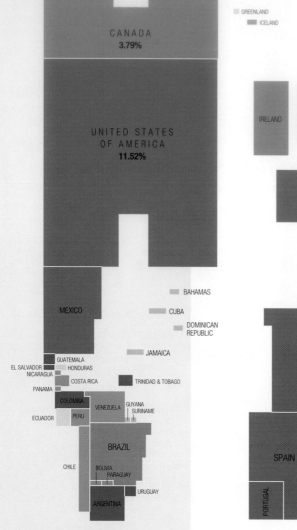

CANADA 3.79%
UNITED STATES OF AMERICA 11.52%
MEXICO
BAHAMAS
CUBA
DOMINICAN REPUBLIC
JAMAICA
GUATEMALA
EL SALVADOR
HONDURAS
NICARAGUA
COSTA RICA
TRINIDAD & TOBAGO
PANAMA
COLOMBIA
VENEZUELA
GUYANA
SURINAME
ECUADOR
PERU
BRAZIL
CHILE
BOLIVIA
PARAGUAY
URUGUAY
ARGENTINA
GREENLAND
ICELAND
NORWAY
SWEDEN
FINLAND
DENMARK
IRELAND
UK 4.76%
NETHERLANDS 3.85%
GERMANY 10.08%
BELGIUM 3.32%
FRANCE 5.65%
SPAIN
PORTUGAL
ITALY 4.56%

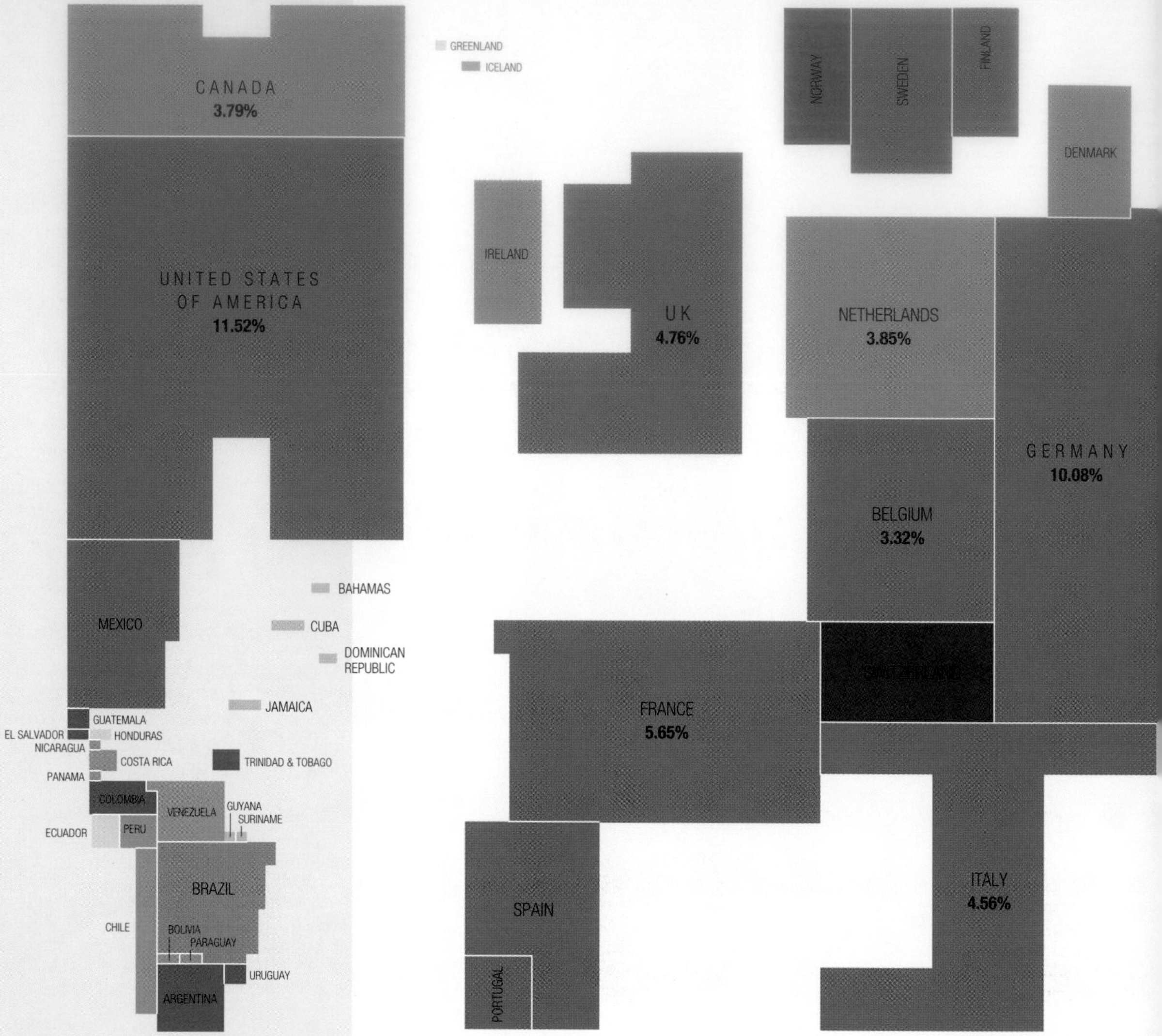

Statistics on manufacturing and trade are an expression of economic power. That power is concentrated in North America (primarily the USA), Western Europe (primarily the 15 countries of the European Union), and East Asia (primarily Japan). The three zones of economic power accounted for about 70 percent of the world's exports in 1980, and about 85 percent in 1996.

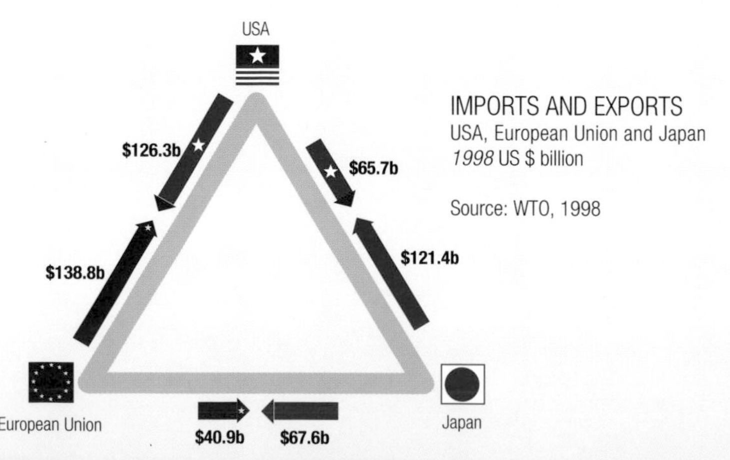
USA
$126.3b
$65.7b
$138.8b
$121.4b
European Union
Japan
$40.9b
$67.6b

IMPORTS AND EXPORTS
USA, European Union and Japan
1998 US $ billion

Source: WTO, 1998

Trade and Industry

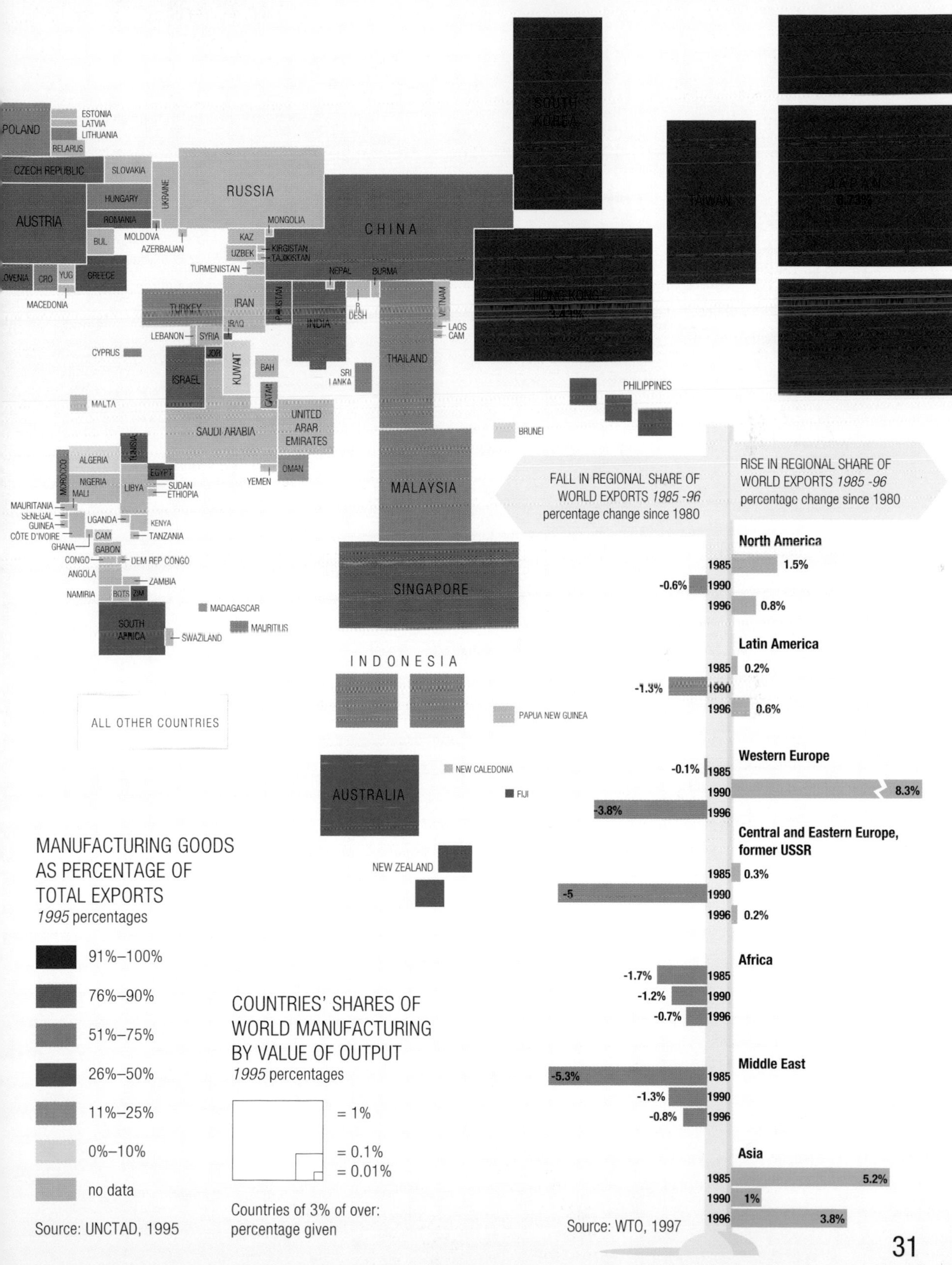

POLAND
ESTONIA
LATVIA
LITHUANIA
BELARUS
CZECH REPUBLIC
SLOVAKIA
UKRAINE
RUSSIA
HUNGARY
AUSTRIA
ROMANIA
MONGOLIA
CHINA
SOUTH KOREA
TAIWAN
JAPAN
8.73%
BUL
MOLDOVA
AZERBAIJAN
KAZ
UZBEK
KIRGISTAN
TAJIKISTAN
TURMENISTAN
OVENIA
CRO
YUG
GREECE
MACEDONIA
NEPAL
BURMA
TURKEY
IRAN
IRAQ
PAKISTAN
INDIA
B DESH
VIETNAM
LAOS
CAM
HONG KONG
LEBANON
SYRIA
JOR
CYPRUS
ISRAEL
KUWAIT
BAH
QATAR
SRI LANKA
THAILAND
PHILIPPINES
MALTA
SAUDI ARABIA
UNITED ARAB EMIRATES
BRUNEI
OMAN
YEMEN
ALGERIA
TUNISIA
MOROCCO
NIGERIA
MALI
LIBYA
EGYPT
SUDAN
ETHIOPIA
MALAYSIA
MAURITANIA
SENEGAL
GUINEA
CÔTE D'IVOIRE
GHANA
UGANDA
KENYA
CAM
TANZANIA
GABON
CONGO
DEM REP CONGO
ANGOLA
ZAMBIA
NAMIBIA
BOTS
ZIM
SINGAPORE
MADAGASCAR
SOUTH AFRICA
MAURITIUS
SWAZILAND
INDONESIA
ALL OTHER COUNTRIES
PAPUA NEW GUINEA
NEW CALEDONIA
FIJI
AUSTRALIA
NEW ZEALAND
MANUFACTURING GOODS AS PERCENTAGE OF TOTAL EXPORTS
1995 percentages
91%–100%
76%–90%
51%–75%
26%–50%
11%–25%
0%–10%
no data
Source: UNCTAD, 1995
COUNTRIES' SHARES OF WORLD MANUFACTURING BY VALUE OF OUTPUT
1995 percentages
= 1%
= 0.1%
= 0.01%
Countries of 3% of over: percentage given
FALL IN REGIONAL SHARE OF WORLD EXPORTS 1985 -96
percentage change since 1980
RISE IN REGIONAL SHARE OF WORLD EXPORTS 1985 -96
percentage change since 1980
North America
1985 1.5%
-0.6% 1990
1996 0.8%
Latin America
1985 0.2%
-1.3% 1990
1996 0.6%
Western Europe
-0.1% 1985
1990 8.3%
-3.8% 1996
Central and Eastern Europe, former USSR
1985 0.3%
-5 1990
1996 0.2%
Africa
-1.7% 1985
-1.2% 1990
-0.7% 1996
Middle East
-5.3% 1985
-1.3% 1990
-0.8% 1996
Asia
1985 5.2%
1990 1%
1996 3.8%
Source: WTO, 1997

Tourists are money-making imports. In the name of exotic holidays and unspoiled locations, the travel and holiday pages of glossy magazines encourage the better-off to find new luxurious enclaves in poor countries. But mass tourism requires a well-developed infrastructure of services, based on a solid record of investment. As a result, while the pattern of the tourist trade and earnings is a little more egalitarian than the distribution of trade and manufacturing power (see **Trade and Industry**, pp.30-1), most tourist expenditure is concentrated in the same regions where most other kinds of wealth are concentrated.

Although international visitors contribute money to the national economy of the country they visit, they are often a burden on local societies. The very curiosity that takes tourists far and wide can threaten the natural and architectural beauties they go to visit. In extreme circumstances, tourism becomes so potent a symbol of cultural invasion, that armed groups in Egypt and Algeria have declared tourists to be legitimate targets of war and acted accordingly.

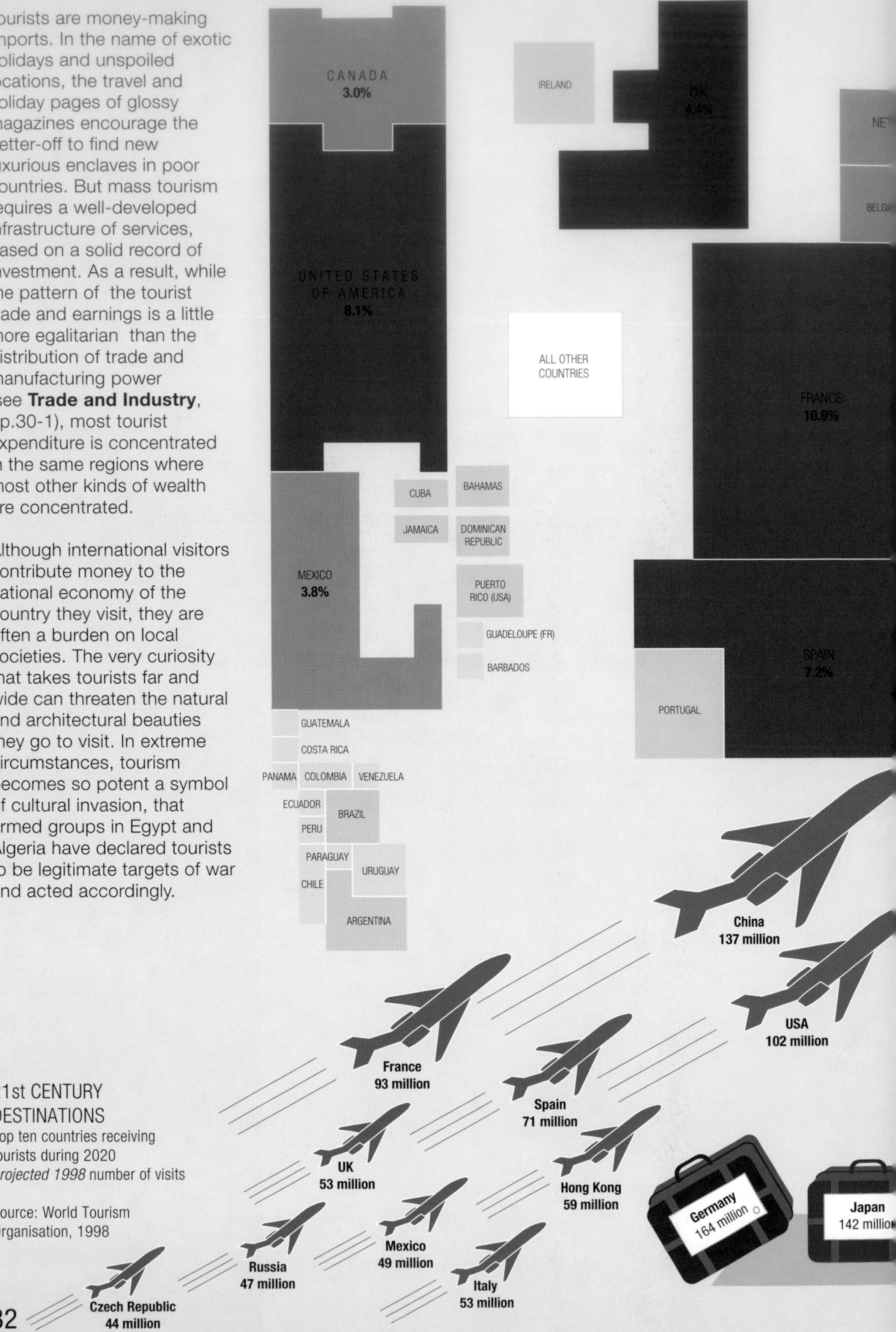
CANADA
3.0%
UNITED STATES OF AMERICA
8.1%
MEXICO
3.8%
CUBA
BAHAMAS
JAMAICA
DOMINICAN REPUBLIC
PUERTO RICO (USA)
GUADELOUPE (FR)
BARBADOS
GUATEMALA
COSTA RICA
PANAMA
COLOMBIA
VENEZUELA
ECUADOR
BRAZIL
PERU
PARAGUAY
URUGUAY
CHILE
ARGENTINA
IRELAND
UK
4.4%
NET
BELGI
ALL OTHER COUNTRIES
FRANCE
10.9%
SPAIN
7.2%
PORTUGAL
China
137 million
USA
102 million
France
93 million
Spain
71 million
UK
53 million
Hong Kong
59 million
Germany
164 million
Japan
142 millio
Mexico
49 million
Russia
47 million
Italy
53 million
Czech Republic
44 million

21st CENTURY DESTINATIONS
Top ten countries receiving tourists during 2020
projected 1998 number of visits

Source: World Tourism Organisation, 1998

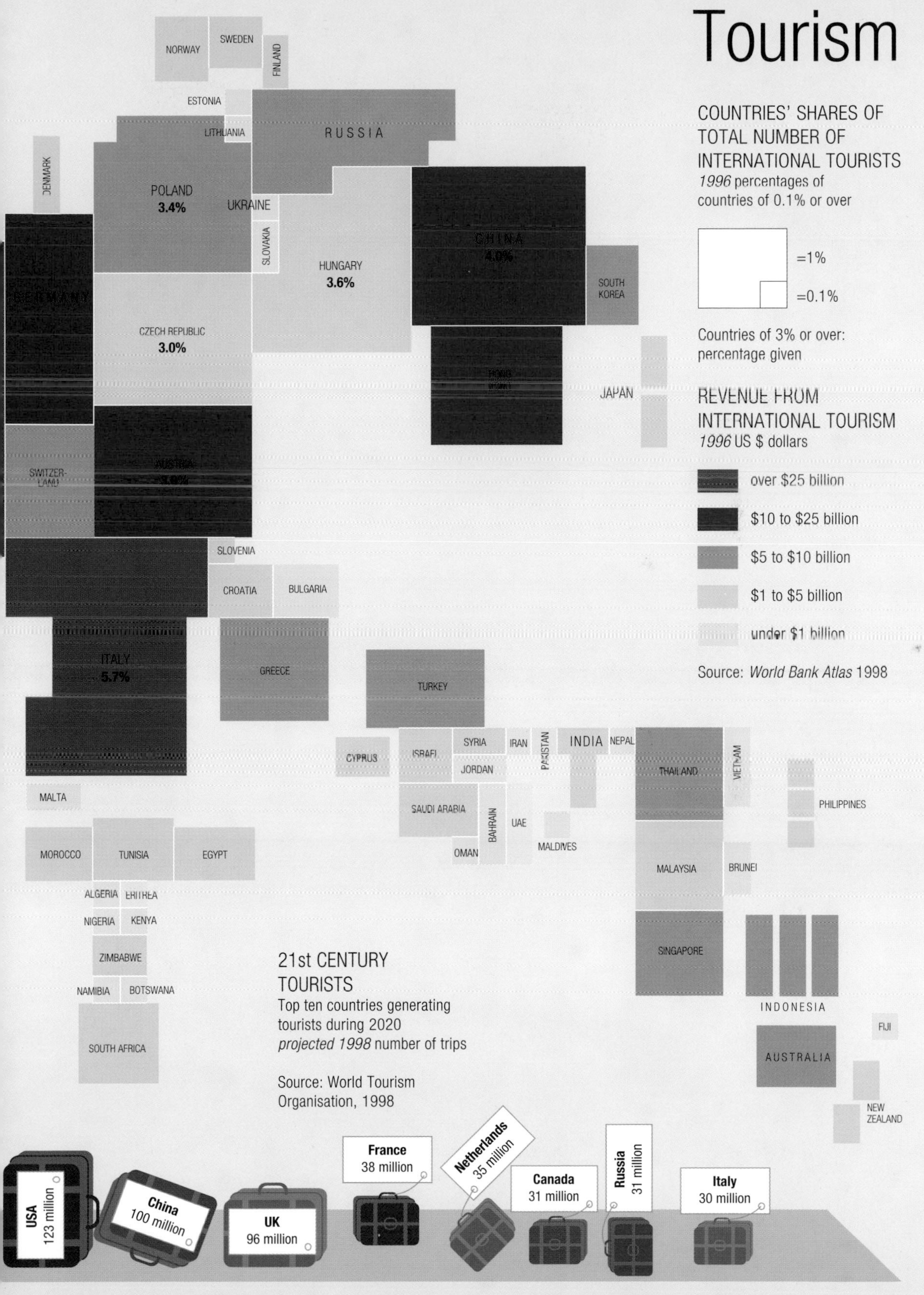

Tourism
COUNTRIES' SHARES OF TOTAL NUMBER OF INTERNATIONAL TOURISTS
1996 percentages of countries of 0.1% or over
=1%
=0.1%
Countries of 3% or over: percentage given
REVENUE FROM INTERNATIONAL TOURISM
1996 US $ dollars
over $25 billion
$10 to $25 billion
$5 to $10 billion
$1 to $5 billion
under $1 billion
Source: *World Bank Atlas* 1998
NORWAY
SWEDEN
FINLAND
ESTONIA
LITHUANIA
RUSSIA
DENMARK
POLAND
3.4%
UKRAINE
SLOVAKIA
HUNGARY
3.6%
CHINA
4.0%
SOUTH KOREA
CZECH REPUBLIC
3.0%
JAPAN
SWITZER-LAND
AUSTRIA
SLOVENIA
CROATIA
BULGARIA
ITALY
5.7%
GREECE
TURKEY
CYPRUS
ISRAEL
SYRIA
JORDAN
IRAN
PAKISTAN
INDIA
NEPAL
THAILAND
VIETNAM
PHILIPPINES
MALTA
SAUDI ARABIA
BAHRAIN
UAE
OMAN
MALDIVES
MALAYSIA
BRUNEI
MOROCCO
TUNISIA
EGYPT
ALGERIA
ERITREA
NIGERIA
KENYA
ZIMBABWE
NAMIBIA
BOTSWANA
SOUTH AFRICA
SINGAPORE
INDONESIA
FIJI
AUSTRALIA
NEW ZEALAND
21st CENTURY TOURISTS
Top ten countries generating tourists during 2020
projected 1998 number of trips
Source: World Tourism Organisation, 1998
USA 123 million
China 100 million
UK 96 million
France 38 million
Netherlands 35 million
Canada 31 million
Russia 31 million
Italy 30 million

The main driving force in the creation of an integrated global economy has been the influence and power of the transnational corporations (TNCs). They generate 70 percent of international trade and 80 percent of all direct foreign investment. Combining operations across continents and, in many cases, in more than one economic sector at a time, the decisions taken in the largest TNCs have a direct impact on market conditions and employment possibilities.

With few exceptions, TNCs are effectively their own masters, accountable only to their shareholders, and able to face down most governments if there is a confrontation over economic policy. But they are not immune to economic laws and even the giant Japanese conglomerates stumbled in the late-1990s.

There is little doubt where profit lies. The pattern of investment in the global economy reveals extremes of concentration.

In only four countries was annual investment from foreign sources above US $10 billion in the mid-1990s. The total for those four countries, however, was US $170 billion, as US $77 billion flowed into the USA, US $40 billion into China, US $32 billion into the UK, and US $21 billion into France. Foreign investment in several African countries amounted to no more than a few million dollars.

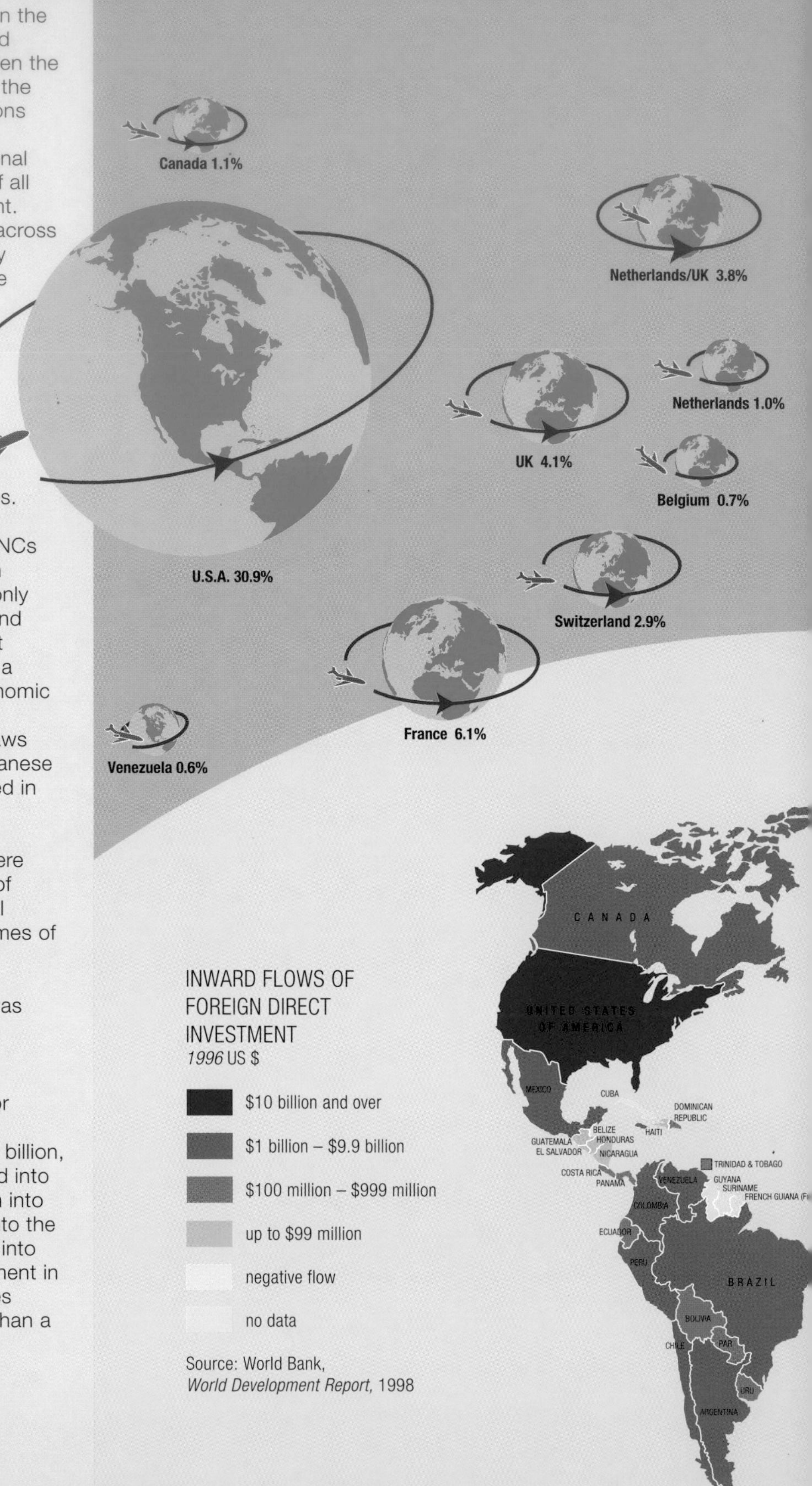
Canada 1.1%
Netherlands/UK 3.8%
Netherlands 1.0%
UK 4.1%
Belgium 0.7%
U.S.A. 30.9%
Switzerland 2.9%
France 6.1%
Venezuela 0.6%
CANADA
UNITED STATES OF AMERICA
MEXICO
CUBA
DOMINICAN REPUBLIC
HAITI
BELIZE
HONDURAS
GUATEMALA
EL SALVADOR
NICARAGUA
TRINIDAD & TOBAGO
COSTA RICA
PANAMA
VENEZUELA
GUYANA
SURINAME
COLOMBIA
ECUADOR
PERU
BRAZIL
BOLIVIA
CHILE
PAR
URU
ARGENTINA
INWARD FLOWS OF FOREIGN DIRECT INVESTMENT
1996 US $
$10 billion and over
$1 billion – $9.9 billion
$100 million – $999 million
up to $99 million
negative flow
no data
Source: World Bank, World Development Report, 1998

Investment

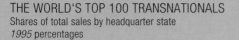

THE WORLD'S TOP 100 TRANSNATIONALS

Shares of total sales by headquarter state
1995 percentages

Total sales in 1995: $4,177.6 billion

Source: UN, *World Investment Report: Transnational Corporations, Market Structure and Competitive Policy*, 1998

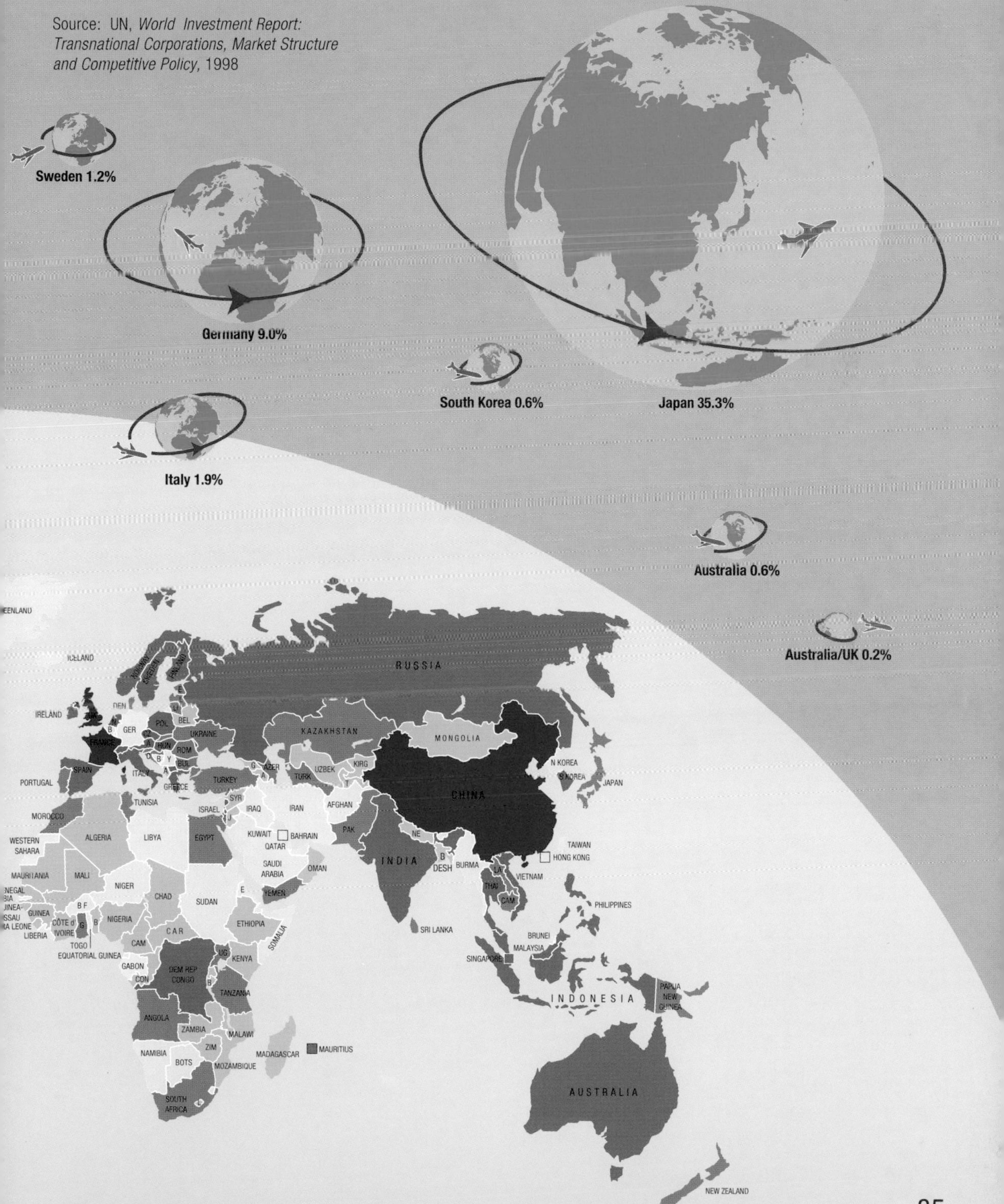

Sweden 1.2%

Germany 9.0%

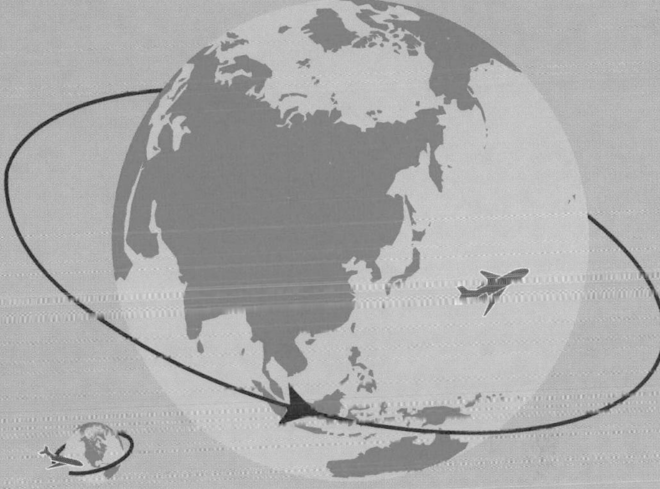

South Korea 0.6%

Japan 35.3%

Italy 1.9%

Australia 0.6%

Australia/UK 0.2%

For governments, as for people, debt starts with spending too much and borrowing to make ends meet. Loans may avoid the problem rather than solve it.

Deficits accumulate, debt grows, and soon the first and largest call on hard-earned income is the debt itself.

Governments deep in debt can only pay the interest (or service the debt). They cannot repay the debt itself. The debt burden is measured by the debt service ratio, which tells how much of income earned from exports is spent on interest payment.

The flow of debt payments from the poor countries to the rich is still larger than the flow of aid from rich to poor. Few countries meet the United Nations' target that rich countries should spend 0.7 percent of their annual income on aid.

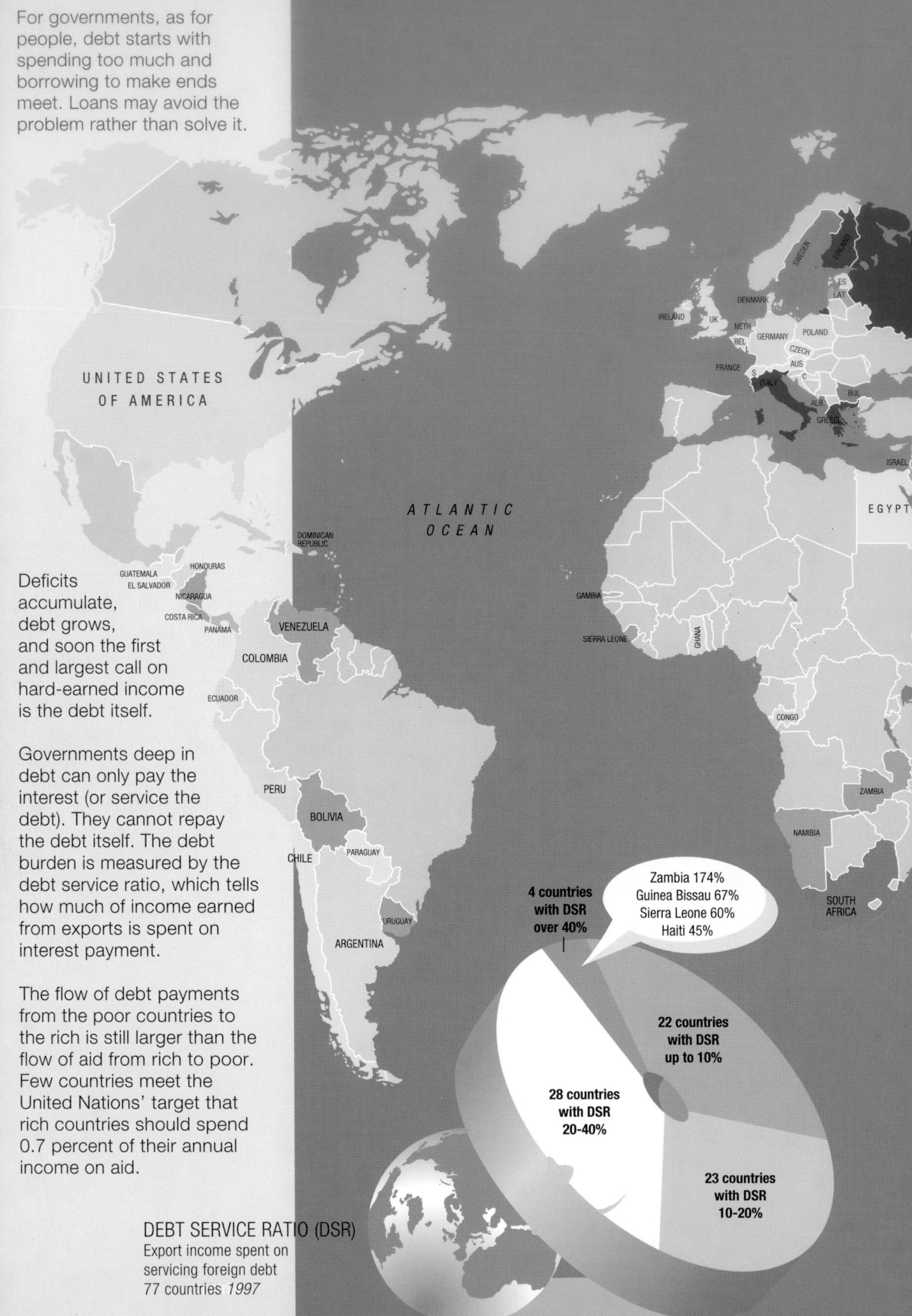
UNITED STATES OF AMERICA
ATLANTIC OCEAN
DOMINICAN REPUBLIC
GUATEMALA
HONDURAS
EL SALVADOR
NICARAGUA
COSTA RICA
PANAMA
VENEZUELA
COLOMBIA
ECUADOR
PERU
BOLIVIA
CHILE
PARAGUAY
URUGUAY
ARGENTINA
IRELAND
UK
DENMARK
SWEDEN
FINLAND
ES
LAT
NETH
BEL
L
GERMANY
POLAND
CZECH
AUS
FRANCE
S
C
ITALY
ALB
BUL
GREECE
ISRAEL
EGYPT
GAMBIA
SIERRA LEONE
GHANA
CONGO
ZAMBIA
NAMIBIA
SOUTH AFRICA
4 countries with DSR over 40%
Zambia 174%
Guinea Bissau 67%
Sierra Leone 60%
Haiti 45%
22 countries with DSR up to 10%
28 countries with DSR 20-40%
23 countries with DSR 10-20%

DEBT SERVICE RATIO (DSR)
Export income spent on servicing foreign debt
77 countries *1997*

Sources: UNDP, *Human Development Report*, 1998

Debt

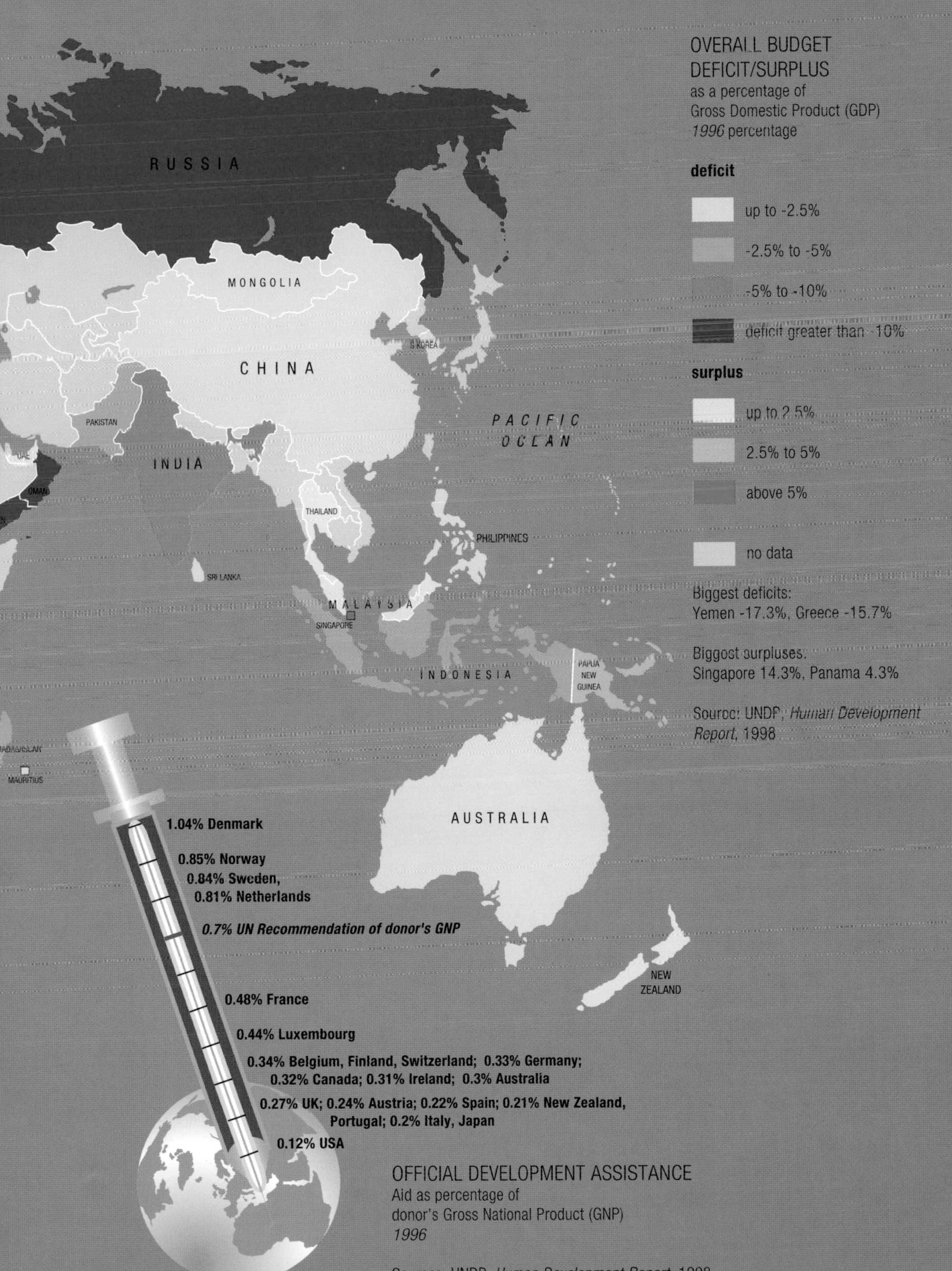

OVERALL BUDGET DEFICIT/SURPLUS
as a percentage of
Gross Domestic Product (GDP)
1996 percentage
deficit
up to -2.5%
-2.5% to -5%
-5% to -10%
deficit greater than -10%
surplus
up to 2.5%
2.5% to 5%
above 5%
no data
Biggest deficits:
Yemen -17.3%, Greece -15.7%
Biggest surpluses:
Singapore 14.3%, Panama 4.3%
Source: UNDP, Human Development Report, 1998
RUSSIA
MONGOLIA
CHINA
S KOREA
PAKISTAN
INDIA
UAE
OMAN
THAILAND
PACIFIC OCEAN
PHILIPPINES
SRI LANKA
MALAYSIA
SINGAPORE
INDONESIA
PAPUA NEW GUINEA
MAURITIUS
AUSTRALIA
NEW ZEALAND
1.04% Denmark
0.85% Norway
0.84% Sweden,
0.81% Netherlands
0.7% UN Recommendation of donor's GNP
0.48% France
0.44% Luxembourg
0.34% Belgium, Finland, Switzerland; 0.33% Germany;
0.32% Canada; 0.31% Ireland; 0.3% Australia
0.27% UK; 0.24% Austria; 0.22% Spain; 0.21% New Zealand,
Portugal; 0.2% Italy, Japan
0.12% USA
OFFICIAL DEVELOPMENT ASSISTANCE
Aid as percentage of
donor's Gross National Product (GNP)
1996
Sources: UNDP, Human Development Report, 1998

Gross National Product (GNP) is the most commonly-used indicator of a nation's wealth. It measures the consumption of goods (things people grow, make or extract from the ground and then sell) and services (things people do for money). The more a country consumes, the richer it is. How that wealth is distributed is another matter entirely.

The world's wealth is concentrated among the advanced economies. In a comparative worldview, Africa is almost lost to sight and most of Asia, the largest and most populous continent, is sharply reduced in scale. Measured by average personal income, the contrasts are just as striking. More than half the world's population gets by, sort of, on about two dollars a day.

The measure of purchasing power illustrates how much people from different countries would be able to spend if they were buying the same goods in the same supermarket.

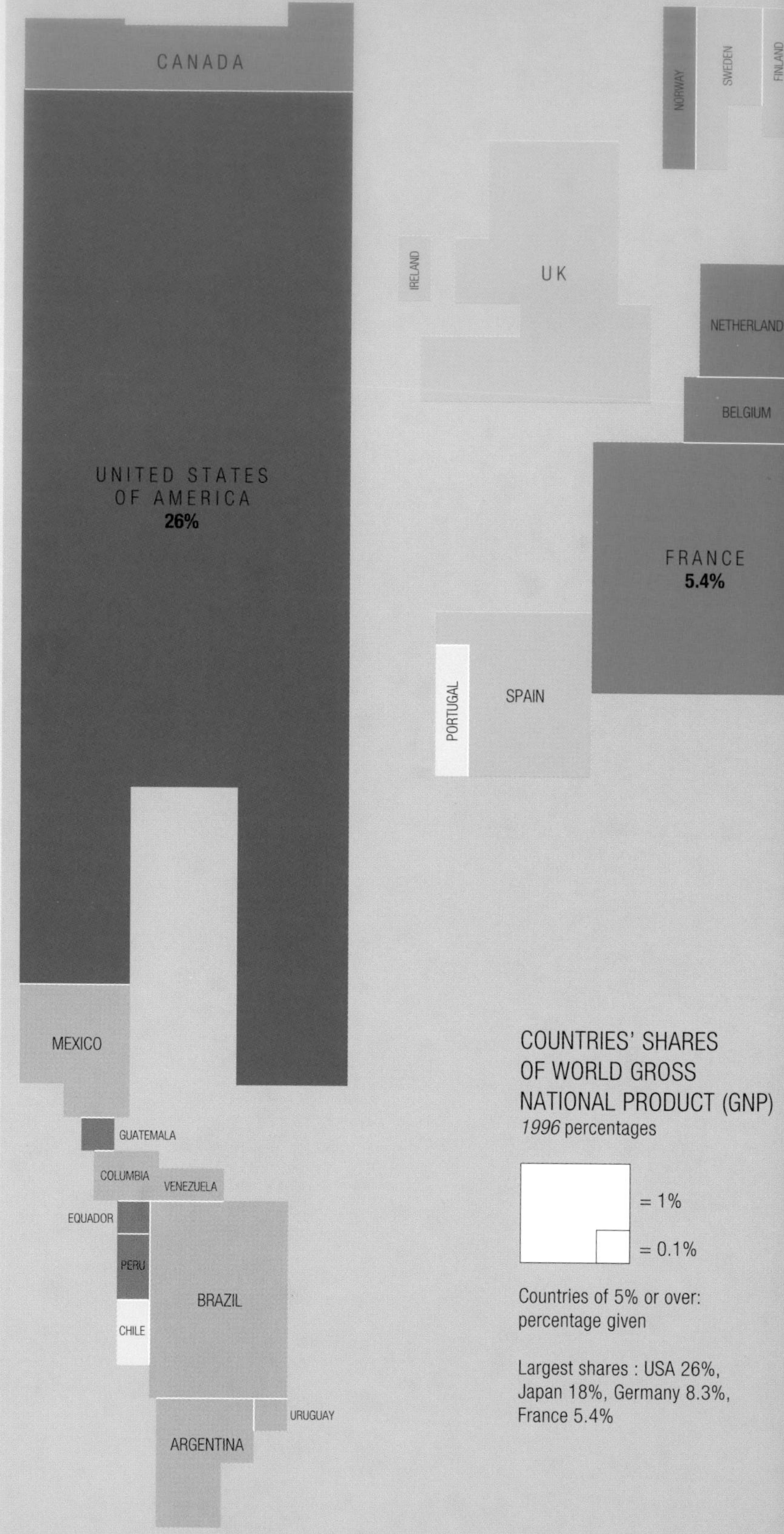
CANADA
UNITED STATES OF AMERICA
26%
MEXICO
GUATEMALA
COLUMBIA
VENEZUELA
EQUADOR
PERU
CHILE
BRAZIL
URUGUAY
ARGENTINA
NORWAY
SWEDEN
FINLAND
IRELAND
UK
NETHERLANDS
BELGIUM
FRANCE
5.4%
PORTUGAL
SPAIN
= 1%
= 0.1%

COUNTRIES' SHARES OF WORLD GROSS NATIONAL PRODUCT (GNP)
1996 percentages

Countries of 5% or over: percentage given

Largest shares : USA 26%, Japan 18%, Germany 8.3%, France 5.4%

National Income

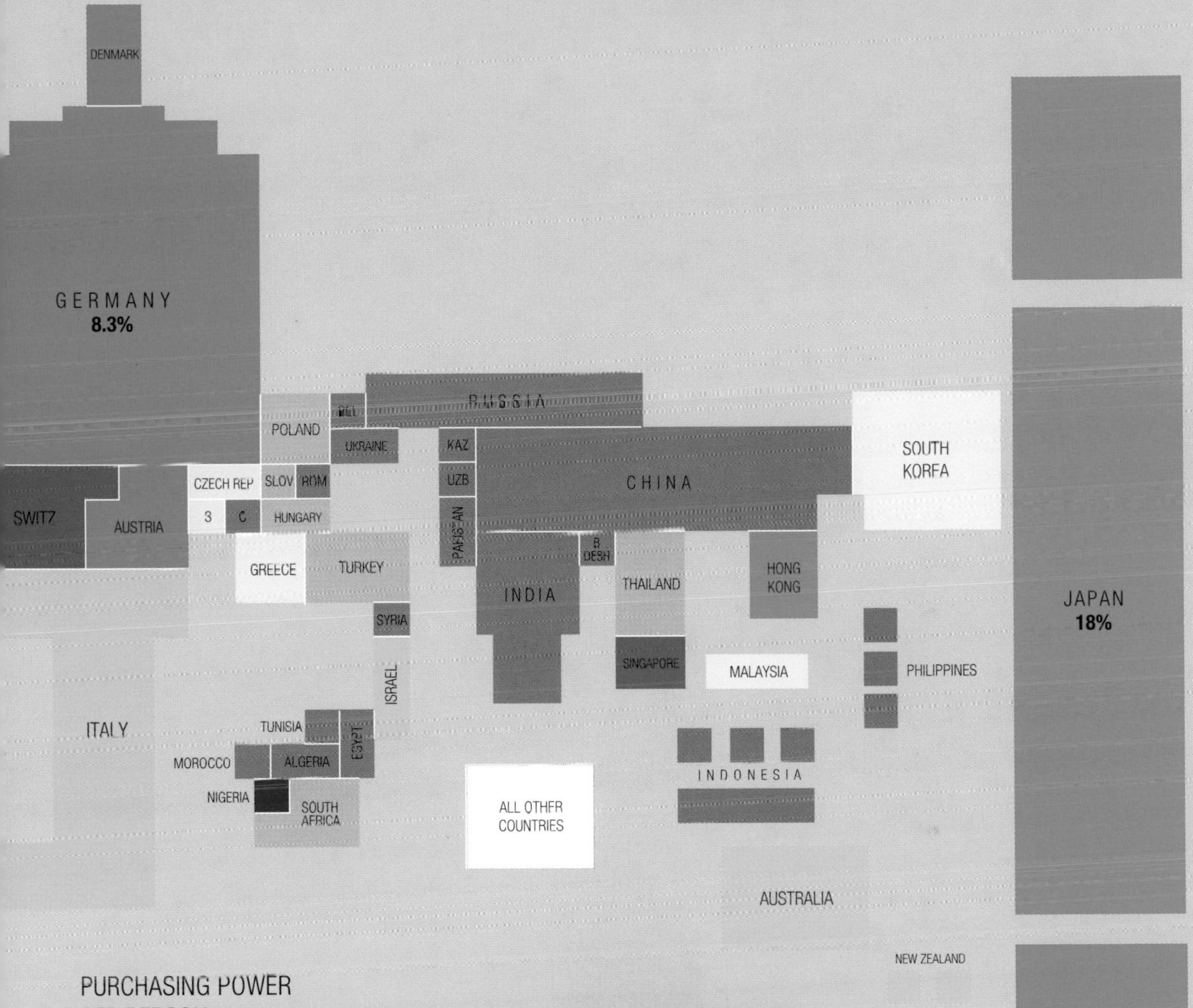

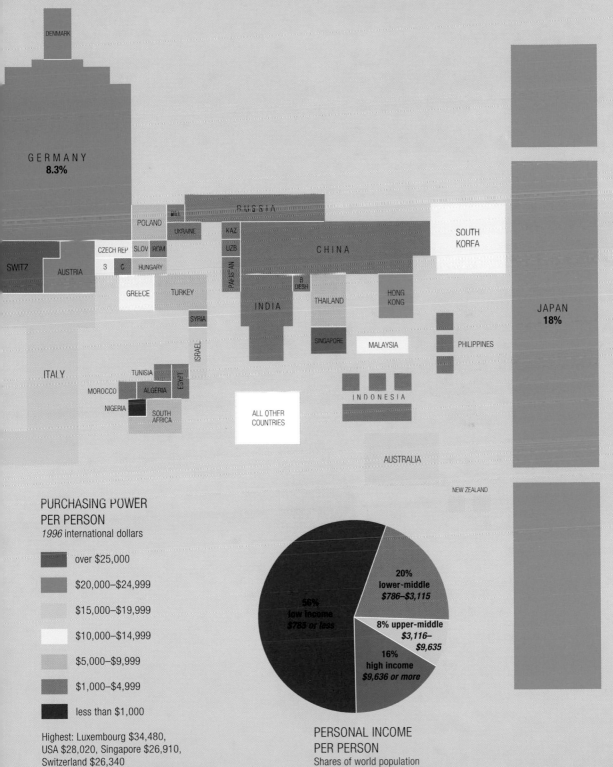

DENMARK

GERMANY
8.3%

POLAND
BEL
RUSSIA
UKRAINE
KAZ
UZB
PAKISTAN
CHINA
SOUTH KOREA
SWITZ
AUSTRIA
CZECH REP
SLOV
ROM
HUNGARY
GREECE
TURKEY
B DESH
INDIA
THAILAND
HONG KONG
JAPAN
18%
SYRIA
ISRAEL
SINGAPORE
MALAYSIA
PHILIPPINES
ITALY
TUNISIA
EGYPT
MOROCCO
ALGERIA
NIGERIA
SOUTH AFRICA
ALL OTHER COUNTRIES
INDONESIA
AUSTRALIA
NEW ZEALAND

PURCHASING POWER
PER PERSON
1996 international dollars

- over $25,000
- $20,000–$24,999
- $15,000–$19,999
- $10,000–$14,999
- $5,000–$9,999
- $1,000–$4,999
- less than $1,000

Highest: Luxembourg $34,480,
USA $28,020, Singapore $26,910,
Switzerland $26,340
Lowest: Ethiopia and Mozambique $500,
Sierra Leone $510, Burundi $590

Source: *World Bank Atlas 1998*

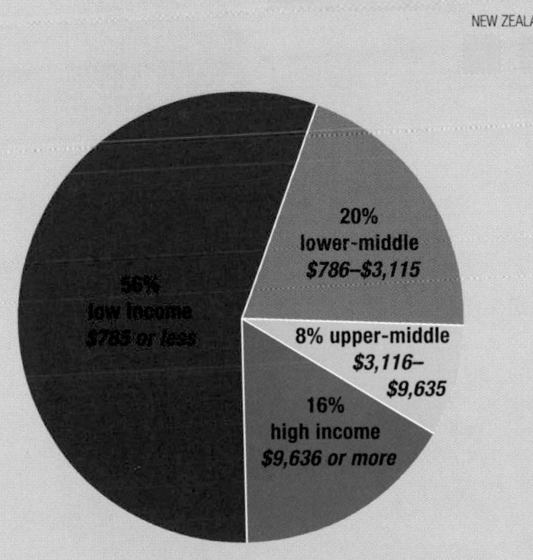

56% low income $785 or less
20% lower-middle $786–$3,115
8% upper-middle $3,116–$9,635
16% high income $9,636 or more

PERSONAL INCOME
PER PERSON
Shares of world population
in each income group
1996 percentages

Source: *World Bank Atlas 1998*

Part Three Work

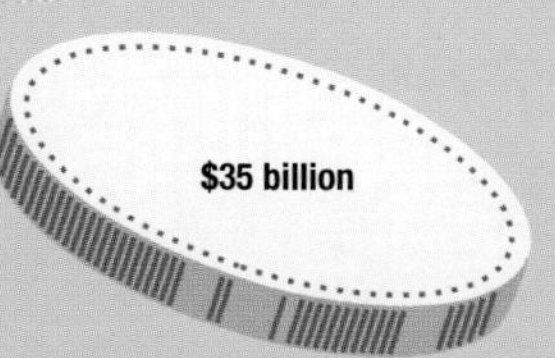
$35 billion

BUSINESS ENTERTAINMENT
IN JAPAN *1997*

Source: UNDP, 1998

With the first development of modern heavy industry in the nineteenth century, there started to be more jobs in manufacturing than in agriculture. In the final two decades of the twentieth century, the next stage has been reached: as the most important source of employment, industry is giving way to the service sector, including the growing information economy. The balance of employment between the three broad sectors of agriculture, industry and services is a quick guide to how economically advanced a country is.

In all sectors, the work of people is continually being reinforced and often replaced by the work of machines. Robotics and computerization mean that fewer workers can fulfill more tasks. The range of tasks that need to be performed by humans is narrowing daily.

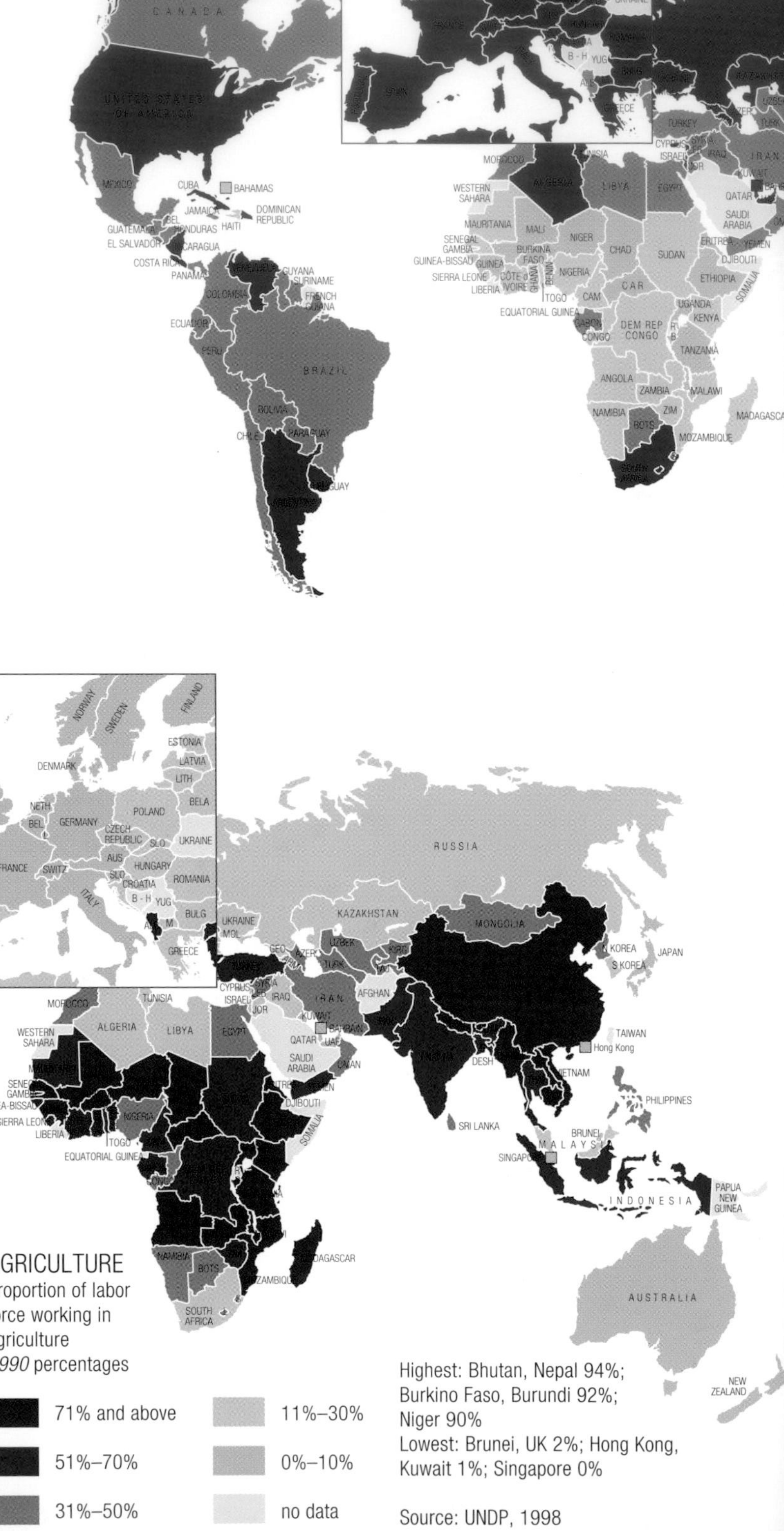
ICELAND
CANADA
UNITED STATES OF AMERICA
MEXICO
CUBA
BAHAMAS
JAMAICA
DOMINICAN REPUBLIC
HAITI
GUATEMALA
BEL
HONDURAS
EL SALVADOR
NICARAGUA
COSTA RICA
PANAMA
VENEZUELA
GUYANA
SURINAME
FRENCH GUIANA
COLOMBIA
ECUADOR
PERU
BRAZIL
BOLIVIA
PARAGUAY
CHILE
URUGUAY
ARGENTINA
NORWAY
SWEDEN
FINLAND
ESTONIA
LATVIA
LITH
DENMARK
IRELAND
U.K.
NETH
BEL
GERMANY
POLAND
BELA
CZECH REPUBLIC
SLO
UKRAINE
FRANCE
SWITZ
AUS
HUNGARY
SLO
CROATIA
ROMANIA
B-H
YUG
ITALY
BULG
PORTUGAL
SPAIN
GREECE
MOL
RUSSIA
KAZAKHSTAN
MONGOLIA
UZBEK
TURK
KYRG
GEO
AZER
TURKEY
CYPRUS
SYRIA
ISRAEL
JOR
IRAQ
IRAN
AFGHAN
KUWAIT
BAHRAIN
QATAR
UAE
SAUDI ARABIA
OMAN
YEMEN
MOROCCO
TUNISIA
ALGERIA
LIBYA
EGYPT
WESTERN SAHARA
MAURITANIA
MALI
NIGER
SENEGAL
GAMBIA
GUINEA-BISSAU
GUINEA
BURKINA FASO
CHAD
SUDAN
ERITREA
DJIBOUTI
SIERRA LEONE
LIBERIA
CÔTE D'IVOIRE
GHANA
TOGO
BENIN
NIGERIA
CAM
CAR
ETHIOPIA
SOMALIA
EQUATORIAL GUINEA
GABON
CONGO
DEM REP CONGO
UGANDA
KENYA
TANZANIA
ANGOLA
ZAMBIA
MALAWI
NAMIBIA
ZIM
BOTS
MOZAMBIQUE
MADAGASCAR
SOUTH AFRICA
INDIA
DESH
SRI LANKA
N KOREA
S KOREA
JAPAN
TAIWAN
Hong Kong
VIETNAM
PHILIPPINES
BRUNEI
MALAYSIA
SINGAPORE
INDONESIA
PAPUA NEW GUINEA
AUSTRALIA
NEW ZEALAND
AGRICULTURE
Proportion of labor force working in agriculture
1990 percentages
71% and above
51%–70%
31%–50%
11%–30%
0%–10%
no data
Highest: Bhutan, Nepal 94%; Burkino Faso, Burundi 92%; Niger 90%
Lowest: Brunei, UK 2%; Hong Kong, Kuwait 1%; Singapore 0%
Source: UNDP, 1998

Jobs

MONGOLIA
KOREA
JAPAN
CHINA
TAIWAN
Hong Kong
BURMA
VIETNAM
THAI
CAM
PHILIPPINES
SRI LANKA
BRUNEI
SINGAPORE
INDONESIA
PAPUA NEW GUINEA
NEW ZEALAND

INDUSTRY

Proportion of labor force working in industry
1990 percentages

- 36% and above
- 26%–35%
- 16%–25%
- 6%–15%
- 0%–5%
- no data

Highest: Romania 47%; Slovenia 46%; Czech Republic 45%; Russia 42%
Lowest: Nepal 0%; Bhutan 1%; Burkino Faso, Guinea, Guinea-Bissau, Mali 2%

Source: UNDP, 1998

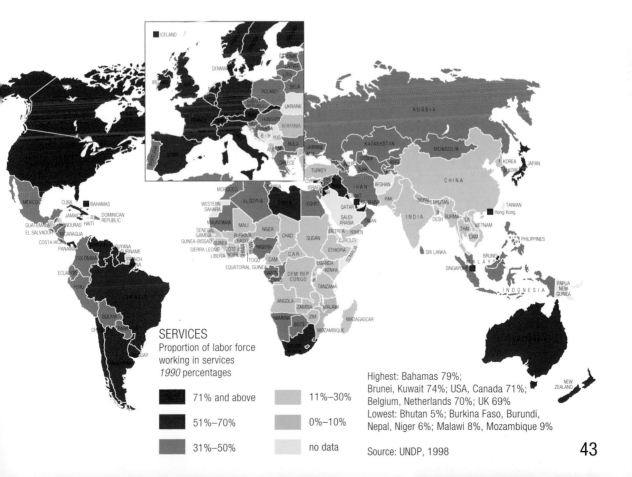

SERVICES

Proportion of labor force working in services
1990 percentages

- 71% and above
- 51%–70%
- 31%–50%
- 11%–30%
- 0%–10%
- no data

Highest: Bahamas 79%; Brunei, Kuwait 74%; USA, Canada 71%; Belgium, Netherlands 70%; UK 69%
Lowest: Bhutan 5%; Burkina Faso, Burundi, Nepal, Niger 6%; Malawi 8%, Mozambique 9%

Source: UNDP, 1998

The global economy requires large numbers of diligent, unskilled or semi-skilled, low-paid workers. An increasing proportion of them is female.

Between women and men in the labor market, there are many countries where the terms are slowly becoming more equal. In a few countries, the amount of paid maternity leave that is available for new mothers approaches the amount of leave they need. In some countries, some women are finding an almost fair share of places in management. But in most of the world, women are still expected to do more than men in raising children and still get paid less for working more.

GREENLAND
CANADA
UNITED STATES OF AMERICA
MEXICO
22%
CUBA
BAHAMAS
DOMINICAN REPUBLIC
JAMAICA
HAITI
BELIZE
HONDURAS
GUATEMALA
EL SALVADOR
NICARAGUA
COSTA RICA
PANAMA
BARBADOS
TRINIDAD & TOBAGO
GUYANA
SURINAME
FRENCH GUIANA (Fr)
VENEZUELA
COLOMBIA
ECUADOR
PERU
BRAZIL
BOLIVIA
PARAGUAY
CHILE
ARGENTINA
URUGUAY
CAPE VERDE
WESTERN SAHARA
GAMBIA
GUINEA-BISSAU
SIERRA LEONE

MANAGEMENT

Women as a proportion of administrators and managers in selected countries
latest available date percentages

Source: UNDP, 1998

Italy
54%
Australia
USA
43%
Canada
42%
Poland
35%
UK
33%
Spain
32%
Switzerland
28%
Czech Republic
27%
Germany
26%
Austria
24%
Mali
Netherlands
20%
China
Egypt
Papua New Guinea
12%
Mozambique
11%
France
Japan
9%
India
2%

Women Working

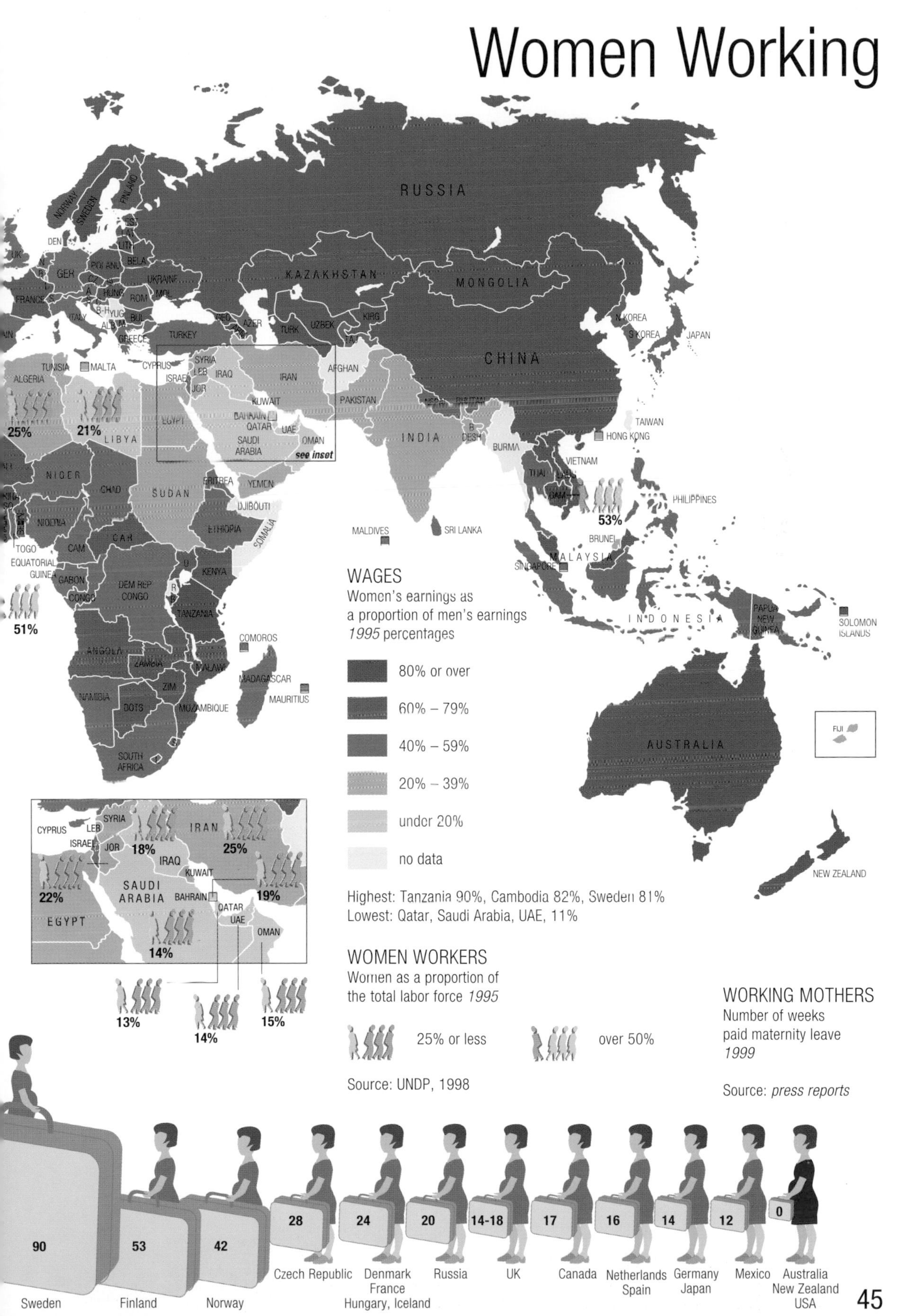

RUSSIA
KAZAKHSTAN
MONGOLIA
CHINA
N KOREA
S KOREA
JAPAN
NORWAY
SWEDEN
FINLAND
DEN
UK
GER
POLAND
BELA
UKRAINE
FRANCE
ITALY
HUNG
ROM
MOL
BUL
GREECE
TURKEY
GEO
AZER
TURK
UZBEK
KIRG
AFGHAN
PAKISTAN
IRAN
IRAQ
SYRIA
LEB
ISRAEL
JOR
KUWAIT
BAHRAIN
QATAR
UAE
SAUDI ARABIA
OMAN
see inset
INDIA
NEPAL
BHUTAN
B DESH
BURMA
TAIWAN
HONG KONG
VIETNAM
THAI
LAOS
CAM
PHILIPPINES
53%
MALDIVES
SRI LANKA
BRUNEI
MALAYSIA
SINGAPORE
INDONESIA
PAPUA NEW GUINEA
SOLOMON ISLANDS
AUSTRALIA
FIJI
NEW ZEALAND
TUNISIA
MALTA
CYPRUS
ALGERIA
25%
21%
LIBYA
EGYPT
NIGER
CHAD
SUDAN
ERITREA
YEMEN
DJIBOUTI
ETHIOPIA
SOMALIA
NIGERIA
CAR
CAM
TOGO
EQUATORIAL GUINEA
GABON
CONGO
DEM REP CONGO
KENYA
TANZANIA
51%
COMOROS
ANGOLA
ZAMBIA
MALAWI
MADAGASCAR
MAURITIUS
ZIM
NAMIBIA
BOTS
MOZAMBIQUE
SOUTH AFRICA
CYPRUS
LEB
SYRIA
ISRAEL
JOR
18%
IRAN
25%
IRAQ
KUWAIT
22%
SAUDI ARABIA
BAHRAIN
19%
QATAR
UAE
EGYPT
OMAN
14%
13%
14%
15%
WAGES
Women's earnings as a proportion of men's earnings 1995 percentages
80% or over
60% – 79%
40% – 59%
20% – 39%
under 20%
no data
Highest: Tanzania 90%, Cambodia 82%, Sweden 81%
Lowest: Qatar, Saudi Arabia, UAE, 11%
WOMEN WORKERS
Women as a proportion of the total labor force 1995
25% or less
over 50%
Source: UNDP, 1998
WORKING MOTHERS
Number of weeks paid maternity leave 1999
Source: press reports
90
Sweden
53
Finland
42
Norway
28
Czech Republic
24
Denmark
France
Hungary, Iceland
20
Russia
14-18
UK
17
Canada
16
Netherlands
Spain
14
Germany
Japan
12
Mexico
0
Australia
New Zealand
USA

Full employment is no longer a real goal of economic policy. If everybody has a job, there is less of the flexibility in the labor market that is deemed to be essential to economic growth. National economic success requires a degree of personal economic insecurity. Mass unemployment is now endemic in most of the poorer countries of the world and in some of the richer ones too, though statistical uncertainties make comparisons difficult. Long-term unemployment is a particular economic blight, because it dis-qualifies people for work, getting them out of working habits and making them strangers to work discipline.

It can be difficult for young people to find a worthwhile place in the labor market, and the more time passes after the end of formal education before they find a place, the harder it gets.

Towards the end of working life it can also be difficult to find worthwhile work. Many companies find a variety of reasons for not employing a person who only has 10 to 15 years left of working life, while hiring people who anyway risk losing their jobs in a few years due to the ups and downs of market economics.

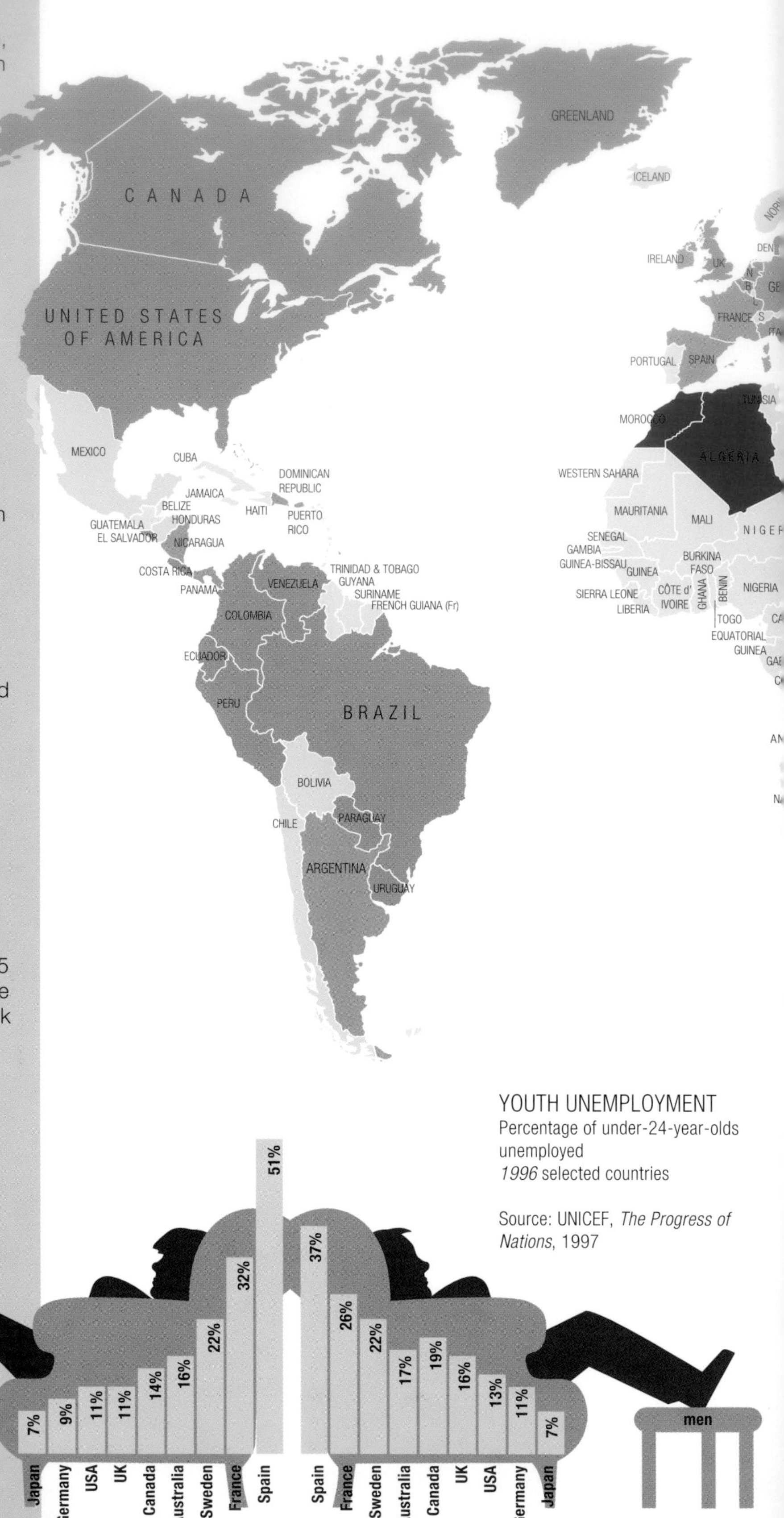
CANADA
UNITED STATES OF AMERICA
GREENLAND
ICELAND
IRELAND
UK
FRANCE
PORTUGAL
SPAIN
MOROCCO
ALGERIA
WESTERN SAHARA
MAURITANIA
MALI
SENEGAL
GAMBIA
GUINEA-BISSAU
GUINEA
SIERRA LEONE
LIBERIA
CÔTE d' IVOIRE
BURKINA FASO
GHANA
BENIN
TOGO
NIGERIA
EQUATORIAL GUINEA
MEXICO
CUBA
JAMAICA
BELIZE
HONDURAS
HAITI
DOMINICAN REPUBLIC
PUERTO RICO
GUATEMALA
EL SALVADOR
NICARAGUA
COSTA RICA
PANAMA
TRINIDAD & TOBAGO
GUYANA
SURINAME
FRENCH GUIANA (Fr)
VENEZUELA
COLOMBIA
ECUADOR
PERU
BRAZIL
BOLIVIA
PARAGUAY
CHILE
ARGENTINA
URUGUAY
YOUTH UNEMPLOYMENT
Percentage of under-24-year-olds unemployed
1996 selected countries
Source: UNICEF, *The Progress of Nations*, 1997
women
Japan 7%
Germany 9%
USA 11%
UK 11%
Canada 14%
Australia 16%
Sweden 22%
France 32%
Spain 51%
men
Spain 37%
France 26%
Sweden 22%
Australia 17%
Canada 19%
UK 16%
USA 13%
Germany 11%
Japan 7%

Unemployment

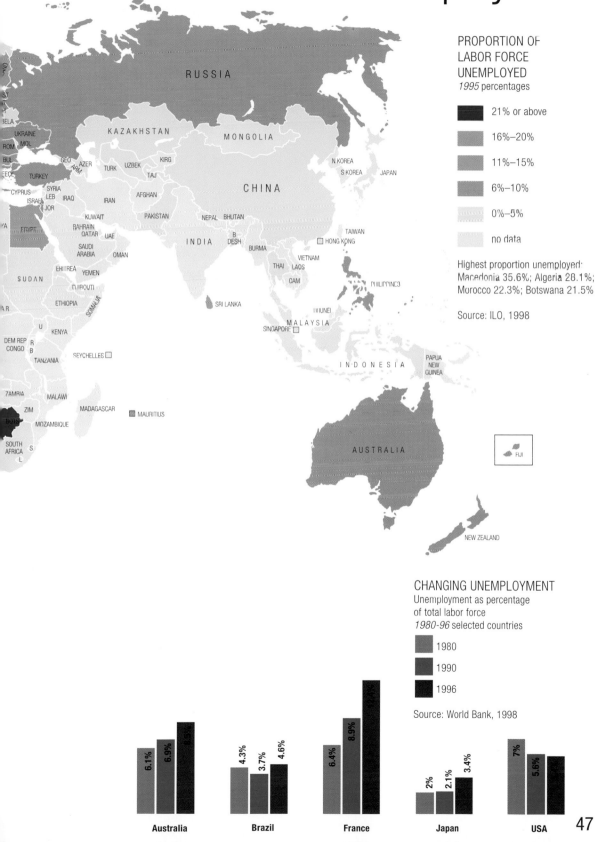

PROPORTION OF LABOR FORCE UNEMPLOYED
1995 percentages

- 21% or above
- 16%–20%
- 11%–15%
- 6%–10%
- 0%–5%
- no data

Highest proportion unemployed: Macedonia 35.6%; Algeria 28.1%; Morocco 22.3%; Botswana 21.5%

Source: ILO, 1998

CHANGING UNEMPLOYMENT
Unemployment as percentage of total labor force
1980-96 selected countries

	1980	1990	1996
Australia	6.1%	6.9%	[illegible]
Brazil	4.3%	3.7%	4.6%
France	6.4%	8.9%	[illegible]
Japan	2%	2.1%	3.4%
USA	7%	5.6%	[illegible]

Source: World Bank, 1998

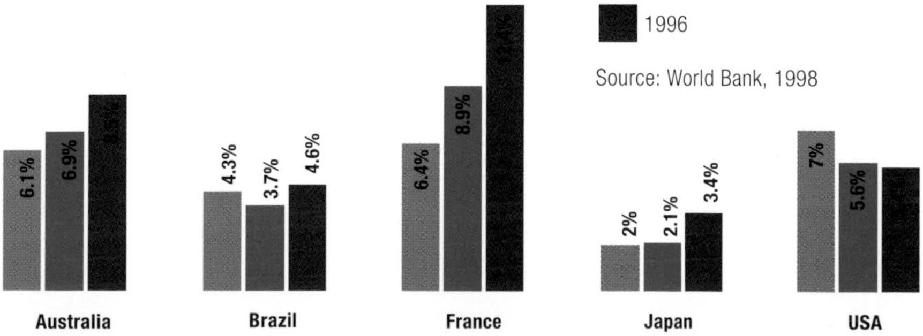

Would-be workers travel abroad under a dual push and pull effect.

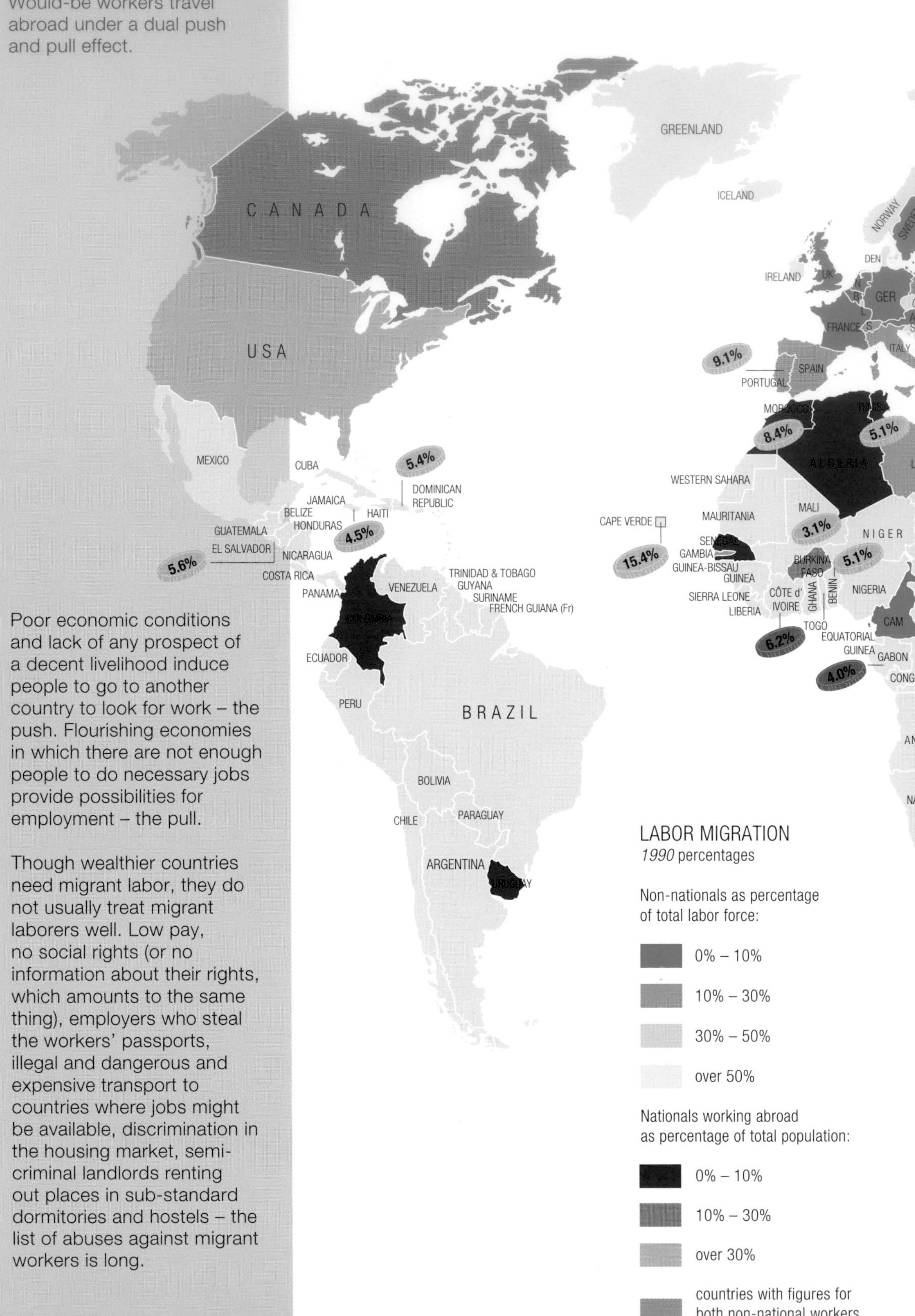
CANADA
USA
MEXICO
CUBA
GREENLAND
ICELAND
NORWAY
SWEDEN
DEN
IRELAND
UK
GER
FRANCE
ITALY
SPAIN
PORTUGAL
9.1%
MOROCCO
8.4%
5.1%
ALGERIA
LIBY
WESTERN SAHARA
MAURITANIA
MALI
3.1%
NIGER
CHAD
CAPE VERDE
15.4%
SENEGAL
GAMBIA
GUINEA-BISSAU
GUINEA
SIERRA LEONE
LIBERIA
CÔTE d' IVOIRE
6.2%
GHANA
TOGO
BENIN
BURKINA FASO
5.1%
NIGERIA
CAM
EQUATORIAL GUINEA
GABON
4.0%
CONGO
ANGOLA
NAMIBIA
5.4%
DOMINICAN REPUBLIC
JAMAICA
HAITI
BELIZE
HONDURAS
4.5%
GUATEMALA
EL SALVADOR
5.6%
NICARAGUA
COSTA RICA
PANAMA
TRINIDAD & TOBAGO
GUYANA
SURINAME
FRENCH GUIANA (Fr)
VENEZUELA
COLOMBIA
ECUADOR
PERU
BRAZIL
BOLIVIA
PARAGUAY
CHILE
ARGENTINA
URUGUAY
LABOR MIGRATION
1990 percentages
Non-nationals as percentage of total labor force:
0% – 10%
10% – 30%
30% – 50%
over 50%
Nationals working abroad as percentage of total population:
0% – 10%
10% – 30%
over 30%
countries with figures for both non-national workers and nationals working abroad

Poor economic conditions and lack of any prospect of a decent livelihood induce people to go to another country to look for work – the push. Flourishing economies in which there are not enough people to do necessary jobs provide possibilities for employment – the pull.

Though wealthier countries need migrant labor, they do not usually treat migrant laborers well. Low pay, no social rights (or no information about their rights, which amounts to the same thing), employers who steal the workers' passports, illegal and dangerous and expensive transport to countries where jobs might be available, discrimination in the housing market, semi-criminal landlords renting out places in sub-standard dormitories and hostels – the list of abuses against migrant workers is long.

Working Abroad

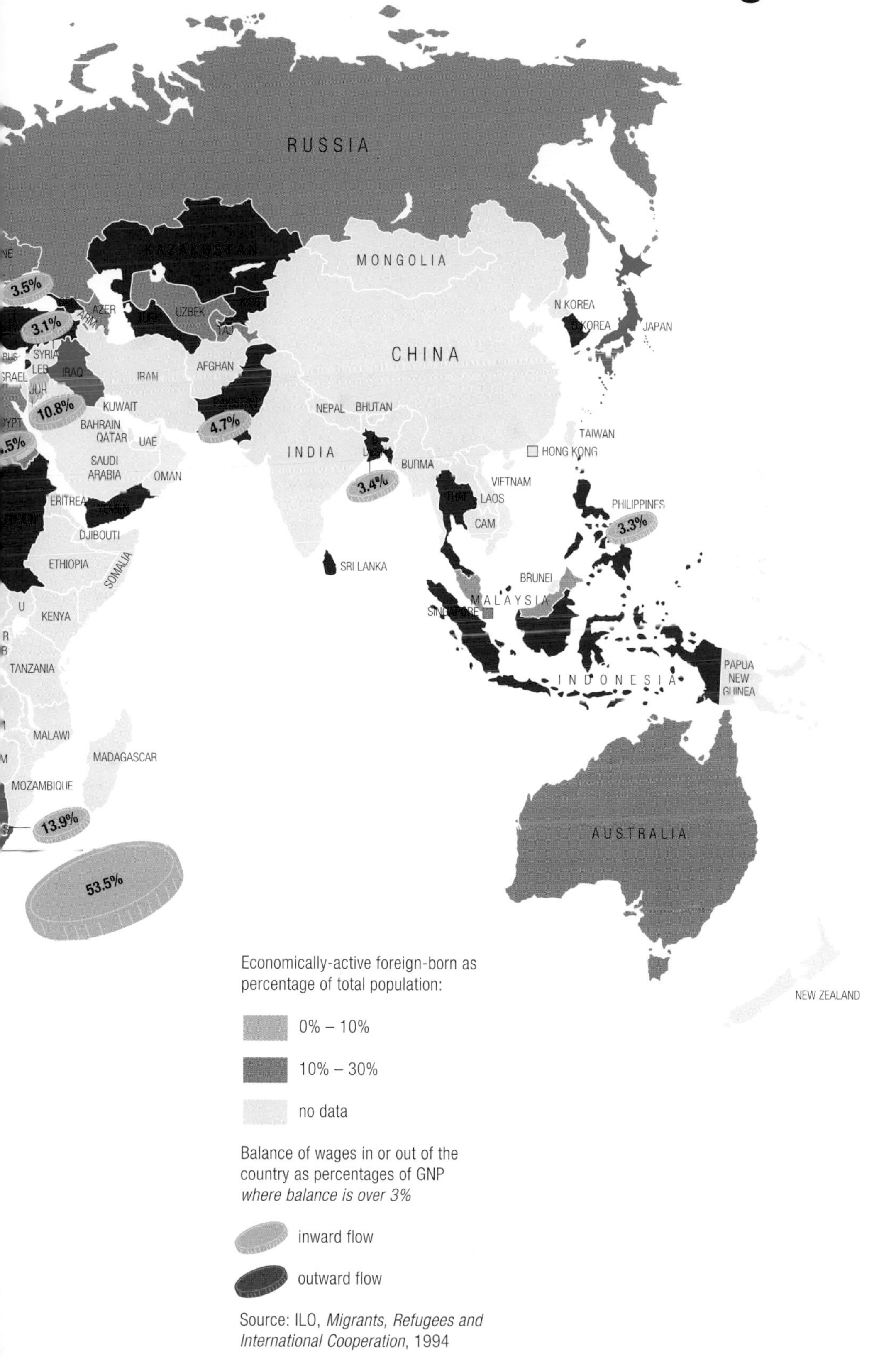
RUSSIA
MONGOLIA
CHINA
N KOREA
S KOREA
JAPAN
AZER
UZBEK
TAJ
AFGHAN
SYRIA
LEB
ISRAEL
IRAQ
IRAN
KUWAIT
BAHRAIN
QATAR
UAE
SAUDI ARABIA
OMAN
ERITREA
DJIBOUTI
ETHIOPIA
SOMALIA
KENYA
TANZANIA
MALAWI
MADAGASCAR
MOZAMBIQUE
NEPAL
BHUTAN
INDIA
BURMA
SRI LANKA
TAIWAN
HONG KONG
VIETNAM
LAOS
CAM
PHILIPPINES
BRUNEI
MALAYSIA
SINGAPORE
INDONESIA
PAPUA NEW GUINEA
AUSTRALIA
NEW ZEALAND
3.5%
3.1%
10.8%
4.7%
3.4%
3.3%
13.9%
53.5%

Economically-active foreign-born as percentage of total population:

0% – 10%

10% – 30%

no data

Balance of wages in or out of the country as percentages of GNP *where balance is over 3%*

inward flow

outward flow

Source: ILO, *Migrants, Refugees and International Cooperation*, 1994

Part Four Politics

THE WORLD'S PRIORITIES

Source: UNDP, 1998

Estimated cost of
providing basic
education for all

$6 billion

Military spending
in the world

$780 billion

The precondition for democracy is the ability to hold elections between competitive parties that are free to air their arguments and have equal access to public media, in which no ballot boxes are stuffed, no dead people miraculously turn out to vote, and nobody threatens you to make sure you vote the right way.

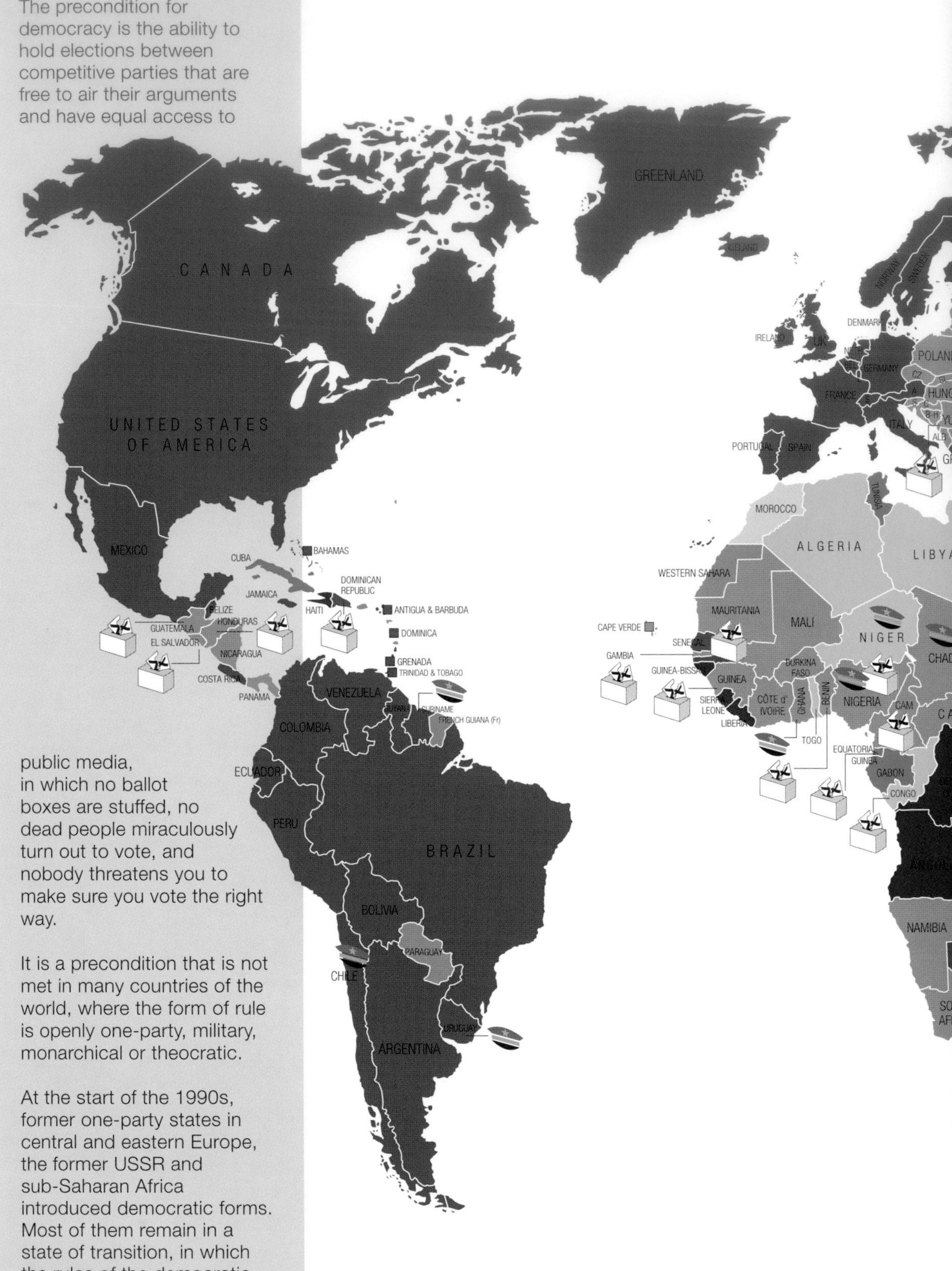
CANADA
GREENLAND
UNITED STATES OF AMERICA
MEXICO
CUBA
BAHAMAS
DOMINICAN REPUBLIC
JAMAICA
HAITI
BELIZE
HONDURAS
GUATEMALA
EL SALVADOR
NICARAGUA
COSTA RICA
PANAMA
ANTIGUA & BARBUDA
DOMINICA
GRENADA
TRINIDAD & TOBAGO
VENEZUELA
GUYANA
FRENCH GUIANA (Fr)
COLOMBIA
ECUADOR
PERU
BRAZIL
BOLIVIA
PARAGUAY
CHILE
URUGUAY
ARGENTINA
NORWAY
SWEDEN
DENMARK
IRELAND
UK
GERMANY
POLAND
CZ
HUNG
FRANCE
ITALY
SPAIN
MOROCCO
TUNISIA
ALGERIA
LIBYA
WESTERN SAHARA
MAURITANIA
MALI
NIGER
CHAD
CAPE VERDE
GAMBIA
GUINEA
BURKINA FASO
NIGERIA
LIBERIA
CÔTE d' IVOIRE
GHANA
TOGO
BENIN
CAM
EQUATORIAL GUINEA
GABON
CONGO
ANGOLA
NAMIBIA

It is a precondition that is not met in many countries of the world, where the form of rule is openly one-party, military, monarchical or theocratic.

At the start of the 1990s, former one-party states in central and eastern Europe, the former USSR and sub-Saharan Africa introduced democratic forms. Most of them remain in a state of transition, in which the rules of the democratic game are inconsistently respected.

Political Systems

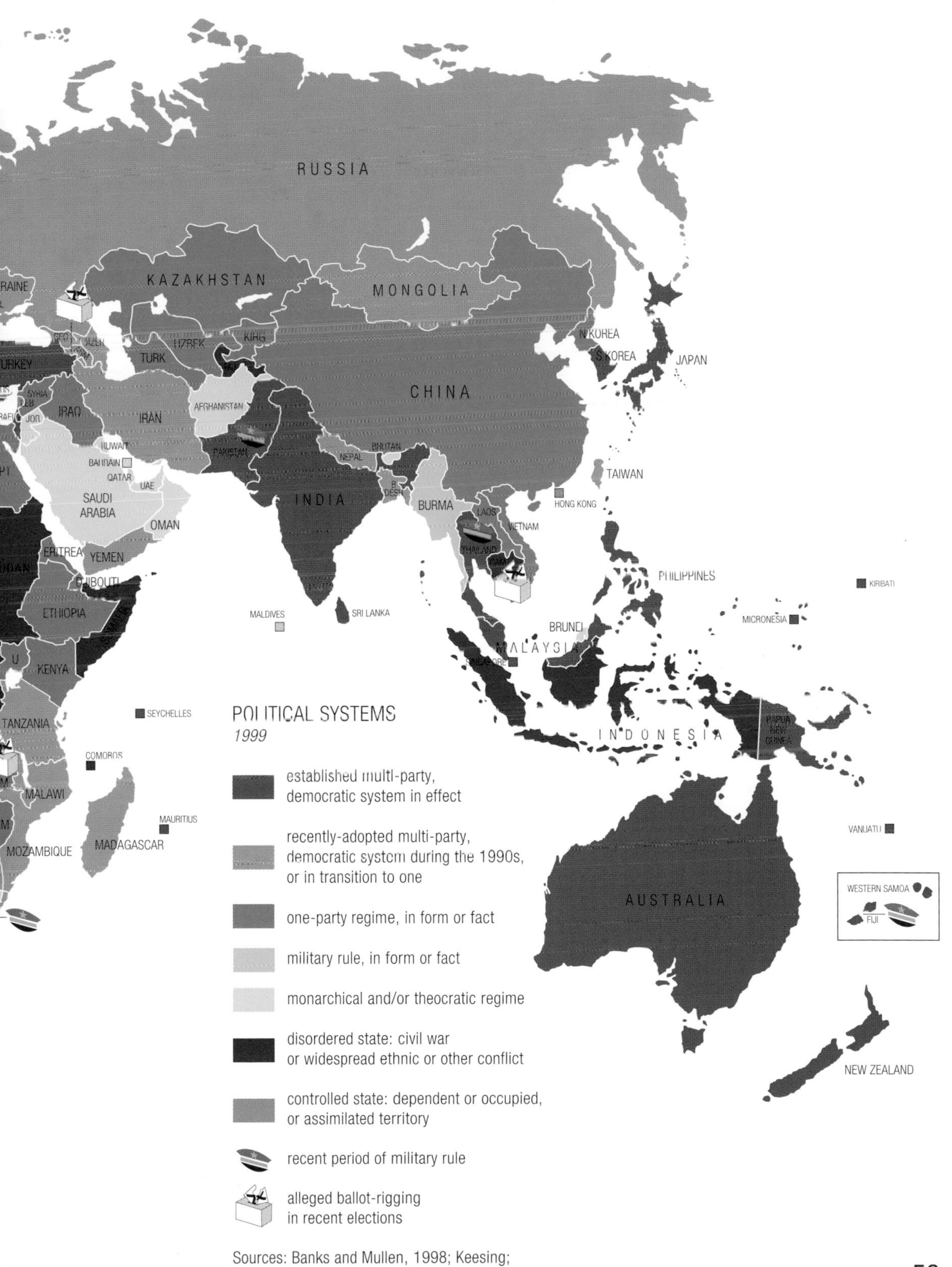
RUSSIA
KAZAKHSTAN
MONGOLIA
CHINA
N KOREA
S KOREA
JAPAN
TURK
KIRG
AFGHANISTAN
IRAQ
IRAN
JOR
SYRIA
KUWAIT
BAHRAIN
QATAR
UAE
SAUDI ARABIA
OMAN
YEMEN
ERITREA
DJIBOUTI
ETHIOPIA
KENYA
TANZANIA
MALAWI
MOZAMBIQUE
MADAGASCAR
COMOROS
MAURITIUS
SEYCHELLES
PAKISTAN
NEPAL
BHUTAN
B DESH
INDIA
BURMA
LAOS
VIETNAM
THAILAND
TAIWAN
HONG KONG
PHILIPPINES
MALDIVES
SRI LANKA
BRUNEI
MALAYSIA
INDONESIA
PAPUA NEW GUINEA
MICRONESIA
KIRIBATI
VANUATU
WESTERN SAMOA
FIJI
AUSTRALIA
NEW ZEALAND
POLITICAL SYSTEMS
1999
established multi-party, democratic system in effect
recently-adopted multi-party, democratic system during the 1990s, or in transition to one
one-party regime, in form or fact
military rule, in form or fact
monarchical and/or theocratic regime
disordered state: civil war or widespread ethnic or other conflict
controlled state: dependent or occupied, or assimilated territory
recent period of military rule
alleged ballot-rigging in recent elections

Sources: Banks and Mullen, 1998; Keesing; Kidron and Segal, 1995; press reports

In the late-1990s, known military spending had decreased to about two-thirds of its level in 1985, at the peak of the Cold War. Although there were some states whose arms' expenditure rose against the global trend, most governments took the opportunity to reduce their national military burdens.

In 1985 the world spent US $390 per person on the military; by 1997 it was US $240. In 1985 the world devoted just under 7 percent of annual economic output to the military; by 1997 it was barely over 4 percent.

The big cuts came in the first half of the 1990s. By 1996 military spending had largely stabilized, although at the end of the 20th century there were some signs of rearmament as the major powers' military stockpiles began to need re-equipping and new generations of weapon systems became available.

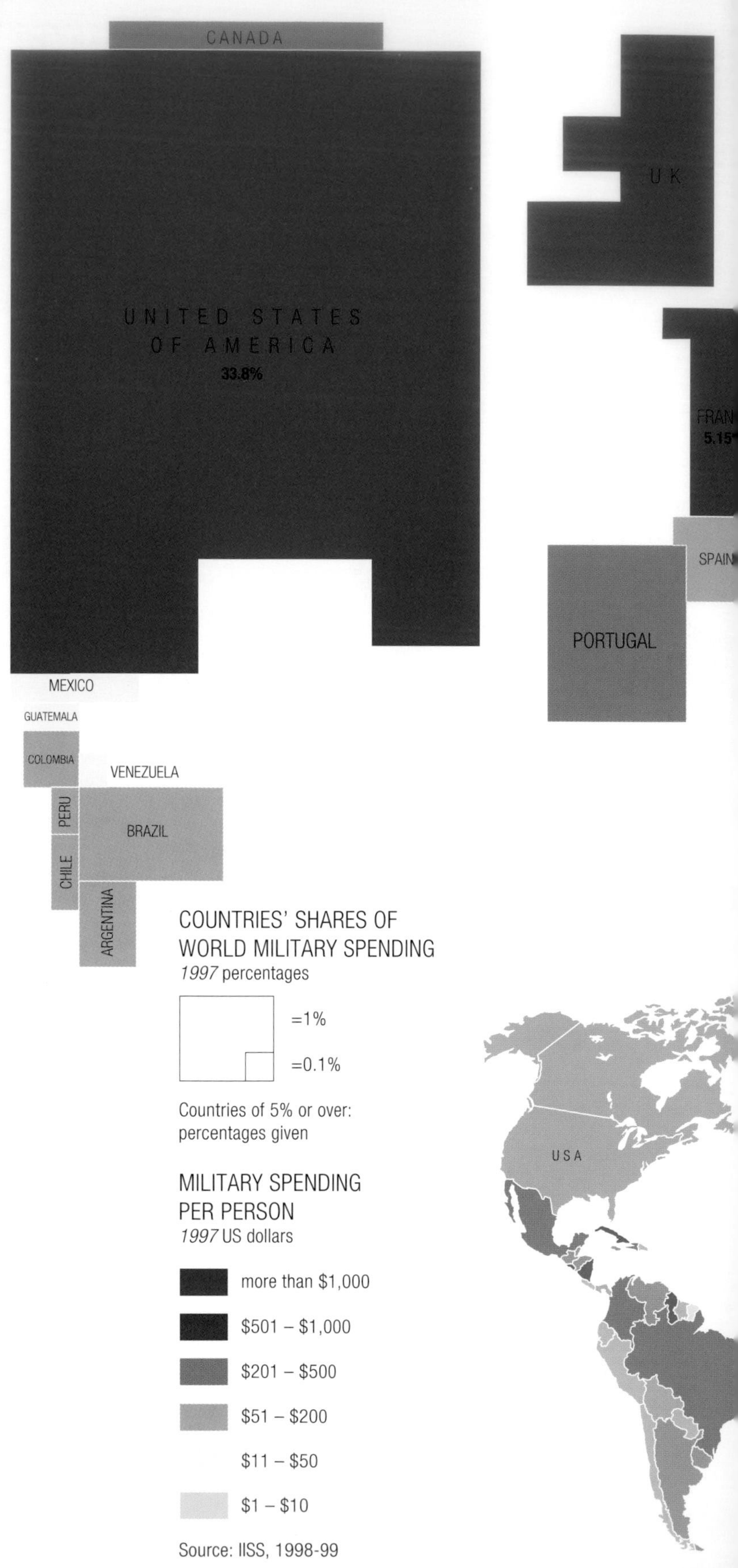
CANADA
UK
UNITED STATES OF AMERICA
33.8%
FRAN
5.15
SPAIN
PORTUGAL
MEXICO
GUATEMALA
COLOMBIA
VENEZUELA
PERU
BRAZIL
CHILE
ARGENTINA
COUNTRIES' SHARES OF WORLD MILITARY SPENDING
1997 percentages
=1%
=0.1%
Countries of 5% or over: percentages given
MILITARY SPENDING PER PERSON
1997 US dollars
more than $1,000
$501 – $1,000
$201 – $500
$51 – $200
$11 – $50
$1 – $10
Source: IISS, 1998-99
USA

Military Spending

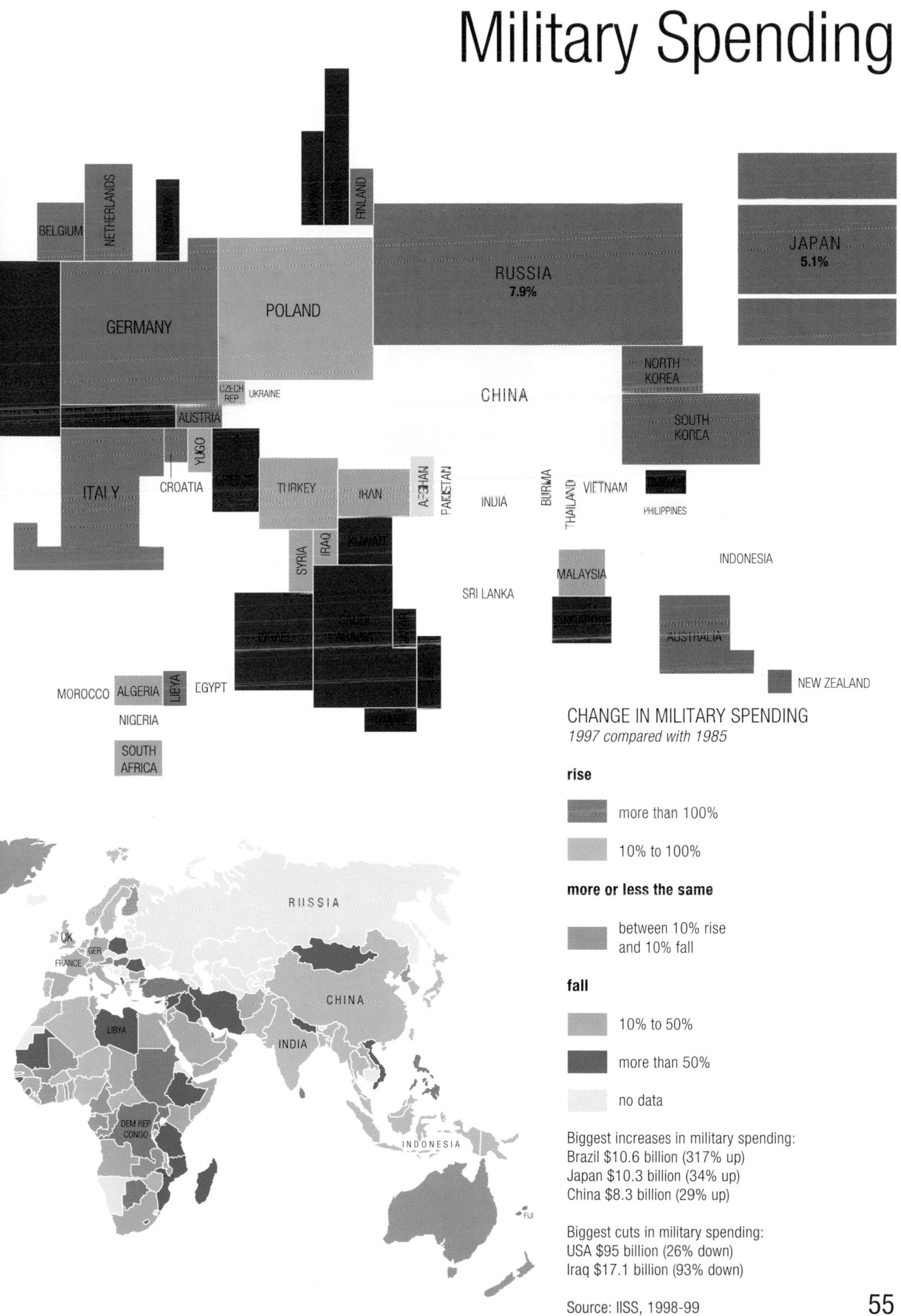

BELGIUM
NETHERLANDS
FINLAND
JAPAN
5.1%
RUSSIA
7.9%
GERMANY
POLAND
CZECH REP
UKRAINE
CHINA
NORTH KOREA
SOUTH KOREA
AUSTRIA
YUGO
ITALY
CROATIA
TURKEY
IRAN
PAKISTAN
INDIA
BURMA
THAILAND
VIETNAM
PHILIPPINES
SYRIA
IRAQ
INDONESIA
MALAYSIA
SRI LANKA
AUSTRALIA
NEW ZEALAND
MOROCCO
ALGERIA
LIBYA
EGYPT
NIGERIA
SOUTH AFRICA
CHANGE IN MILITARY SPENDING
1997 compared with 1985
rise
more than 100%
10% to 100%
more or less the same
between 10% rise and 10% fall
fall
10% to 50%
more than 50%
no data
UK
GER
FRANCE
RUSSIA
CHINA
LIBYA
INDIA
DEM REP CONGO
INDONESIA
FIJI

Biggest increases in military spending:
Brazil $10.6 billion (317% up)
Japan $10.3 billion (34% up)
China $8.3 billion (29% up)

Biggest cuts in military spending:
USA $95 billion (26% down)
Iraq $17.1 billion (93% down)

Source: IISS, 1998-99

The number of military personnel in the late 1990s is almost 20 percent fewer than in 1985, at the peak of the Cold War. In part this is the result of arms reductions and demobilization, but it is also because the increasingly sophisticated military technology used by the major powers requires fewer people to get the same firepower.

The military profession is traditionally the manly profession. Some national forces recruit women, although in most countries they are confined to support roles rather than being trained for combat.

The regular, uniformed military of the state are not the only armed force in many countries. Irregular forces are often highly motivated and as well-trained as most of the government forces they fight against. Some irregular forces, however, are little different from bandits, and some augment their strength by recruiting children. There are thought to be in excess of 200,000 soldiers aged under 15, serving in regions where there is war, or a high risk of it.

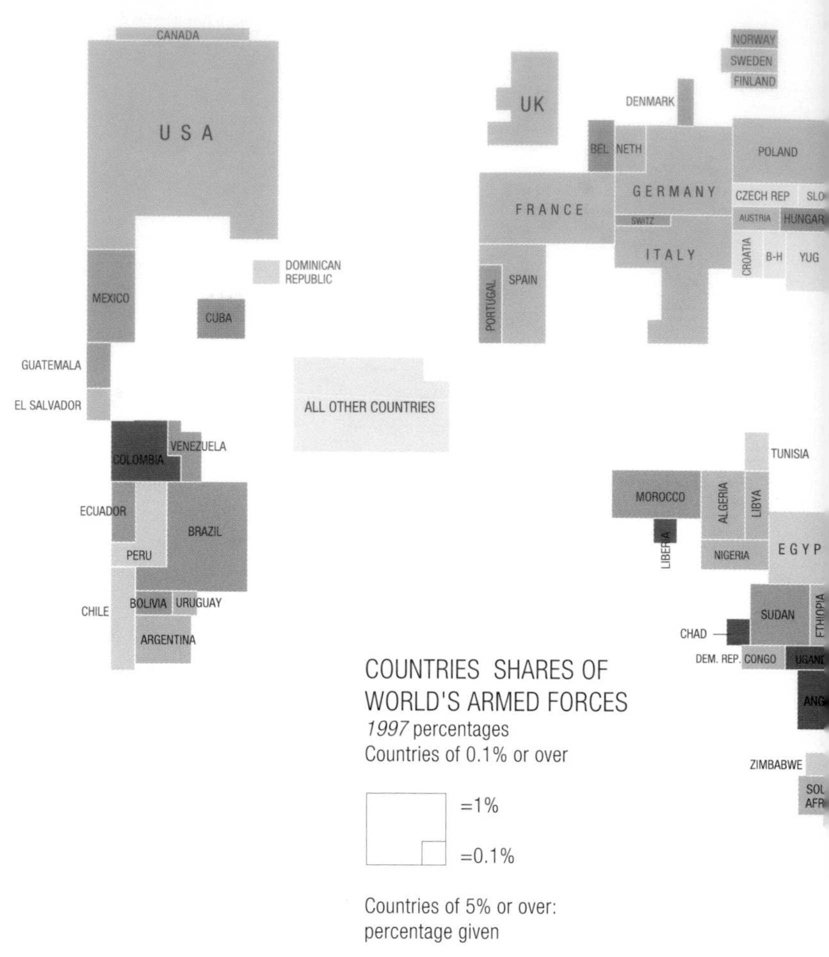
CANADA
USA
MEXICO
CUBA
DOMINICAN REPUBLIC
GUATEMALA
EL SALVADOR
COLOMBIA
VENEZUELA
ECUADOR
PERU
BRAZIL
CHILE
BOLIVIA
URUGUAY
ARGENTINA
ALL OTHER COUNTRIES
UK
DENMARK
NORWAY
SWEDEN
FINLAND
BEL
NETH
GERMANY
POLAND
FRANCE
CZECH REP
AUSTRIA
HUNGAR
SWITZ
ITALY
CROATIA
B-H
YUG
PORTUGAL
SPAIN
TUNISIA
MOROCCO
ALGERIA
LIBYA
LIBERIA
NIGERIA
EGYP
SUDAN
ETHIOPIA
CHAD
DEM. REP. CONGO
ZIMBABWE

COUNTRIES SHARES OF WORLD'S ARMED FORCES

1997 percentages

Countries of 0.1% or over

=1%

=0.1%

Countries of 5% or over: percentage given

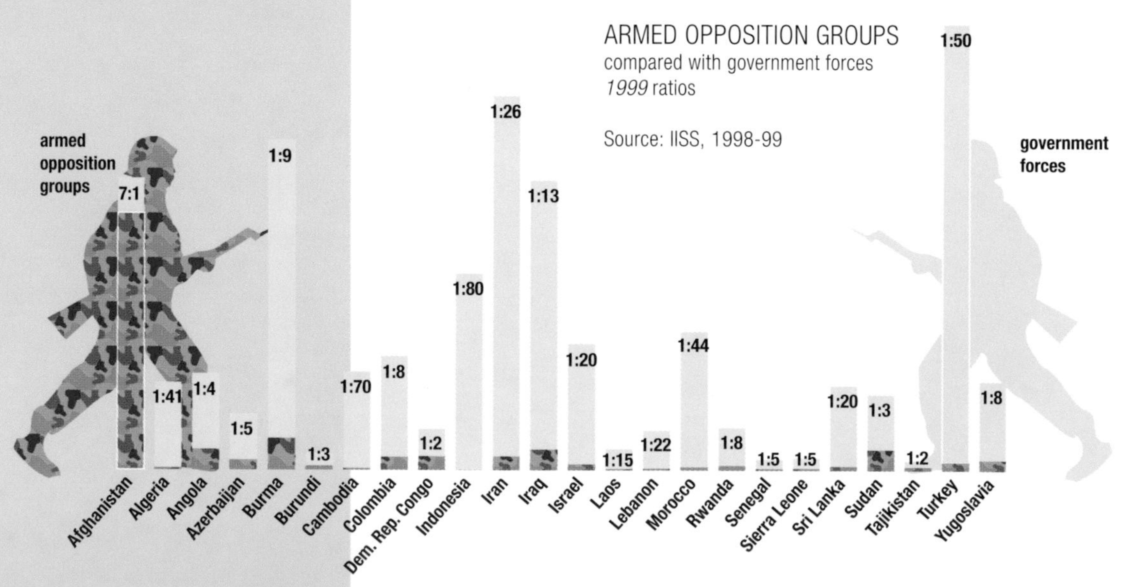
armed opposition groups
government forces
7:1
1:41
1:4
1:5
1:9
1:3
1:70
1:8
1:2
1:80
1:26
1:13
1:20
1:15
1:22
1:44
1:8
1:5
1:5
1:20
1:3
1:2
1:50
1:8
Afghanistan
Algeria
Angola
Azerbaijan
Burma
Burundi
Cambodia
Colombia
Dem. Rep. Congo
Indonesia
Iran
Iraq
Israel
Laos
Lebanon
Morocco
Rwanda
Senegal
Sierra Leone
Sri Lanka
Sudan
Tajikistan
Turkey
Yugoslavia

ARMED OPPOSITION GROUPS

compared with government forces

1999 ratios

Source: IISS, 1998-99

Armed Forces

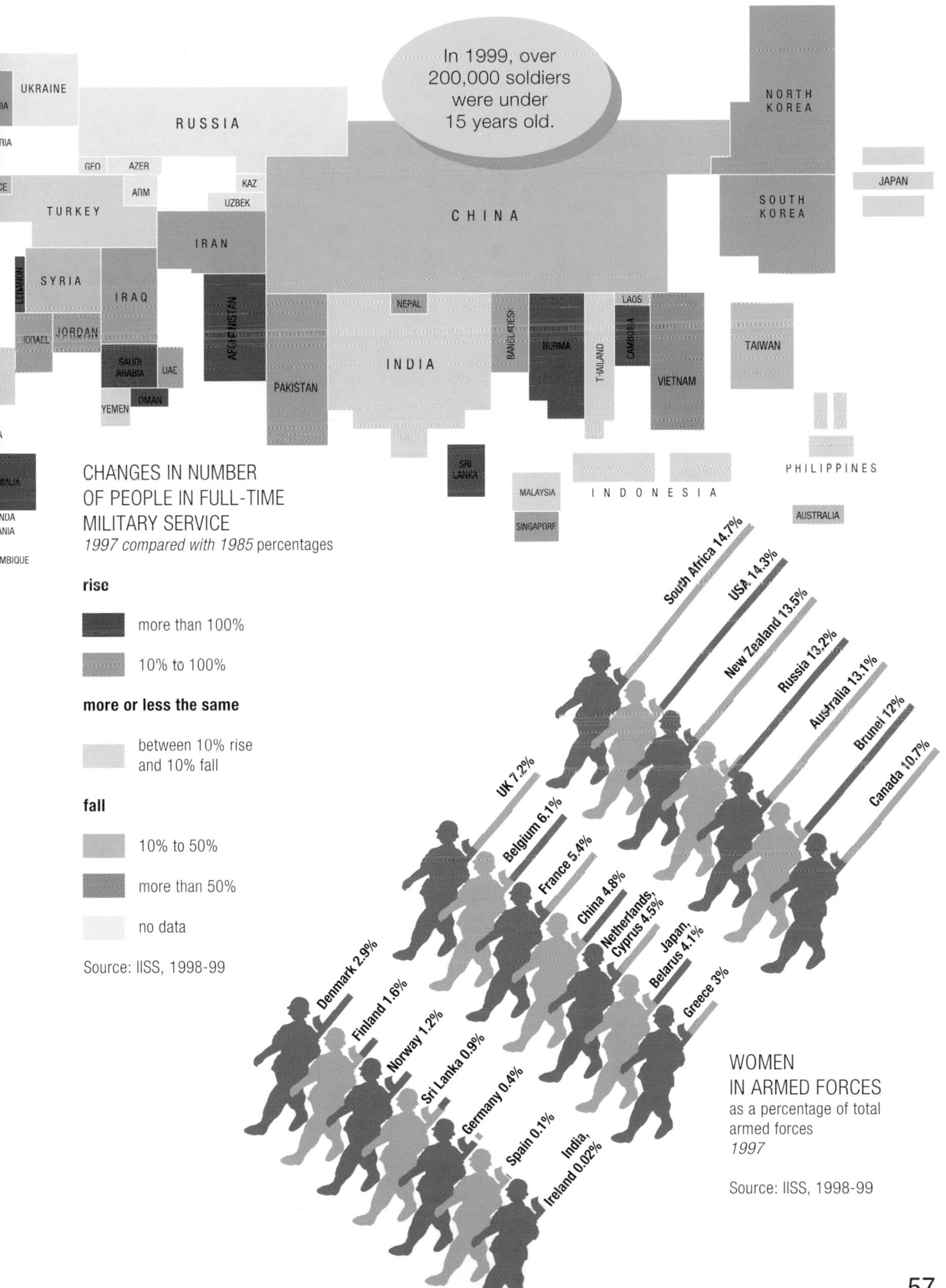

In 1999, over 200,000 soldiers were under 15 years old.
UKRAINE
RUSSIA
GEO
AZER
ARM
KAZ
UZBEK
TURKEY
IRAN
CHINA
NORTH KOREA
SOUTH KOREA
JAPAN
SYRIA
IRAQ
LEBANON
ISRAEL
JORDAN
AFGHANISTAN
SAUDI ARABIA
UAE
OMAN
YEMEN
PAKISTAN
NEPAL
INDIA
BANGLADESH
BURMA
THAILAND
LAOS
CAMBODIA
VIETNAM
TAIWAN
SRI LANKA
MALAYSIA
SINGAPORE
INDONESIA
PHILIPPINES
AUSTRALIA
CHANGES IN NUMBER OF PEOPLE IN FULL-TIME MILITARY SERVICE
1997 compared with 1985 percentages
rise
more than 100%
10% to 100%
more or less the same
between 10% rise and 10% fall
fall
10% to 50%
more than 50%
no data
Source: IISS, 1998-99
South Africa 14.7%
USA 14.3%
New Zealand 13.5%
Russia 13.2%
Australia 13.1%
Brunei 12%
Canada 10.7%
UK 7.2%
Belgium 6.1%
France 5.4%
China 4.8%
Netherlands, Cyprus 4.5%
Japan, Belarus 4.1%
Greece 3%
Denmark 2.9%
Finland 1.6%
Norway 1.2%
Sri Lanka 0.9%
Germany 0.4%
Spain 0.1%
India, Ireland 0.02%
WOMEN IN ARMED FORCES
as a percentage of total armed forces
1997
Source: IISS, 1998-99

Most armed conflicts in the 1990s are within states rather than between them; fewer than 10 percent of the decade's wars were classic inter-state clashes. However, outside powers often get involved, supporting this or that faction, or attempting to impose a peace settlement in the name of regional security and stability.

About one-third of today's wars have lasted more than 20 years. Most of them are carried out at relatively low-intensity for most of the time, often confined to one or two remote areas of a state. They are unlikely to catch the eye of the global news media unless a major humanitarian crisis erupts.

Wars are predominantly found in poorer countries with unfair economic and political systems. Although the most ethnically-mixed countries are not always the most war-prone, when economic and political injustices are at the expense of one ethnic group against another, the chances of war are high.

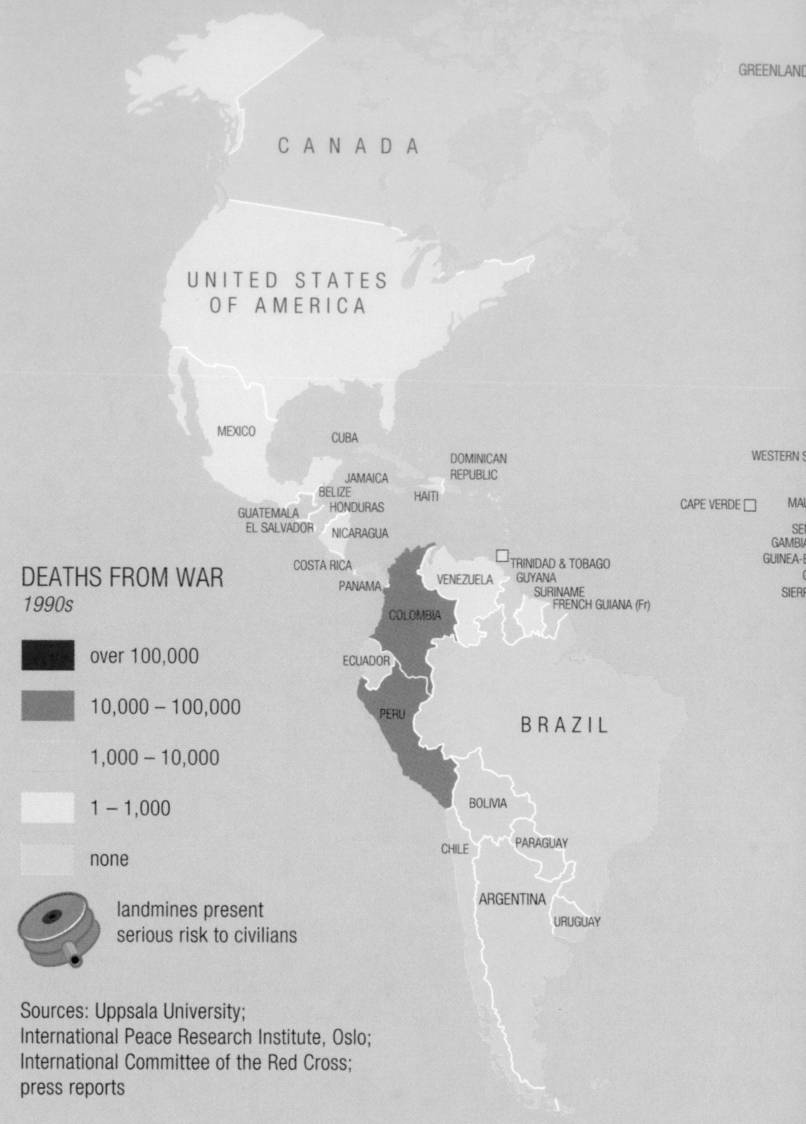
GREENLAND
CANADA
UNITED STATES OF AMERICA
MEXICO
CUBA
DOMINICAN REPUBLIC
JAMAICA
BELIZE
HAITI
HONDURAS
GUATEMALA
EL SALVADOR
NICARAGUA
COSTA RICA
PANAMA
TRINIDAD & TOBAGO
GUYANA
SURINAME
FRENCH GUIANA (Fr)
VENEZUELA
COLOMBIA
ECUADOR
PERU
BRAZIL
BOLIVIA
PARAGUAY
CHILE
ARGENTINA
URUGUAY
WESTERN SA
CAPE VERDE
MAUR
SENE
GAMBIA
GUINEA-BIS
GU
SIERRA
L
DEATHS FROM WAR
1990s
over 100,000
10,000 – 100,000
1,000 – 10,000
1 – 1,000
none
landmines present serious risk to civilians

Sources: Uppsala University; International Peace Research Institute, Oslo; International Committee of the Red Cross; press reports

NUMBER OF WARS BY REGION

1990–97

Sources: Uppsala University; International Peace Research Institute, Oslo

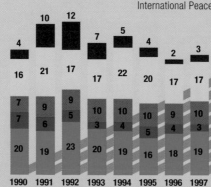

	1990	1991	1992	1993	1994	1995	1996	1997
Europe	4	10	12	7	5	4	2	3
Sub-Saharan Africa	16	21	17	17	22	20	17	17
North Africa and Middle East	7	9	9	10	10	10	9	10
Central and South America	7	6	5	3	4	5	4	3
Asia and Pacific	20	19	23	20	19	16	18	19

War

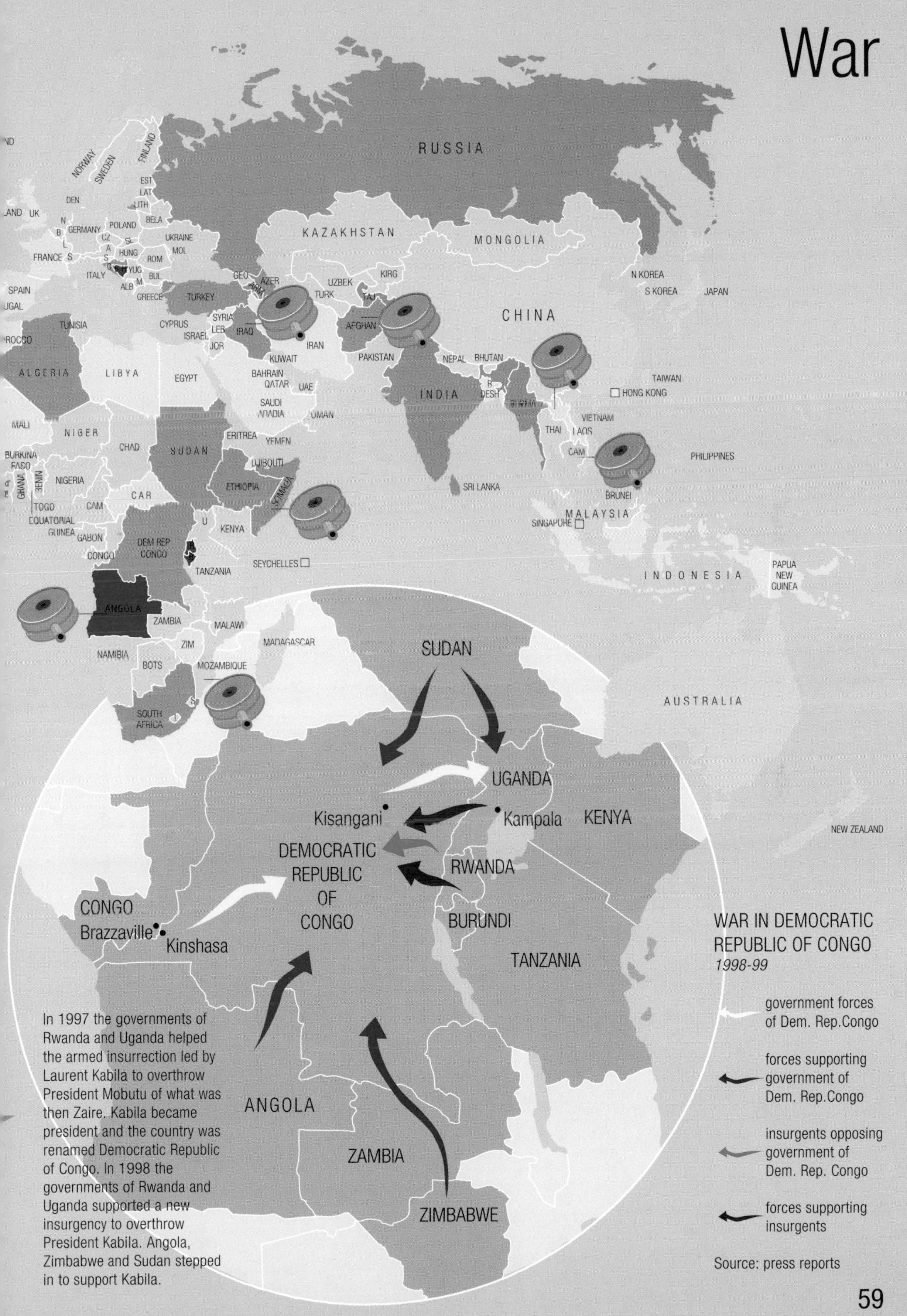
RUSSIA
NORWAY
SWEDEN
FINLAND
EST
LAT
LITH
DEN
UK
BELA
N
B
GERMANY
POLAND
CZ
SL
A
HUNG
UKRAINE
MOL
FRANCE
S
ROM
ITALY
YUG
BUL
ALB
M
GREECE
TURKEY
GEO
ARM
AZER
SPAIN
KAZAKHSTAN
UZBEK
TURK
KIRG
TAJ
MONGOLIA
N KOREA
S KOREA
JAPAN
CHINA
TUNISIA
CYPRUS
SYRIA
LEB
ISRAEL
JOR
IRAQ
IRAN
AFGHAN
PAKISTAN
KUWAIT
BAHRAIN
QATAR
UAE
SAUDI
OMAN
NEPAL
BHUTAN
INDIA
B DESH
BURMA
TAIWAN
HONG KONG
VIETNAM
THAI
LAOS
CAM
PHILIPPINES
SRI LANKA
BRUNEI
MALAYSIA
SINGAPORE
ALGERIA
LIBYA
EGYPT
MALI
NIGER
CHAD
SUDAN
ERITREA
YEMEN
DJIBOUTI
ETHIOPIA
SOMALIA
BURKINA FASO
GHANA
BENIN
NIGERIA
TOGO
CAR
CAM
EQUATORIAL GUINEA
GABON
CONGO
DEM REP CONGO
U
KENYA
TANZANIA
SEYCHELLES
INDONESIA
PAPUA NEW GUINEA
ANGOLA
ZAMBIA
MALAWI
MADAGASCAR
NAMIBIA
ZIM
BOTS
MOZAMBIQUE
SOUTH AFRICA
AUSTRALIA
NEW ZEALAND
SUDAN
UGANDA
Kisangani
Kampala
KENYA
DEMOCRATIC REPUBLIC OF CONGO
RWANDA
BURUNDI
CONGO
Brazzaville
Kinshasa
TANZANIA
ANGOLA
ZAMBIA
ZIMBABWE
WAR IN DEMOCRATIC REPUBLIC OF CONGO
1998-99
government forces of Dem. Rep.Congo
forces supporting government of Dem. Rep.Congo
insurgents opposing government of Dem. Rep. Congo
forces supporting insurgents
Source: press reports

In 1997 the governments of Rwanda and Uganda helped the armed insurrection led by Laurent Kabila to overthrow President Mobutu of what was then Zaire. Kabila became president and the country was renamed Democratic Republic of Congo. In 1998 the governments of Rwanda and Uganda supported a new insurgency to overthrow President Kabila. Angola, Zimbabwe and Sudan stepped in to support Kabila.

During the Cold War, United Nations' peacekeeping operations were launched approximately once every two and half years.

CANADA
UNITED STATES OF AMERICA
MEXICO
CUBA
JAMAICA
BELIZE
HONDURAS
GUATEMALA
EL SALVADOR
NICARAGUA
COSTA RICA
PANAMA
HAITI
DOMINICAN REPUBLIC
ANTIGUA & BARBUDA
TRINIDAD & TOBAGO
VENEZUELA
GUYANA
SURINAME
FRENCH GUIANA
COLOMBIA
ECUADOR
PERU
BRAZIL
BOLIVIA
CHILE
PARAGUAY
ARGENTINA
URUGUAY
CAPE VERDE
IRELAND
UK
DENMARK
NORWAY
SWEDEN
FINLAND
ESTONIA
LATVIA
LITHUANIA
BELARUS
NETH
BEL
L
GERMANY
POLAND
CZECH REPUBLIC
SLOVAKIA
UKRAINE
FRANCE
SWITZ
AUSTRIA
HUNGARY
ROMANIA
SLO
CROATIA
B - H
YUG
ITALY
BULGARIA
M
ALB
GREECE
PORTUGAL
SPAIN
TUNISIA
MALTA
MOROCCO
ALGERIA
LIBYA
WESTERN SAHARA
MAURITANIA
MALI
NIGER
CHAD
SENEGAL
GAMBIA
GUINEA-BISSAU
GUINEA
SIERRA LEONE
LIBERIA
BURKINA FASO
CÔTE d' IVOIRE
GHANA
TOGO
BENIN
NIGERIA
CAMEROON
EQUATORIAL GUINEA
CAR
GABON
CONGO
DEM REP CONGO
ANGOLA
ZAMBIA
NAMIBIA
BOTSWANA
SOUTH AFRICA
UN

Since the Cold War the rate of new peacekeeping operations has been about one every three months.

Traditional-style peacekeeping occurs with the agreement of all parties to a conflict after a peace agreement or ceasefire – when there is a peace to keep. Peacekeeping forces carry small arms only and use them only if under fire and as a last resort.

In 1992 the UN expanded the idea of peace operations to include preventive action and peace enforcement, for which fully-equipped armed forces could be required. Not all peacekeeping forces are under UN control.

Peacekeeping

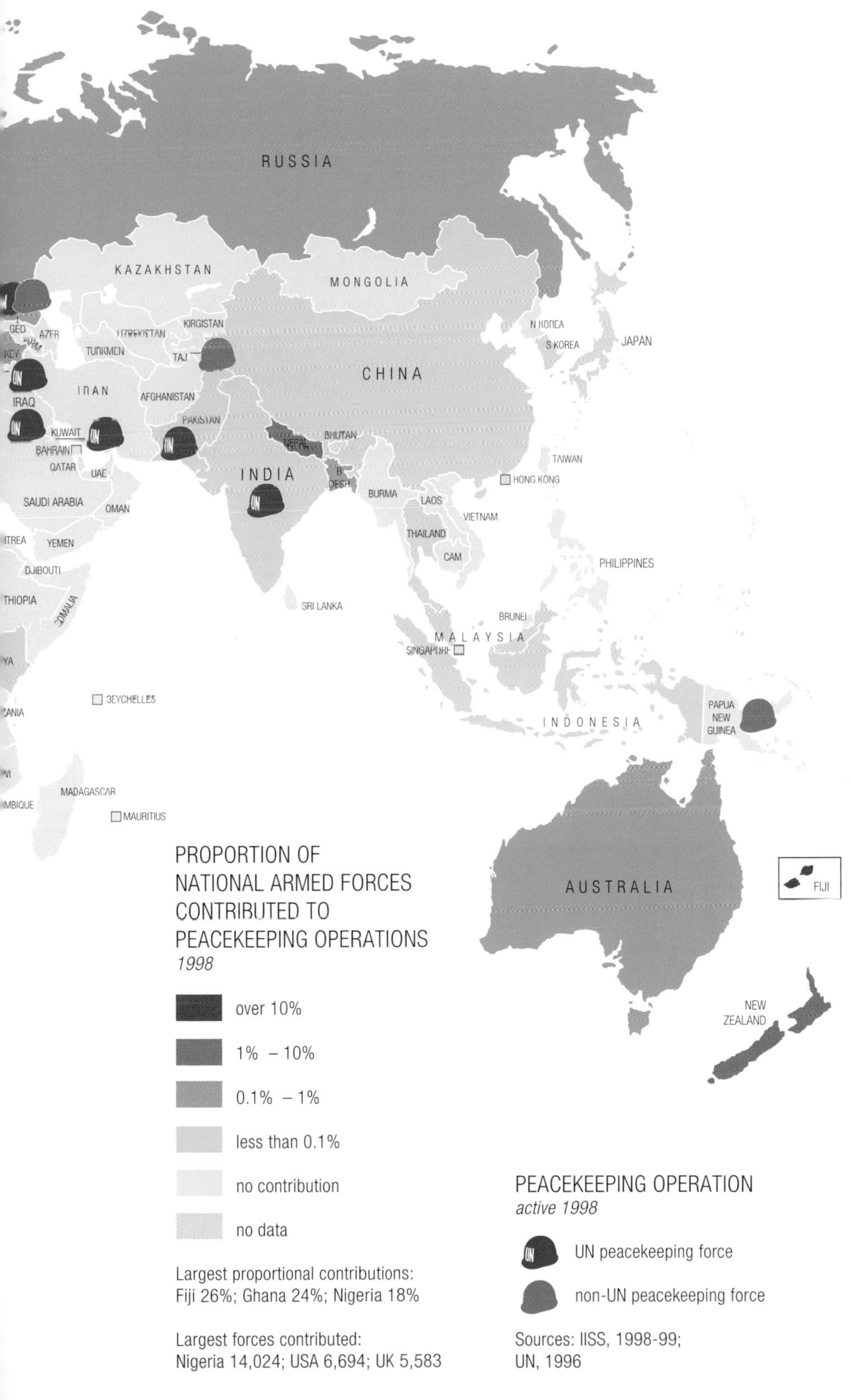

RUSSIA
KAZAKHSTAN
MONGOLIA
KIRGISTAN
TURKMEN
TAJ
IRAN
AFGHANISTAN
CHINA
S KOREA
JAPAN
IRAQ
KUWAIT
BAHRAIN
QATAR
UAE
SAUDI ARABIA
OMAN
BHUTAN
INDIA
TAIWAN
HONG KONG
BURMA
LAOS
VIETNAM
THAILAND
CAM
YEMEN
DJIBOUTI
PHILIPPINES
SRI LANKA
BRUNEI
MALAYSIA
SEYCHELLES
INDONESIA
PAPUA NEW GUINEA
MADAGASCAR
MAURITIUS
AUSTRALIA
FIJI
NEW ZEALAND
PROPORTION OF NATIONAL ARMED FORCES CONTRIBUTED TO PEACEKEEPING OPERATIONS
1998
over 10%
1% – 10%
0.1% – 1%
less than 0.1%
no contribution
no data
Largest proportional contributions:
Fiji 26%; Ghana 24%; Nigeria 18%
Largest forces contributed:
Nigeria 14,024; USA 6,694; UK 5,583
PEACEKEEPING OPERATION
active 1998
UN peacekeeping force
non-UN peacekeeping force
Sources: IISS, 1998-99;
UN, 1996

Most refugees are fleeing from war, and from the abuse of human rights and the threat to their lives that war produces. Many refugees are victims of war not by accident, but as the result of planning, as was seen in Bosnia between 1992 and 1995, and Kosovo in 1998 and 1999.

In 1980 there were approximately 22 million refugees worldwide, including those who do not cross international borders as well as those who do. By the early 1990s, this figure had almost doubled. By 1997, it had declined a little to just over 35 million.

In 1997, about 750,000 refugees returned to their countries of origin voluntarily. About 50,000 were forced to return by countries that were determined not to be their hosts.

Most refugees are produced and hosted in poor countries, and paid for by the rich. Refugee camps are often hot spots for epidemics.

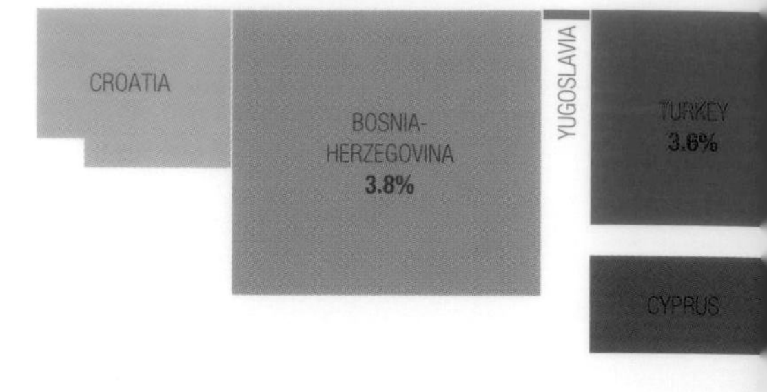
CROATIA
BOSNIA-HERZEGOVINA
3.8%
YUGOSLAVIA
TURKEY
3.6%
CYPRUS

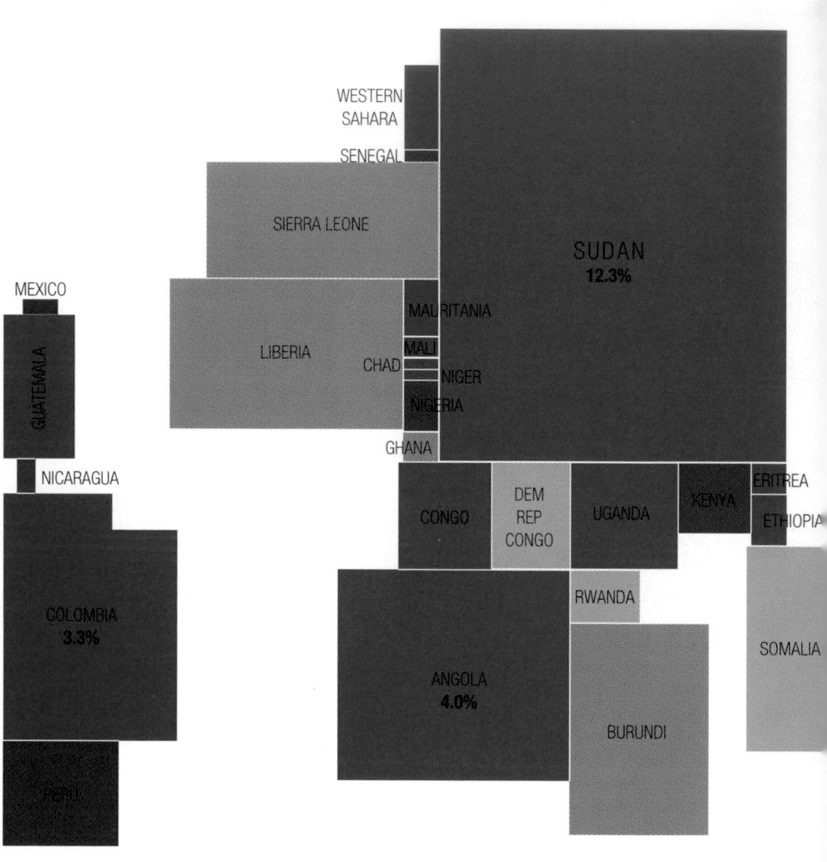
WESTERN SAHARA
SENEGAL
SIERRA LEONE
SUDAN
12.3%
MEXICO
GUATEMALA
MAURITANIA
LIBERIA
MALI
CHAD
NIGER
NIGERIA
GHANA
NICARAGUA
CONGO
DEM REP CONGO
UGANDA
KENYA
ERITREA
ETHIOPIA
COLOMBIA
3.3%
RWANDA
SOMALIA
ANGOLA
4.0%
BURUNDI
PERU

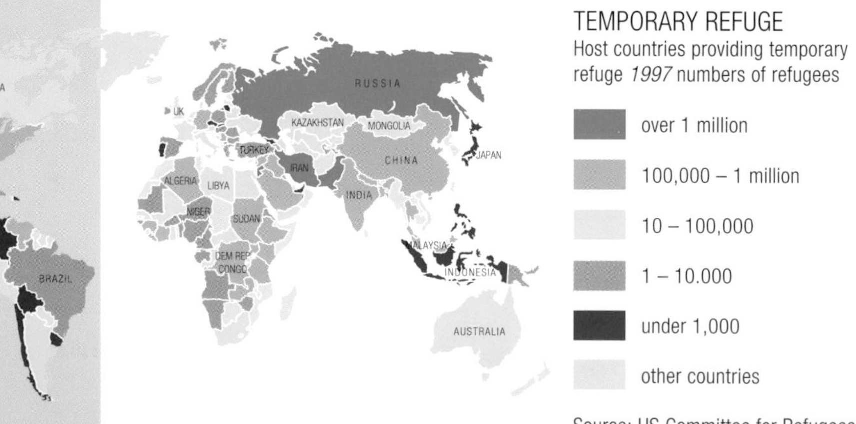
CANADA
USA
BRAZIL
UK
RUSSIA
KAZAKHSTAN
MONGOLIA
TURKEY
IRAN
CHINA
JAPAN
ALGERIA
LIBYA
INDIA
NIGER
SUDAN
DEM REP CONGO
MALAYSIA
INDONESIA
AUSTRALIA

TEMPORARY REFUGE

Host countries providing temporary refuge *1997* numbers of refugees

- over 1 million
- 100,000 – 1 million
- 10 – 100,000
- 1 – 10.000
- under 1,000
- other countries

Source: US Committee for Refugees, 1998

Refugees

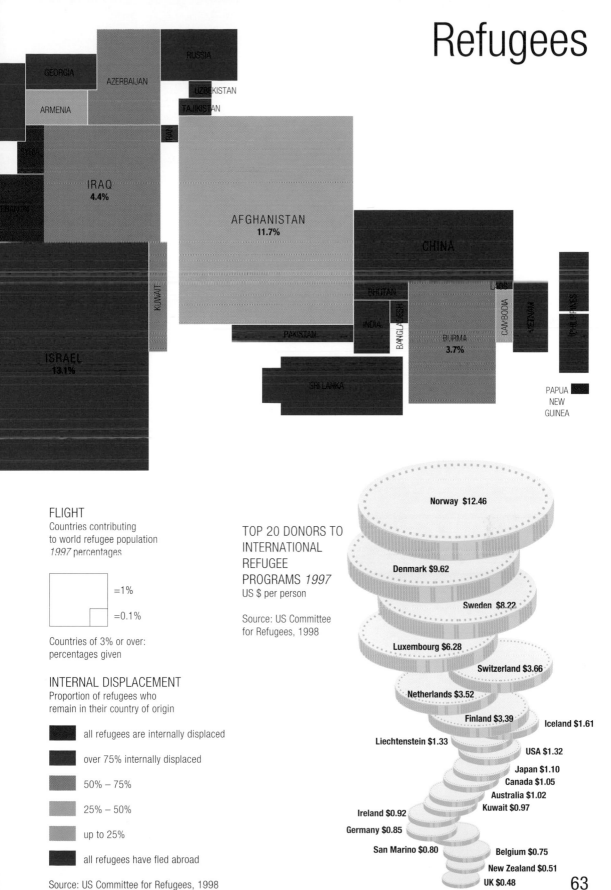

RUSSIA
GEORGIA
AZERBAIJAN
UZBEKISTAN
ARMENIA
TAJIKISTAN
IRAN
SYRIA
IRAQ
4.4%
LEBANON
AFGHANISTAN
11.7%
CHINA
KUWAIT
BHUTAN
LAOS
INDIA
BANGLADESH
CAMBODIA
VIETNAM
PHILIPPINES
PAKISTAN
BURMA
3.7%
ISRAEL
13.1%
SRI LANKA
PAPUA NEW GUINEA

FLIGHT

Countries contributing to world refugee population *1997* percentages

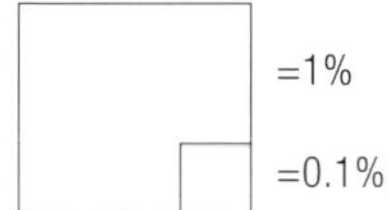

=1%

=0.1%

Countries of 3% or over: percentages given

INTERNAL DISPLACEMENT

Proportion of refugees who remain in their country of origin

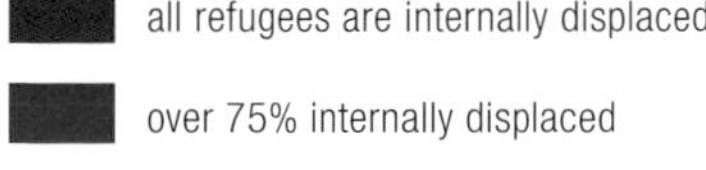

all refugees are internally displaced

over 75% internally displaced

50% – 75%

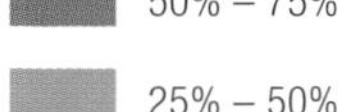

25% – 50%

up to 25%

all refugees have fled abroad

Source: US Committee for Refugees, 1998

TOP 20 DONORS TO INTERNATIONAL REFUGEE PROGRAMS *1997*
US $ per person

Source: US Committee for Refugees, 1998

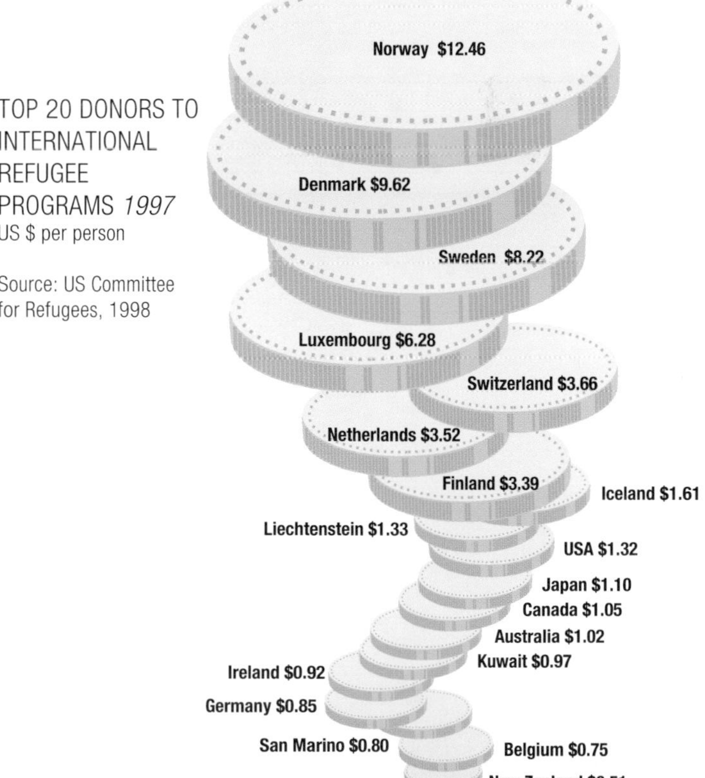
Norway $12.46
Denmark $9.62
Sweden $8.22
Luxembourg $6.28
Switzerland $3.66
Netherlands $3.52
Finland $3.39
Iceland $1.61
Liechtenstein $1.33
USA $1.32
Japan $1.10
Canada $1.05
Australia $1.02
Kuwait $0.97
Ireland $0.92
Germany $0.85
San Marino $0.80
Belgium $0.75
New Zealand $0.51
UK $0.48

The abuse of human rights is becoming more visible, and global awareness of it more focused.

ICELAND
NORWAY
SWEDEN
FINLAND
ESTONIA
LATVIA
LITHUANIA
DENMARK
IRELAND
U K
NETH
BEL
L
GERMANY
POLAND
BELARUS
CZECH REPUBLIC
SLOVAKIA
UKRAINE
FRANCE
SWITZ
AUSTRIA
SLO
HUNGARY
ROMANIA
CROATIA
B - H
YUG
ITALY
BULGARIA
M
PORTUGAL
SPAIN
GREECE
CANADA
UNITED STATES OF AMERICA
TUNISIA
MOROCCO
CUBA
BAHAMAS
DOMINICAN REPUBLIC
JAMAICA
HAITI
BELIZE
HONDURAS
GUATEMALA
EL SALVADOR
NICARAGUA
COSTA RICA
PANAMA
TRINIDAD & TOBAGO
GUYANA
SURINAME
MAURITANIA
MALI
GAMBIA
GUINEA-BISSAU
GUINEA
BURKINA FASO
CÔTE d' IVOIRE
GHANA
BENIN
TOGO
EQUATORIAL GUINEA
CAR
GABON
CHILE
URUGUAY
NAMIBIA
BOTSWANA
LATVIA
YUGOSLAVIA
TUNISIA
CUBA
BAHAMAS
BELIZE
JAMAICA
GUATEMALA
DOMINICA
BARBADOS
TRINIDAD & TOBAGO
GUYANA
LIBERIA
EQUATORIAL GUINEA
CAR
MALAWI

With the decision by the UN Security Council in 1991 to establish "safe havens" for Iraqi Kurds in the northern border region, a threshold was passed: for the first time, the right of a sovereign state to massacre its own citizens was denied.

There is no real evidence, however, that the abuse of human rights is on the decline, or even that there is a slackening in the most extreme abuses of extra-judicial killing and systematic torture.

Abuse of human rights is not only carried out by states, but sometimes by their opponents too, especially amid the bitter enmities of long-lasting civil wars.

Human Rights

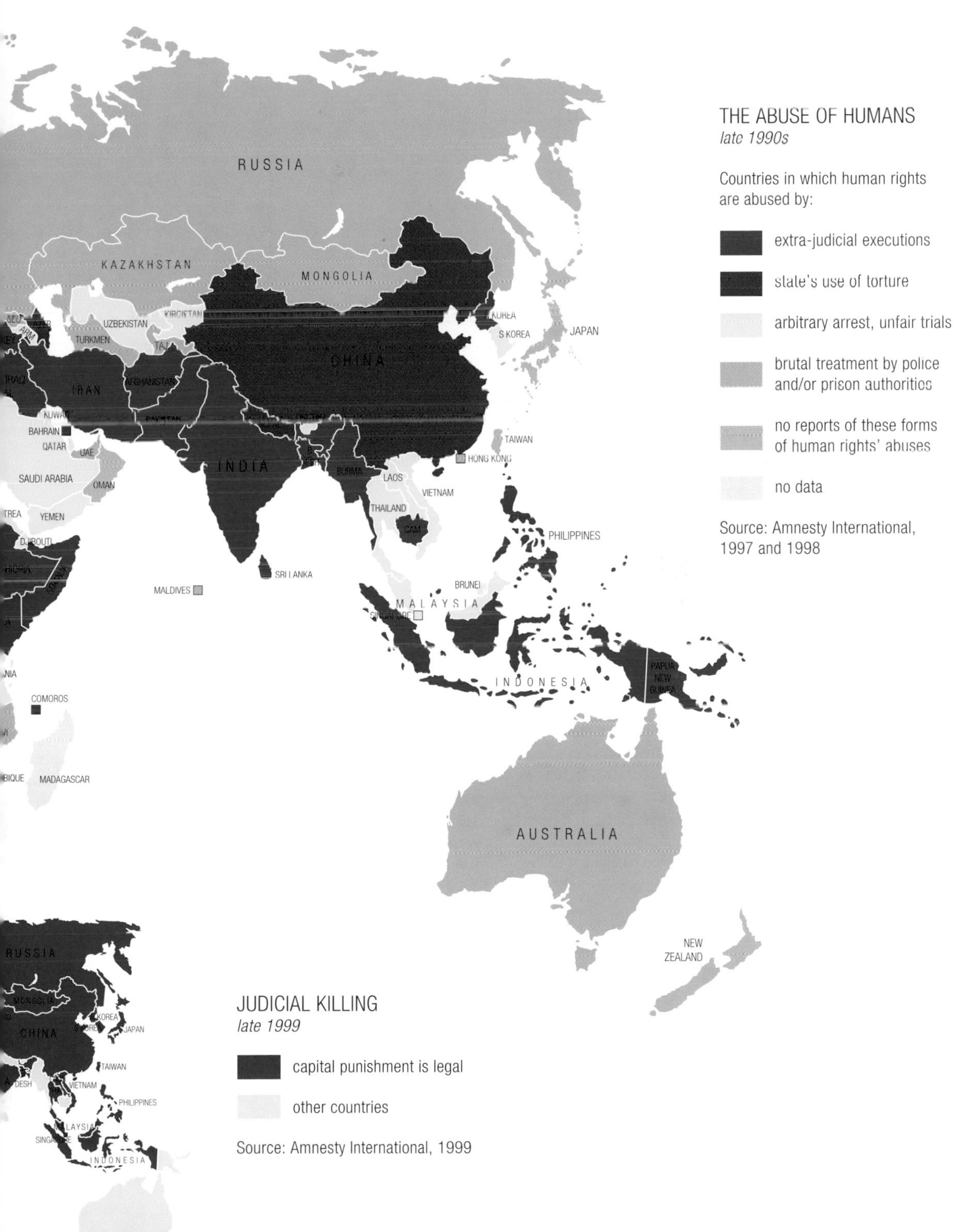
THE ABUSE OF HUMANS
late 1990s
Countries in which human rights are abused by:
extra-judicial executions
state's use of torture
arbitrary arrest, unfair trials
brutal treatment by police and/or prison authorities
no reports of these forms of human rights' abuses
no data
Source: Amnesty International, 1997 and 1998
RUSSIA
KAZAKHSTAN
MONGOLIA
UZBEKISTAN
TURKMEN
IRAN
AFGHANISTAN
CHINA
S KOREA
JAPAN
KUWAIT
BAHRAIN
QATAR
UAE
SAUDI ARABIA
OMAN
YEMEN
DJIBOUTI
INDIA
BURMA
LAOS
VIETNAM
THAILAND
CAM
TAIWAN
HONG KONG
PHILIPPINES
SRI LANKA
MALDIVES
BRUNEI
MALAYSIA
INDONESIA
PAPUA NEW GUINEA
COMOROS
MADAGASCAR
AUSTRALIA
NEW ZEALAND
JUDICIAL KILLING
late 1999
capital punishment is legal
other countries
Source: Amnesty International, 1999
RUSSIA
CHINA
KOREA
JAPAN
TAIWAN
VIETNAM
PHILIPPINES
INDONESIA

Part Five Society

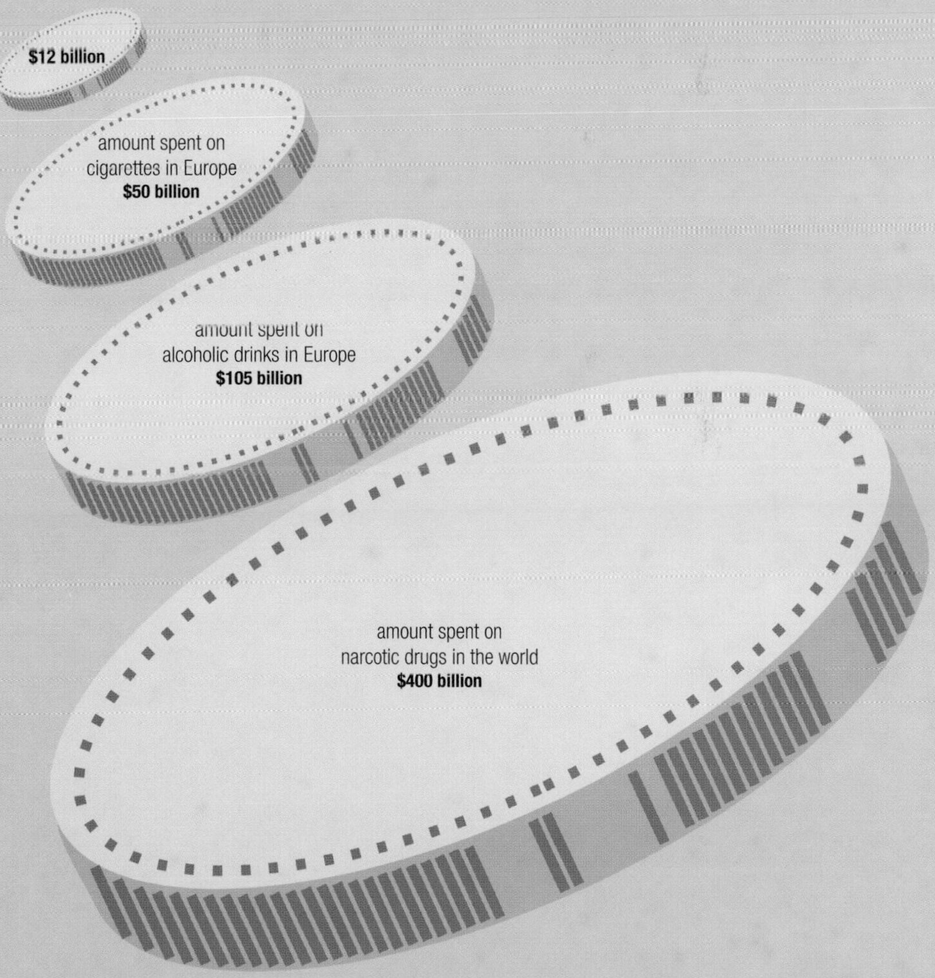

cost of providing
access to reproductive health
services for all women in
developing countries
$12 billion
amount spent on
cigarettes in Europe
$50 billion
amount spent on
alcoholic drinks in Europe
$105 billion
amount spent on
narcotic drugs in the world
$400 billion

Source: UNDP, 1998

The development of a world economy has accelerated the destruction of many groups' native homes. But that does not seem to be eliminating diversity.

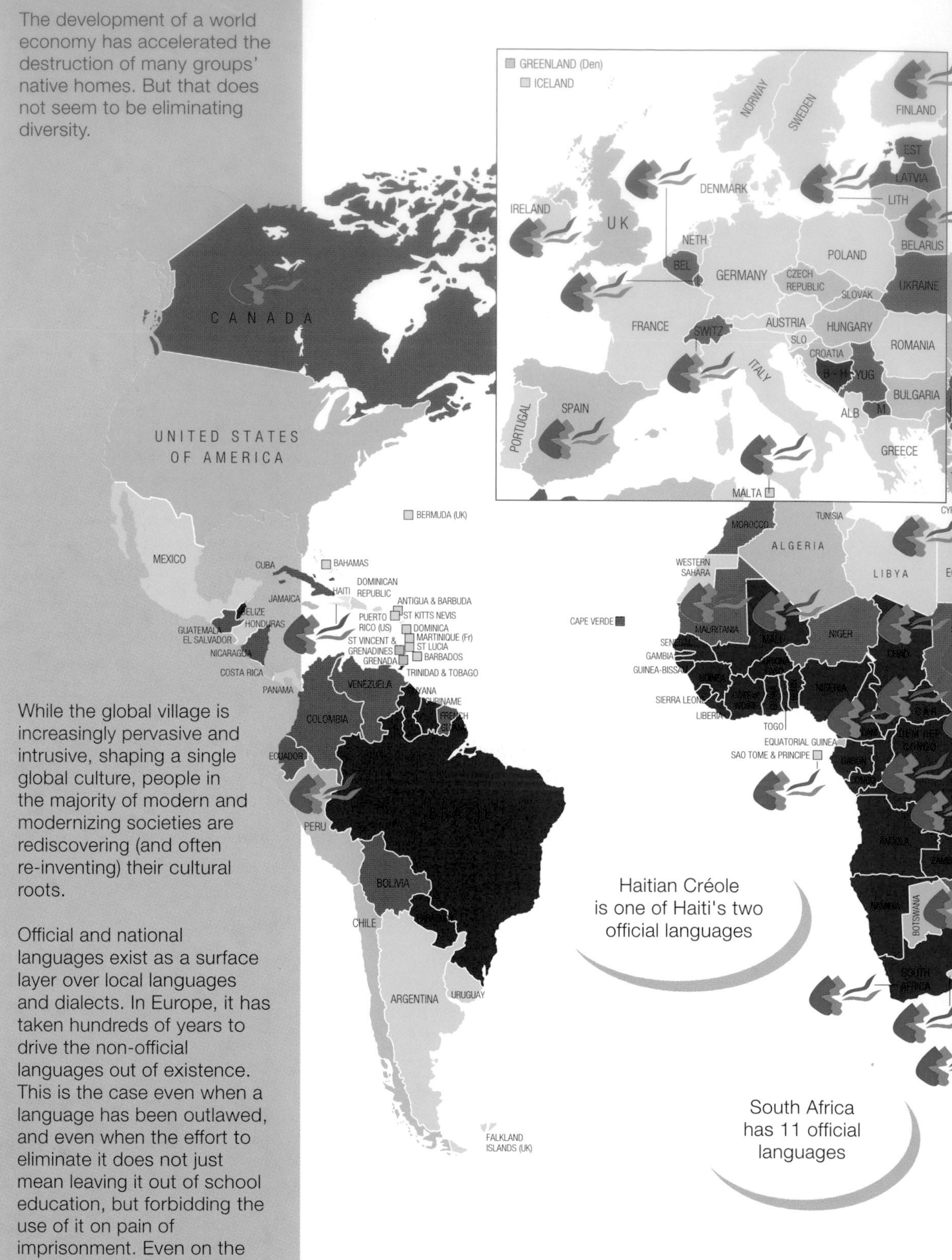
GREENLAND (Den)
ICELAND
NORWAY
SWEDEN
FINLAND
EST
LATVIA
LITH
DENMARK
IRELAND
UK
NETH
BEL
GERMANY
POLAND
BELARUS
CZECH REPUBLIC
SLOVAK
UKRAINE
FRANCE
SWITZ
AUSTRIA
SLO
HUNGARY
ROMANIA
CROATIA
B-H
YUG
ITALY
BULGARIA
PORTUGAL
SPAIN
ALB
M
GREECE
MALTA
CANADA
UNITED STATES OF AMERICA
MEXICO
CUBA
BERMUDA (UK)
BAHAMAS
HAITI
DOMINICAN REPUBLIC
JAMAICA
ANTIGUA & BARBUDA
BELIZE
HONDURAS
PUERTO RICO (US)
ST KITTS NEVIS
GUATEMALA
EL SALVADOR
DOMINICA
MARTINIQUE (Fr)
ST VINCENT & GRENADINES
ST LUCIA
NICARAGUA
GRENADA
BARBADOS
COSTA RICA
TRINIDAD & TOBAGO
PANAMA
VENEZUELA
GUYANA
SURINAME
FRENCH GUIANA
COLOMBIA
ECUADOR
PERU
BOLIVIA
CHILE
ARGENTINA
URUGUAY
FALKLAND ISLANDS (UK)
CAPE VERDE
MOROCCO
TUNISIA
ALGERIA
WESTERN SAHARA
LIBYA
MAURITANIA
MALI
NIGER
CHAD
SENEGAL
GAMBIA
GUINEA-BISSAU
SIERRA LEONE
LIBERIA
NIGERIA
TOGO
EQUATORIAL GUINEA
SAO TOME & PRINCIPE
ANGOLA
BOTSWANA
SOUTH AFRICA
Haitian Créole is one of Haiti's two official languages
South Africa has 11 official languages

While the global village is increasingly pervasive and intrusive, shaping a single global culture, people in the majority of modern and modernizing societies are rediscovering (and often re-inventing) their cultural roots.

Official and national languages exist as a surface layer over local languages and dialects. In Europe, it has taken hundreds of years to drive the non-official languages out of existence. This is the case even when a language has been outlawed, and even when the effort to eliminate it does not just mean leaving it out of school education, but forbidding the use of it on pain of imprisonment. Even on the brink of elimination, local languages can and do revive.

Ethnicity

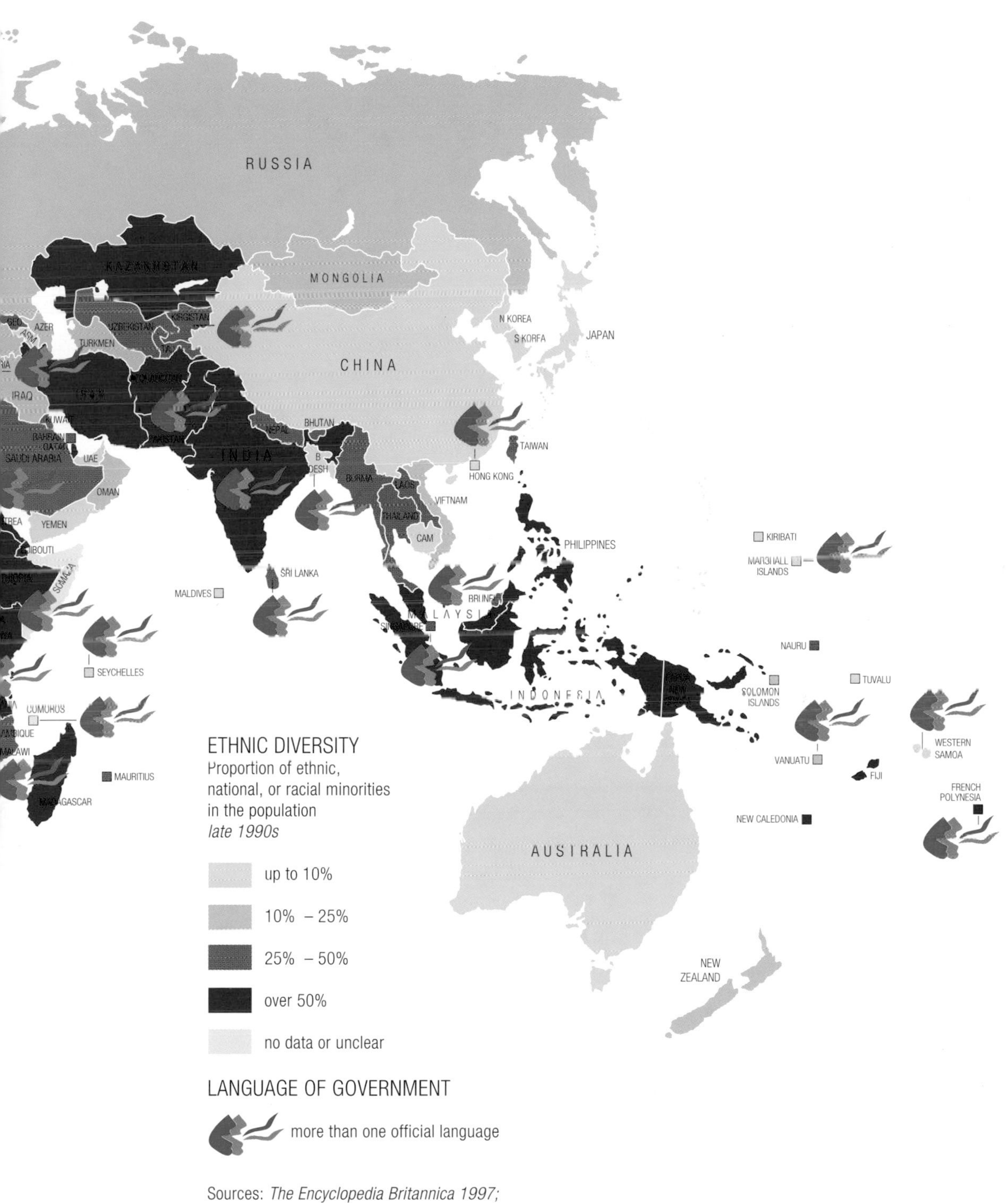
RUSSIA
MONGOLIA
N KOREA
S KOREA
JAPAN
CHINA
AZER
TURKMEN
UZBEKISTAN
IRAQ
BAHRAIN
QATAR
SAUDI ARABIA
UAE
OMAN
YEMEN
BHUTAN
NEPAL
INDIA
B DESH
BURMA
LAOS
THAILAND
VIETNAM
CAM
TAIWAN
HONG KONG
PHILIPPINES
SRI LANKA
MALDIVES
SEYCHELLES
COMOROS
MAURITIUS
INDONESIA
KIRIBATI
MARSHALL ISLANDS
NAURU
SOLOMON ISLANDS
TUVALU
VANUATU
FIJI
WESTERN SAMOA
FRENCH POLYNESIA
NEW CALEDONIA
AUSTRALIA
NEW ZEALAND
ETHNIC DIVERSITY
Proportion of ethnic, national, or racial minorities in the population
late 1990s
up to 10%
10% – 25%
25% – 50%
over 50%
no data or unclear
LANGUAGE OF GOVERNMENT
more than one official language

Sources: *The Encyclopedia Britannica 1997; The Statesman's Year-Book 1996-97*

In many countries many people never learn to read or write.

FINLAND
NORWAY
SWEDEN
ESTONIA
LATVIA
DENMARK
LITHUANIA
IRELAND
UK
NETH
BEL
L
GERMANY
POLAND
BELARUS
CZECH REPUBLIC
SLOVAK
UKRAINE
FRANCE
SWITZ
AUSTRIA
HUNGARY
SLO
CROATIA
ROMANIA
B - H
YUG
ITALY
BUL
PORTUGAL
SPAIN
ALB
M
GREECE
CANADA
UNITED STATES OF AMERICA
MEXICO
ATLANTIC OCEAN
BAHAMAS
CUBA
DOMINICAN REPUBLIC
JAMAICA
HAITI
ANTIGUA & BARBUDA
ST KITTS NEVIS
BELIZE
HONDURAS
GUATEMALA
EL SALVADOR
NICARAGUA
ST VINCENT & GRENADINES
GRENADA
BARBADOS
COSTA RICA
PANAMA
VENEZUELA
TRINIDAD & TOBAGO
GUYANA
SURINAME
FRENCH GUIANA (Fr)
COLOMBIA
ECUADOR
BRAZIL
PERU
BOLIVIA
PARAGUAY
CHILE
ARGENTINA
URUGUAY
CAPE VERDE
TUNISIA
MOROCCO
ALGERIA
LIBYA
WESTERN SAHARA
MAURITANIA
MALI
NIGER
CHAD
SENEGAL
GAMBIA
GUINEA-BISSAU
GUINEA
BURKINA FASO
SIERRA LEONE
LIBERIA
CÔTE d' IVOIRE
GHANA
BENIN
TOGO
NIGERIA
CAR
CAMEROON
EQUATORIAL GUINEA
SAO TOME & PRINCIPE
GABON
CONGO
DEM R CONG
ANGOLA
NAMIBIA
BOTSWANA
SOUTH AFRICA
ILLITERACY
Amongst those of 15 years and older
1995 percentages
over 70%
50.1% – 70%
30.1% – 50%
10.1% – 30%
up to 10%
no data
Highest illiteracy rates: Niger 86%, Somalia 76%
over 70% of illiterate adults are women
more illiterate adults are men than women
Source: UNESCO, 1998

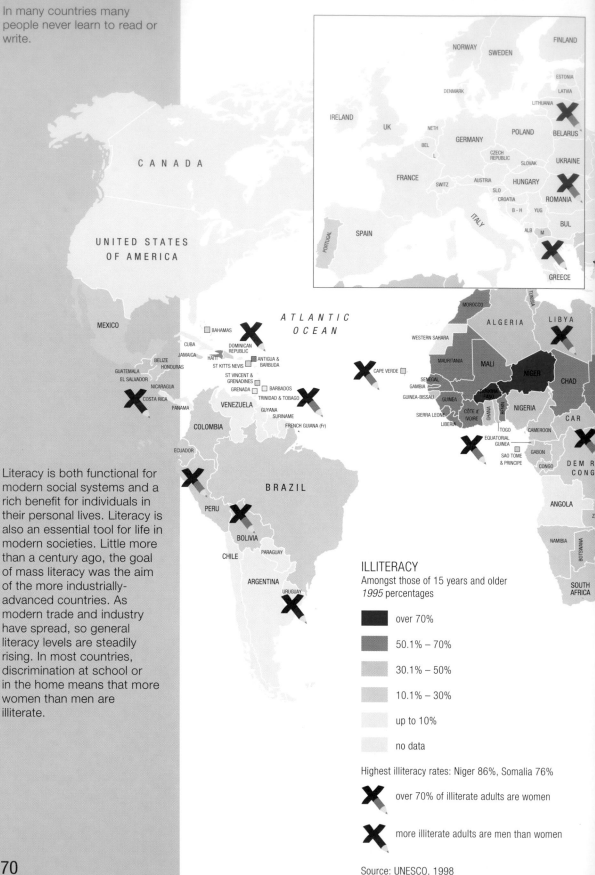

Literacy is both functional for modern social systems and a rich benefit for individuals in their personal lives. Literacy is also an essential tool for life in modern societies. Little more than a century ago, the goal of mass literacy was the aim of the more industrially-advanced countries. As modern trade and industry have spread, so general literacy levels are steadily rising. In most countries, discrimination at school or in the home means that more women than men are illiterate.

Literacy

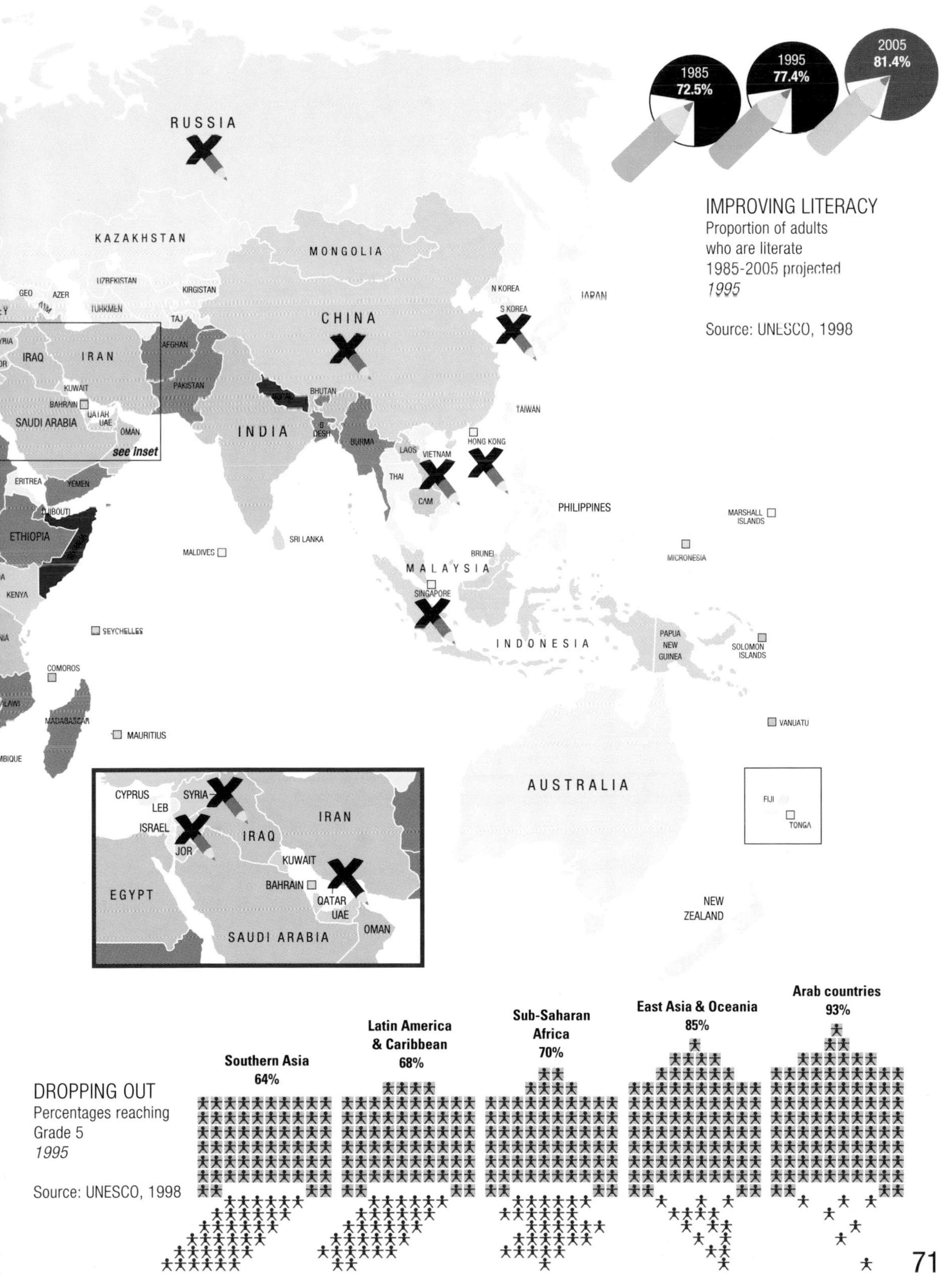

1985
72.5%
1995
77.4%
2005
81.4%
IMPROVING LITERACY
Proportion of adults
who are literate
1985-2005 projected
1995
Source: UNESCO, 1998
RUSSIA
KAZAKHSTAN
MONGOLIA
UZBEKISTAN
KIRGISTAN
GEO
AZER
TURKMEN
TAJ
CHINA
N KOREA
S KOREA
JAPAN
IRAQ
IRAN
AFGHAN
PAKISTAN
KUWAIT
BAHRAIN
QATAR
UAE
SAUDI ARABIA
OMAN
see inset
BHUTAN
TAIWAN
INDIA
B DESH
BURMA
HONG KONG
LAOS
VIETNAM
THAI
CAM
ERITREA
YEMEN
DJIBOUTI
ETHIOPIA
KENYA
PHILIPPINES
MARSHALL ISLANDS
SRI LANKA
MALDIVES
BRUNEI
MALAYSIA
SINGAPORE
MICRONESIA
SEYCHELLES
INDONESIA
PAPUA NEW GUINEA
SOLOMON ISLANDS
COMOROS
MADAGASCAR
MAURITIUS
VANUATU
CYPRUS
LEB
SYRIA
ISRAEL
JOR
IRAQ
IRAN
KUWAIT
BAHRAIN
QATAR
UAE
EGYPT
SAUDI ARABIA
OMAN
AUSTRALIA
FIJI
TONGA
NEW ZEALAND
DROPPING OUT
Percentages reaching
Grade 5
1995
Source: UNESCO, 1998
Southern Asia
64%
Latin America
& Caribbean
68%
Sub-Saharan
Africa
70%
East Asia & Oceania
85%
Arab countries
93%

Nowhere are women as well off as men. In general, the relative position of women is improving, though in Eastern Europe it worsened during the 1990s.

CANADA
UNITED STATES OF AMERICA
MEXICO
CUBA
BAHAMAS
DOMINICAN REPUBLIC
JAMAICA
HAITI
BELIZE
HONDURAS
GUATEMALA
EL SALVADOR
NICARAGUA
COSTA RICA
PANAMA
BARBADOS
TRINIDAD & TOBAGO
VENEZUELA
GUYANA
SURINAME
FRENCH GUIANA
COLOMBIA
ECUADOR
PERU
BRAZIL
BOLIVIA
PARAGUAY
CHILE
ARGENTINA
URUGUAY
NORWAY
SWEDEN
FINLAND
ESTONIA
LATVIA
LITHUANIA
BELARUS
DENMARK
IRELAND
UK
NETH
BEL
GERMANY
POLAND
CZECH REPUBLIC
SLOVAK
UKRAINE
FRANCE
SWITZ
AUSTRIA
HUNGARY
ROMANIA
SLO
CROATIA
B - H
YUG
ITALY
PORTUGAL
SPAIN
ALB
M
BULGARIA
MOL
GREECE
TURKEY
MALTA
CYPRUS
SYRIA
LEB
ISRAEL
JOR
TUNISIA
MOROCCO
ALGERIA
LIBYA
EGYPT
WESTERN SAHARA
MAURITANIA
CAPE VERDE
MALI
NIGER
SENEGAL
GAMBIA
GUINEA-BISSAU
GUINEA
BURKINA FASO
SIERRA LEONE
LIBERIA
CÔTE d' IVOIRE
GHANA
TOGO
BENIN
NIGERIA
CHAD
SUDAN
CAMEROON
EQUATORIAL GUINEA
CAR
GABON
CONGO
DEM REP CONGO
UGANDA
R
TANZANIA
ANGOLA
ZAMBIA
ZIM
NAMIBIA
BOTSWANA
SOUTH AFRICA
WOMEN IN GOVERNMENT
Percentages of seats in parliament held by women
1997 selected countries
Source: UNDP, *Human Development Report 1998*
3%
Pakistan
7%
Brazil, India, Thailand
9%
France
11%
Indonesia, USA
12%
UK
21%
Australia, Canada, China, Spain
26%
Germany
34%
Finland
36%
Norway
40%
Sweden

Discrimination often begins with a family's greater pride in its sons than its daughters. In a few countries, discrimination goes so far that there is evidence of systematic killing of baby girls.

Even in countries with the greatest gender equality, comparatively few women have seats in parliament. Most images of leadership still stress values and demeanor associated with masculinity.

Gender Equality

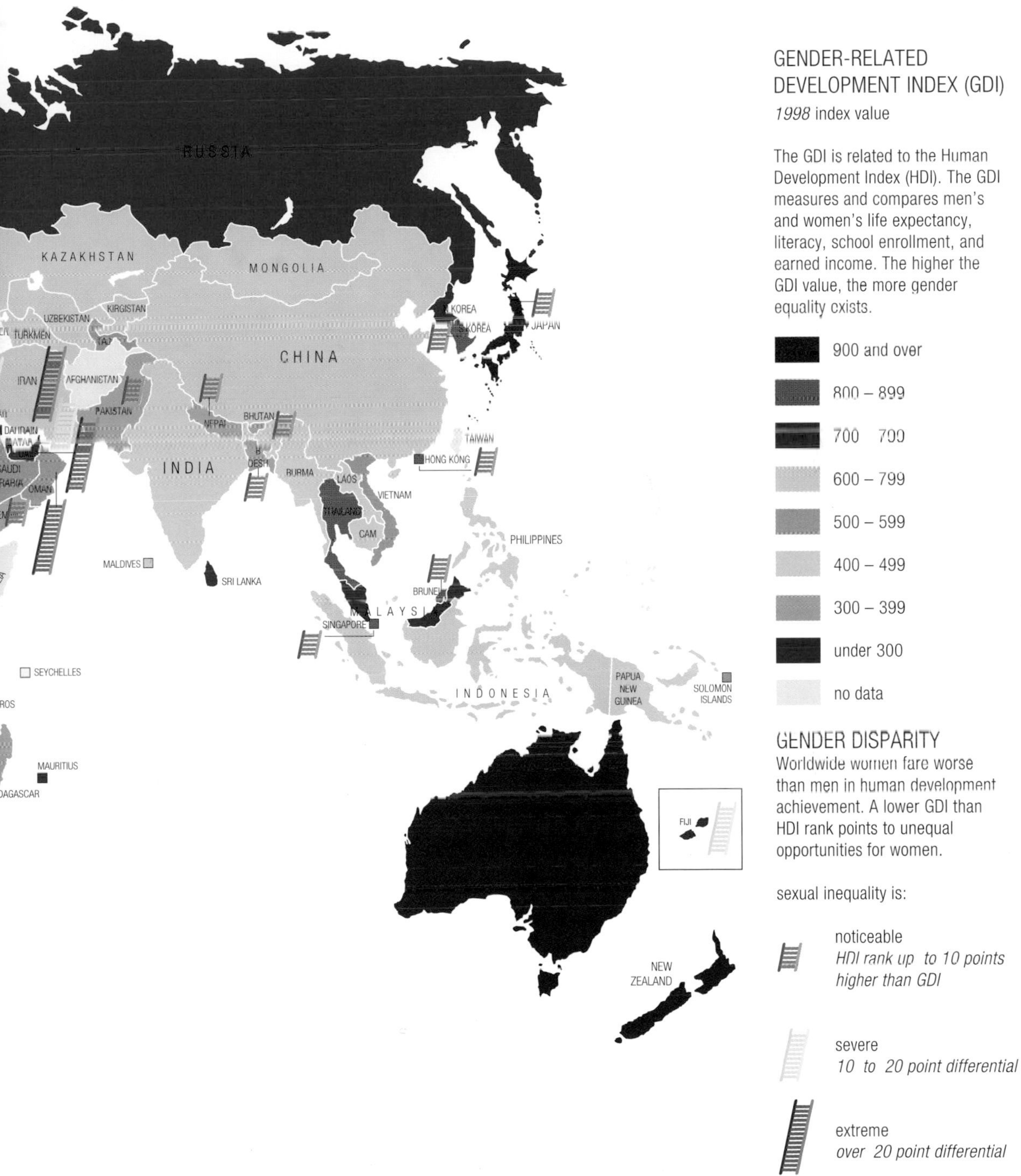
RUSSIA
KAZAKHSTAN
MONGOLIA
UZBEKISTAN
KIRGISTAN
TURKMEN
CHINA
N. KOREA
S. KOREA
JAPAN
IRAN
AFGHANISTAN
PAKISTAN
NEPAL
BHUTAN
BAHRAIN
QATAR
UAE
SAUDI ARABIA
OMAN
INDIA
B DESH
BURMA
TAIWAN
HONG KONG
LAOS
VIETNAM
THAILAND
CAM
PHILIPPINES
MALDIVES
SRI LANKA
BRUNEI
MALAYSIA
SINGAPORE
SEYCHELLES
INDONESIA
PAPUA NEW GUINEA
SOLOMON ISLANDS
MAURITIUS
FIJI
NEW ZEALAND

GENDER-RELATED DEVELOPMENT INDEX (GDI)

1998 index value

The GDI is related to the Human Development Index (HDI). The GDI measures and compares men's and women's life expectancy, literacy, school enrollment, and earned income. The higher the GDI value, the more gender equality exists.

- 900 and over
- 800 – 899
- 700 700
- 600 – 799
- 500 – 599
- 400 – 499
- 300 – 399
- under 300
- no data

GENDER DISPARITY

Worldwide women fare worse than men in human development achievement. A lower GDI than HDI rank points to unequal opportunities for women.

sexual inequality is:

- noticeable *HDI rank up to 10 points higher than GDI*
- severe *10 to 20 point differential*
- extreme *over 20 point differential*

Source: UNDP, *Human Development Report 1998*

Faith is always a matter of individual conscience, often a question of government policy, and in some cases the cornerstone of the state.

The opportunistic deployment of religious symbols for state purposes should not be confused with real spirituality. But the connection between politics and religion is evident everywhere, if in many different forms.

Nearly a quarter of the world's states have formal links to a religion. The meaning of those links varies markedly from state to state. The establishment of one version of one faith as the official religion of a state can mean religious intolerance and even persecution, but in other cases it is compatible with state secularism and religious pluralism in society.

With the dissolution of the USSR and the Soviet bloc in 1991, religious freedom has increased in the 1990s as the number of states intolerant of all religions has declined.

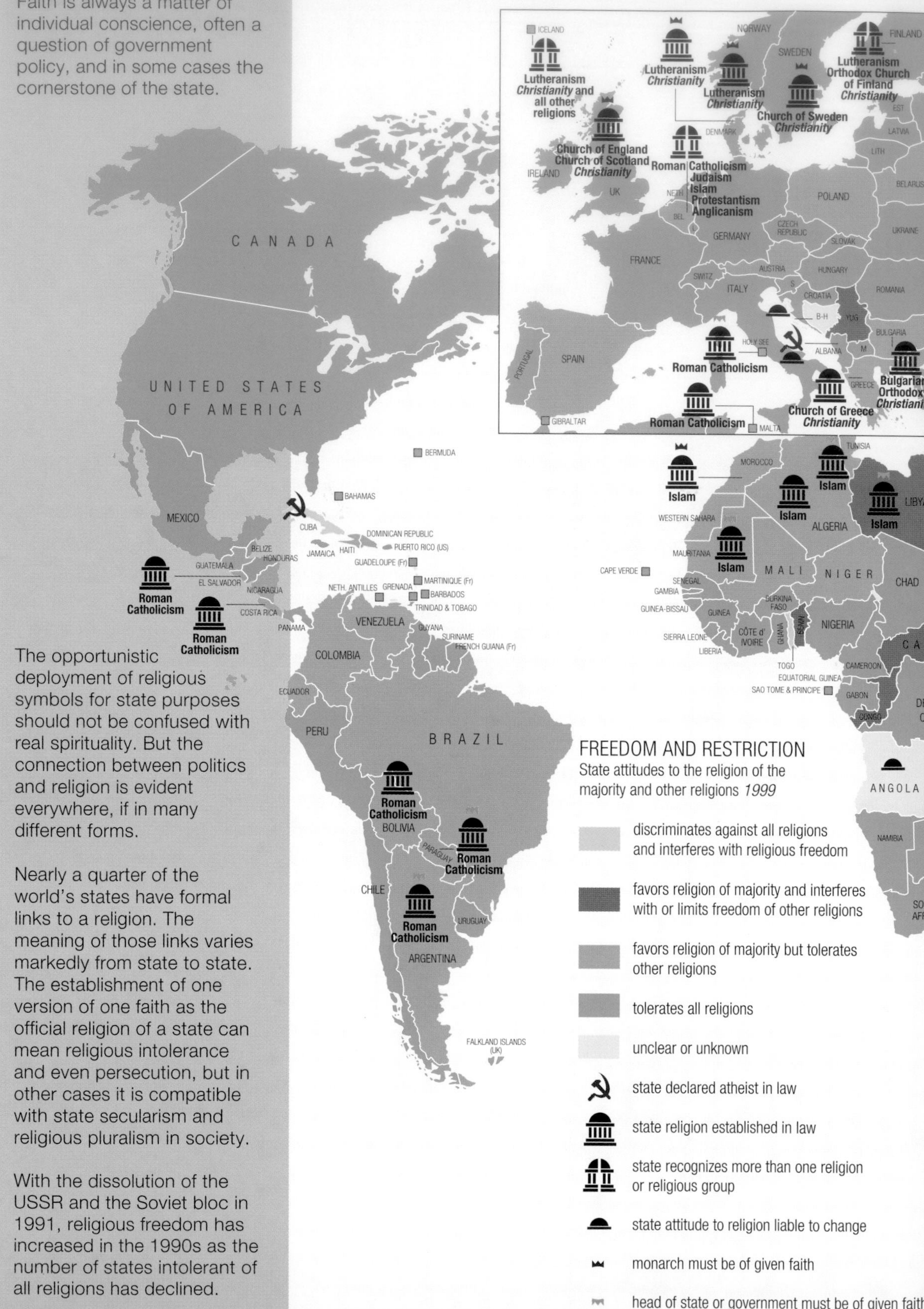

FREEDOM AND RESTRICTION
State attitudes to the religion of the majority and other religions *1999*
discriminates against all religions and interferes with religious freedom
favors religion of majority and interferes with or limits freedom of other religions
favors religion of majority but tolerates other religions
tolerates all religions
unclear or unknown
state declared atheist in law
state religion established in law
state recognizes more than one religion or religious group
state attitude to religion liable to change
monarch must be of given faith
head of state or government must be of given faith
CANADA
UNITED STATES OF AMERICA
MEXICO
BERMUDA
BAHAMAS
CUBA
DOMINICAN REPUBLIC
HAITI
JAMAICA
PUERTO RICO (US)
GUADELOUPE (Fr)
MARTINIQUE (Fr)
BARBADOS
GRENADA
NETH. ANTILLES
TRINIDAD & TOBAGO
BELIZE
HONDURAS
GUATEMALA
EL SALVADOR
NICARAGUA
COSTA RICA
PANAMA
Roman Catholicism
Roman Catholicism
VENEZUELA
GUYANA
SURINAME
FRENCH GUIANA (Fr)
COLOMBIA
ECUADOR
PERU
BRAZIL
Roman Catholicism
BOLIVIA
PARAGUAY
Roman Catholicism
CHILE
Roman Catholicism
URUGUAY
ARGENTINA
FALKLAND ISLANDS (UK)
ICELAND
Lutheranism
Christianity and all other religions
NORWAY
Lutheranism
Christianity
SWEDEN
FINLAND
Lutheranism
Orthodox Church of Finland
Christianity
Lutheranism
Christianity
Church of Sweden
Christianity
DENMARK
EST
LATVIA
LITH
BELARUS
Church of England
Church of Scotland
Christianity
IRELAND
UK
Roman Catholicism
Judaism
Islam
Protestantism
Anglicanism
NETH
BEL
POLAND
GERMANY
CZECH REPUBLIC
SLOVAK
UKRAINE
FRANCE
AUSTRIA
HUNGARY
SWITZ
ROMANIA
ITALY
S
CROATIA
B-H
YUG
BULGARIA
HOLY SEE
ALBANIA
M
PORTUGAL
SPAIN
Roman Catholicism
Bulgarian Orthodoxy
Christianity
GREECE
Church of Greece
Christianity
Roman Catholicism
MALTA
GIBRALTAR
TUNISIA
MOROCCO
Islam
Islam
Islam
Islam
LIBYA
WESTERN SAHARA
ALGERIA
MAURITANIA
Islam
CAPE VERDE
MALI
NIGER
CHAD
SENEGAL
GAMBIA
GUINEA-BISSAU
GUINEA
BURKINA FASO
NIGERIA
SIERRA LEONE
LIBERIA
CÔTE d' IVOIRE
GHANA
BENIN
TOGO
C A R
CAMEROON
EQUATORIAL GUINEA
SAO TOME & PRINCIPE
GABON
CONGO
DEM CON
ANGOLA
NAMIBIA
BOTSWANA
SOUTH AFRICA

Sources: Barrett, 1982; O'Brien and Palmer, 1993

Religion

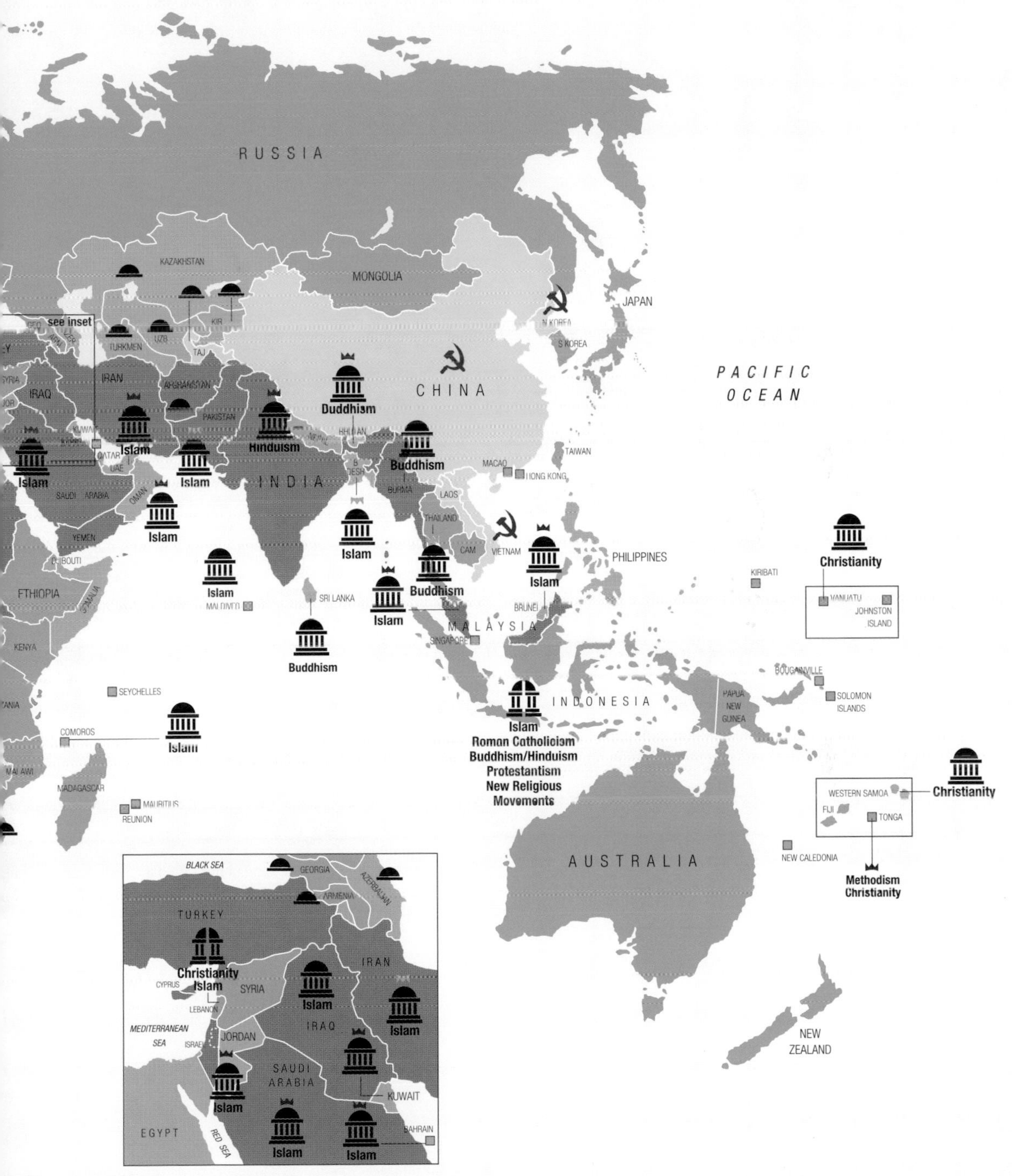

RUSSIA
KAZAKHSTAN
MONGOLIA
see inset
TURKMEN
UZB
TAJ
KIR
IRAN
IRAQ
AFGHANISTAN
PAKISTAN
CHINA
N KOREA
S KOREA
JAPAN
PACIFIC OCEAN
Buddhism
Hinduism
Islam
INDIA
SAUDI ARABIA
OMAN
QATAR
UAE
YEMEN
DJIBOUTI
ETHIOPIA
KENYA
BHUTAN
Buddhism
BURMA
LAOS
THAILAND
CAM
VIETNAM
TAIWAN
MACAO
HONG KONG
PHILIPPINES
Islam
Buddhism
SRI LANKA
MALDIVES
Buddhism
BRUNEI
MALAYSIA
SINGAPORE
INDONESIA
Islam
Roman Catholicism
Buddhism/Hinduism
Protestantism
New Religious Movements
KIRIBATI
Christianity
VANUATU
JOHNSTON ISLAND
BOUGAINVILLE
PAPUA NEW GUINEA
SOLOMON ISLANDS
SEYCHELLES
COMOROS
MADAGASCAR
MAURITIUS
REUNION
MALAWI
AUSTRALIA
WESTERN SAMOA
FIJI
TONGA
Christianity
NEW CALEDONIA
Methodism Christianity
NEW ZEALAND
BLACK SEA
GEORGIA
ARMENIA
AZERBAIJAN
TURKEY
Christianity Islam
CYPRUS
SYRIA
LEBANON
MEDITERRANEAN SEA
ISRAEL
JORDAN
IRAQ
IRAN
SAUDI ARABIA
KUWAIT
BAHRAIN
EGYPT
RED SEA

Some people, religions, political parties, and governments believe that only a narrow range of sexual activities should be allowed.

Others maintain that sexual preference is not an issue for law or government policy.

The legal position does not always indicate the intrusiveness of sexual policing. In some countries, legal tolerance masks discrimination in practice; in others, intolerant laws are seldom applied. But almost everywhere, those whose desire takes them outside the heterosexual norm face pressures – of a subtle social kind if not open and political.

The most extreme form of sexual policing is the social acceptance in some countries of the murder of girls and women who have been raped. Forced out of a particularly narrow version of the heterosexual norm against their will, there is no place left for them. The killer is usually a man in the family.

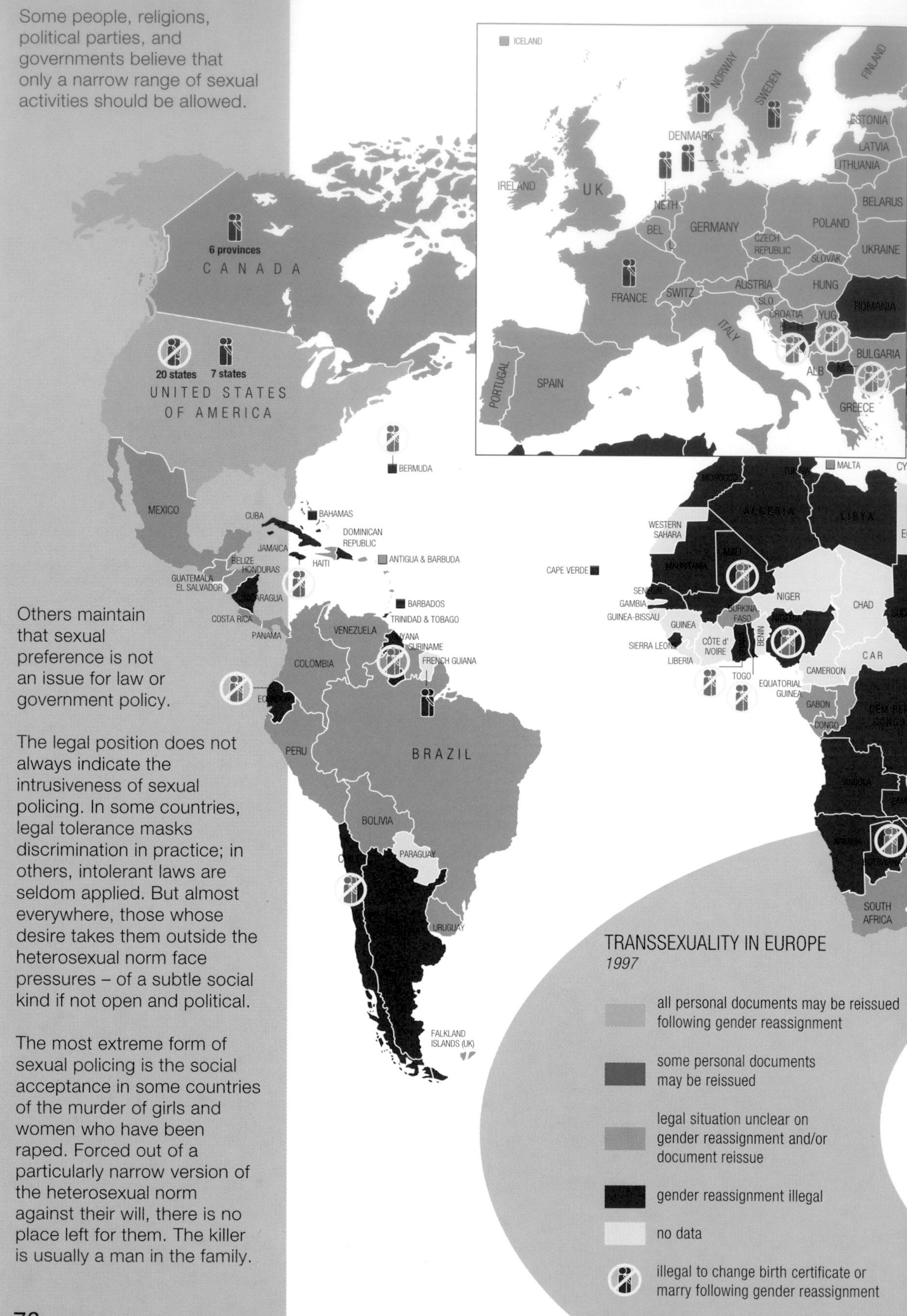
ICELAND
NORWAY
SWEDEN
FINLAND
ESTONIA
LATVIA
LITHUANIA
DENMARK
IRELAND
UK
NETH
BELARUS
BEL
GERMANY
POLAND
CZECH REPUBLIC
SLOVAK
UKRAINE
FRANCE
SWITZ
AUSTRIA
HUNG
SLO
CROATIA
B-H
YUG
ROMANIA
ITALY
BULGARIA
ALB
M
GREECE
PORTUGAL
SPAIN
6 provinces
CANADA
20 states
7 states
UNITED STATES OF AMERICA
BERMUDA
MEXICO
CUBA
BAHAMAS
DOMINICAN REPUBLIC
JAMAICA
HAITI
ANTIGUA & BARBUDA
BELIZE
HONDURAS
GUATEMALA
EL SALVADOR
NICARAGUA
BARBADOS
TRINIDAD & TOBAGO
COSTA RICA
PANAMA
VENEZUELA
GUYANA
SURINAME
FRENCH GUIANA
COLOMBIA
ECUADOR
PERU
BRAZIL
BOLIVIA
PARAGUAY
CHILE
URUGUAY
FALKLAND ISLANDS (UK)
CAPE VERDE
MALTA
MOROCCO
TUNISIA
ALGERIA
LIBYA
WESTERN SAHARA
MAURITANIA
MALI
NIGER
CHAD
SENEGAL
GAMBIA
GUINEA-BISSAU
GUINEA
BURKINA FASO
NIGERIA
SIERRA LEONE
LIBERIA
CÔTE d' IVOIRE
BENIN
TOGO
CAR
CAMEROON
EQUATORIAL GUINEA
GABON
CONGO
DEM REP CONGO
SOUTH AFRICA
TRANSSEXUALITY IN EUROPE
1997
all personal documents may be reissued following gender reassignment
some personal documents may be reissued
legal situation unclear on gender reassignment and/or document reissue
gender reassignment illegal
no data
illegal to change birth certificate or marry following gender reassignment
Source: National Council for Civil Liberties, 1997

Sexual Freedom

LEGAL STATUS OF HOMOSEXUALITY
1997–98

- legal
- illegal or punishable as "immoral"
- different laws in individual states
- unknown
- only male homosexuality targeted in law or practice
- oral and anal sex illegal regardless of gender
- discrimination against homosexuality illegal

Sources: Amnesty International, 1997 and 1998; Hendricks, Tielman and Van der Veen, 1993; Kidron and Segal, 1995

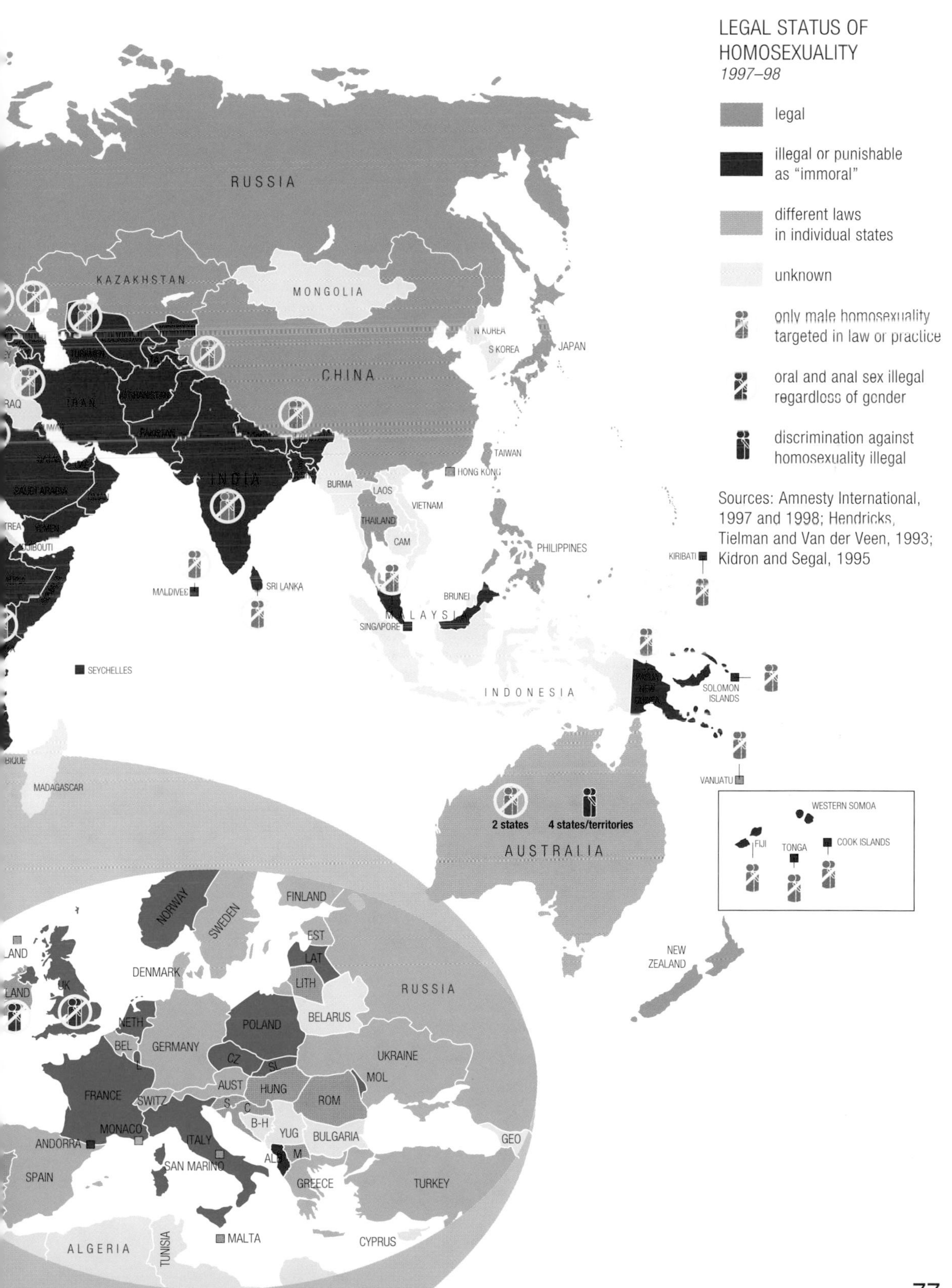

RUSSIA
KAZAKHSTAN
MONGOLIA
CHINA
N KOREA
S KOREA
JAPAN
IRAN
INDIA
TAIWAN
HONG KONG
BURMA
LAOS
VIETNAM
THAILAND
CAM
PHILIPPINES
MALDIVES
SRI LANKA
BRUNEI
MALAYSIA
SINGAPORE
SEYCHELLES
INDONESIA
SOLOMON ISLANDS
KIRIBATI
VANUATU
MADAGASCAR
2 states
4 states/territories
AUSTRALIA
WESTERN SOMOA
FIJI
TONGA
COOK ISLANDS
NEW ZEALAND
NORWAY
SWEDEN
FINLAND
EST
LAT
LITH
DENMARK
UK
RUSSIA
BELARUS
POLAND
NETH
BEL
GERMANY
CZ
SL
L
UKRAINE
MOL
AUST
HUNG
FRANCE
SWITZ
ROM
S
C
B-H
MONACO
YUG
BULGARIA
GEO
ANDORRA
ITALY
AL
M
SAN MARINO
SPAIN
GREECE
TURKEY
ALGERIA
TUNISIA
MALTA
CYPRUS

Increasing acceptance of the use of manufactured contraceptives is one of the great social revolutions of the late twentieth century.

The right of women to abortion as a means of deciding when they will give birth is contested more widely, bitterly and, in some countries such as the USA, violently.

About 70 percent of women reportedly use some kind of contraception, though there remain large areas, especially outside cities, where there is no access to anything except traditional methods. These are often unreliable and sometimes unhealthy, as are some of the modern contraceptive and sterilization methods foisted on the poorer countries.

Though condoms double as a contraceptive and a protection against sexually-transmitted diseases, there are few countries where they are the first choice of contraceptive.

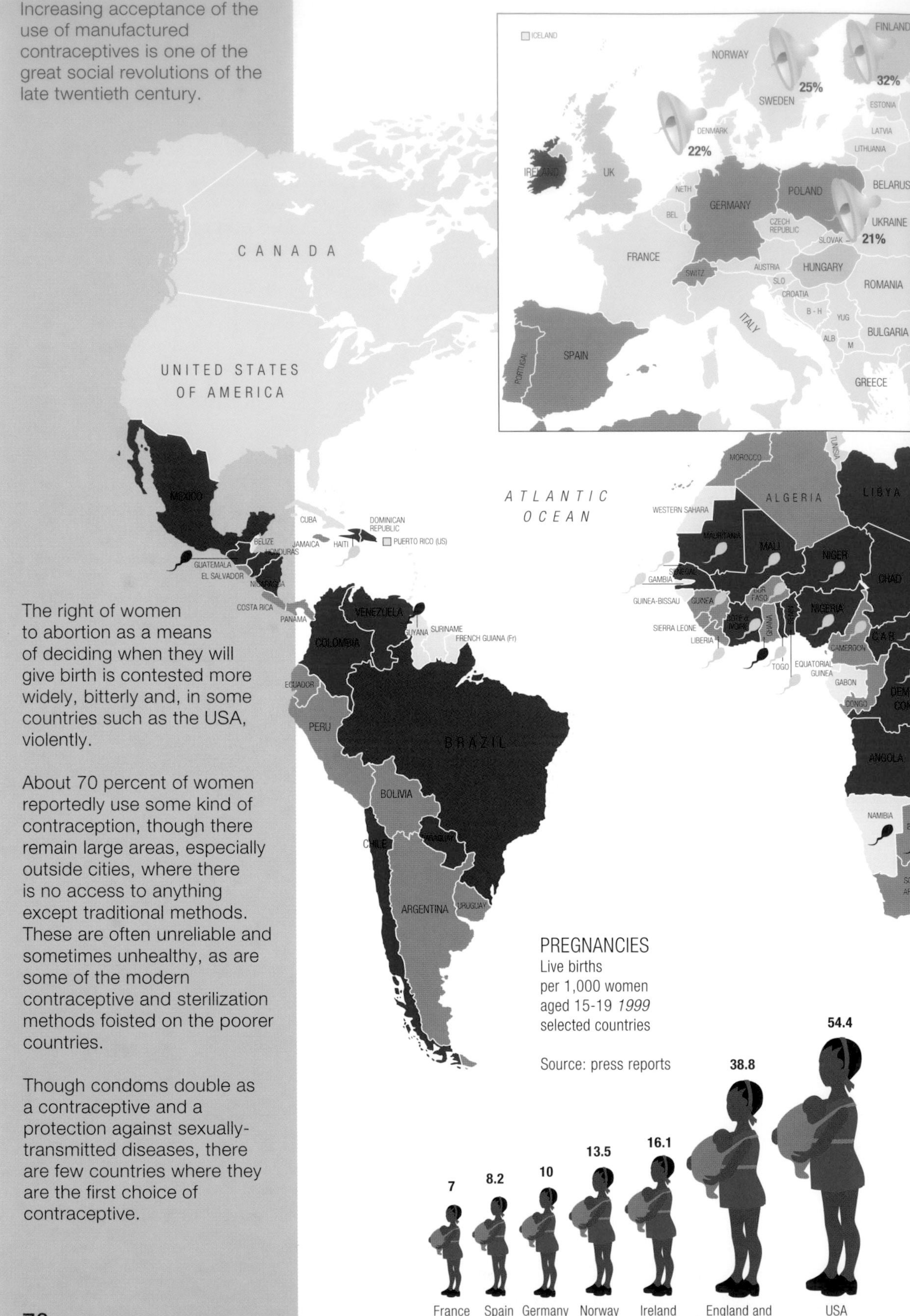
ICELAND
NORWAY
FINLAND
SWEDEN
25%
32%
ESTONIA
DENMARK
22%
LATVIA
LITHUANIA
IRELAND
UK
NETH
GERMANY
POLAND
BELARUS
BEL
CZECH REPUBLIC
UKRAINE
SLOVAK
21%
FRANCE
AUSTRIA
HUNGARY
SWITZ
SLO
CROATIA
ROMANIA
B - H
YUG
ITALY
BULGARIA
ALB
M
PORTUGAL
SPAIN
GREECE
CANADA
UNITED STATES OF AMERICA
MEXICO
CUBA
DOMINICAN REPUBLIC
BELIZE
JAMAICA
HAITI
PUERTO RICO (US)
HONDURAS
GUATEMALA
EL SALVADOR
NICARAGUA
COSTA RICA
PANAMA
ATLANTIC OCEAN
VENEZUELA
GUYANA
SURINAME
FRENCH GUIANA (Fr)
COLOMBIA
ECUADOR
PERU
BRAZIL
BOLIVIA
PARAGUAY
CHILE
ARGENTINA
URUGUAY
MOROCCO
TUNISIA
ALGERIA
LIBYA
WESTERN SAHARA
MAURITANIA
MALI
NIGER
CHAD
GAMBIA
SENEGAL
GUINEA-BISSAU
GUINEA
BUR FASO
NIGERIA
SIERRA LEONE
LIBERIA
CÔTE d'IVOIRE
GHANA
TOGO
BENIN
C.A.R.
CAMEROON
EQUATORIAL GUINEA
GABON
CONGO
DEM REP CONGO
ANGOLA
NAMIBIA
SOUTH AFRICA
PREGNANCIES
Live births
per 1,000 women
aged 15-19 *1999*
selected countries
Source: press reports
7
France
8.2
Spain
10
Germany
13.5
Norway
16.1
Ireland
38.8
England and Wales
54.4
USA

Reproductive Rights

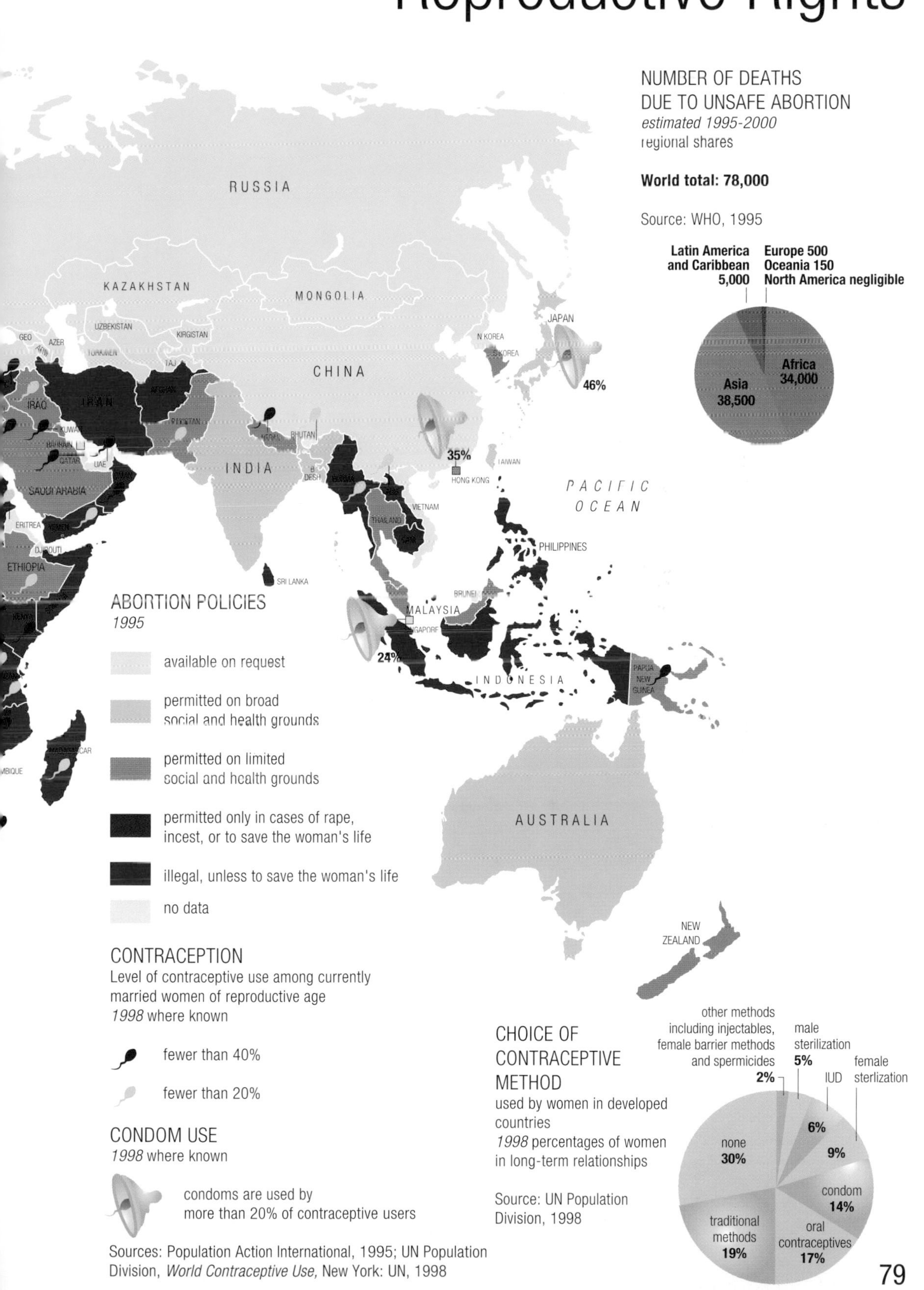

NUMBER OF DEATHS
DUE TO UNSAFE ABORTION
estimated 1995-2000
regional shares
World total: 78,000
Source: WHO, 1995
Latin America and Caribbean 5,000
Europe 500
Oceania 150
North America negligible
Africa 34,000
Asia 38,500
RUSSIA
KAZAKHSTAN
MONGOLIA
CHINA
UZBEKISTAN
KIRGISTAN
GEO
AZER
TAJ
JAPAN
N KOREA
S KOREA
46%
IRAQ
IRAN
AFGHAN
PAKISTAN
NEPAL
BHUTAN
KUWAIT
BAHRAIN
QATAR
UAE
OMAN
SAUDI ARABIA
INDIA
B DESH
BURMA
35%
HONG KONG
TAIWAN
PACIFIC OCEAN
VIETNAM
THAILAND
ERITREA
YEMEN
DJIBOUTI
ETHIOPIA
PHILIPPINES
SRI LANKA
BRUNEI
MALAYSIA
SINGAPORE
24%
INDONESIA
PAPUA NEW GUINEA
KENYA
MADAGASCAR
AUSTRALIA
NEW ZEALAND
ABORTION POLICIES
1995
available on request
permitted on broad social and health grounds
permitted on limited social and health grounds
permitted only in cases of rape, incest, or to save the woman's life
illegal, unless to save the woman's life
no data
CONTRACEPTION
Level of contraceptive use among currently married women of reproductive age
1998 where known
fewer than 40%
fewer than 20%
CONDOM USE
1998 where known
condoms are used by more than 20% of contraceptive users
Sources: Population Action International, 1995; UN Population Division, World Contraceptive Use, New York: UN, 1998
CHOICE OF CONTRACEPTIVE METHOD
used by women in developed countries
1998 percentages of women in long-term relationships
Source: UN Population Division, 1998
other methods including injectables, female barrier methods and spermicides 2%
male sterilization 5%
IUD 6%
female sterlization 9%
condom 14%
oral contraceptives 17%
traditional methods 19%
none 30%

Life expectancy is increasing worldwide. However, in 16 of the world's poorest countries it has fallen.

Many infectious diseases, notably smallpox, have been eradicated but others are spreading. AIDS continues to spread. Over 75 percent of adults newly-infected with HIV infections are heterosexual.

Tuberculosis is increasing. This is partly in the shadow of AIDS – those weakened by HIV/AIDS are more vulnerable to the disease – and partly due to increasing poverty worldwide, especially in cities.

Non-communicable diseases increase with wealth. As economies modernize and grow, more of the population adopts a Western lifestyle. As people smoke more, choose high-fat foods, and exercise less, they become more vulnerable to the main lifestyle illnesses: heart disease, cancer, and diabetes.

In the USA, 10% of new adult HIV infections are among the over-50s.

Worldwide 1.1 million children have HIV/AIDS. Over 95% of them are in sub-Saharan Africa.

GREENLAND
ICE
CANADA
USA
MEXICO
CUBA
BAHAMAS
DOMINICAN REPUBLIC
JAMAICA
HAITI
BELIZE
HONDURAS
GUATEMALA
EL SALVADOR
NICARAGUA
COSTA RICA
PANAMA
BARBADOS
TRINIDAD & TOBAGO
GUYANA
SURINAME
FRENCH GUIANA (Fr)
VENEZUELA
COLOMBIA
ECUADOR
PERU
BRAZIL
BOLIVIA
CHILE
PARAGUAY
ARGENTINA
URUGUAY
SENEGAL
GAMBIA
GUINEA-BISSAU

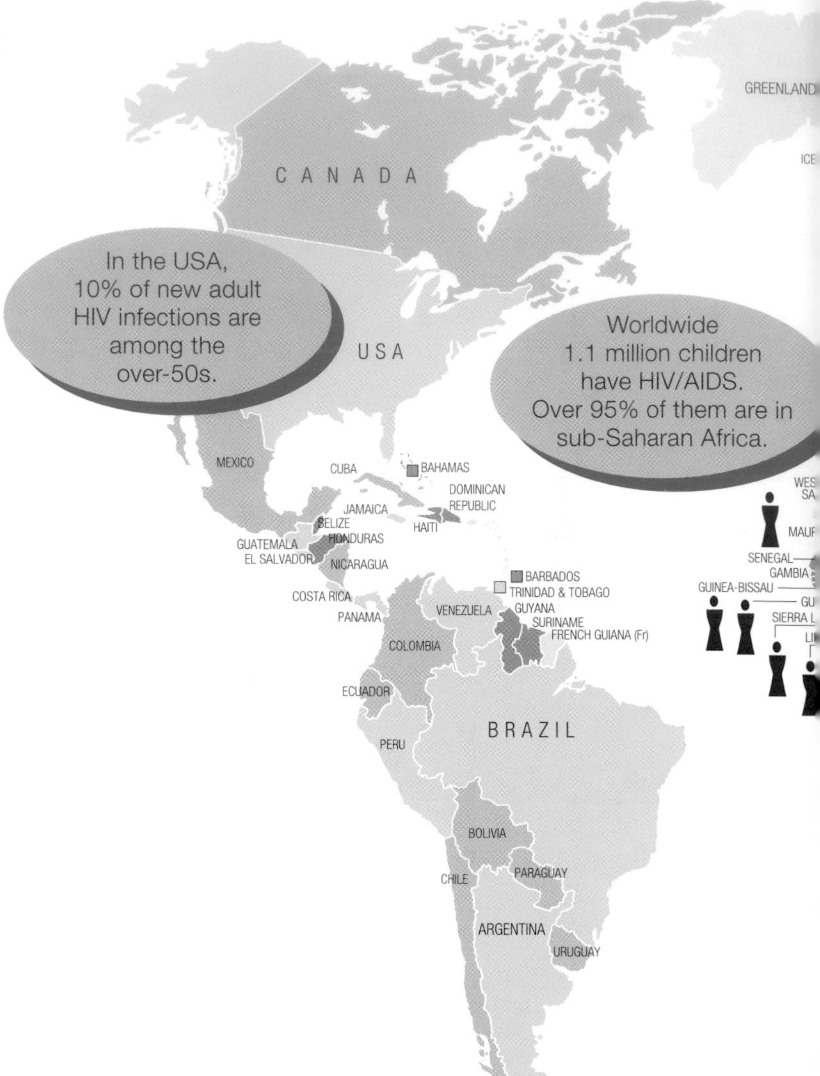

DIABETES EXPECTED TO INCREASE

2050 projected compared with 1997

Source: WHO, 1999

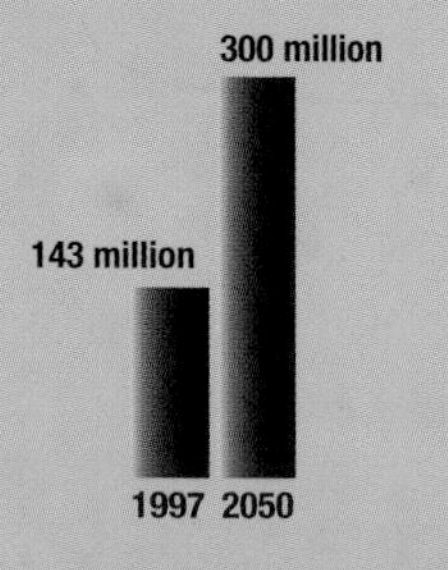
143 million
300 million
1997
2050

THE BIG KILLERS

Causes of death *1997* percentages

world total deaths 52,200,000

Source: WHO

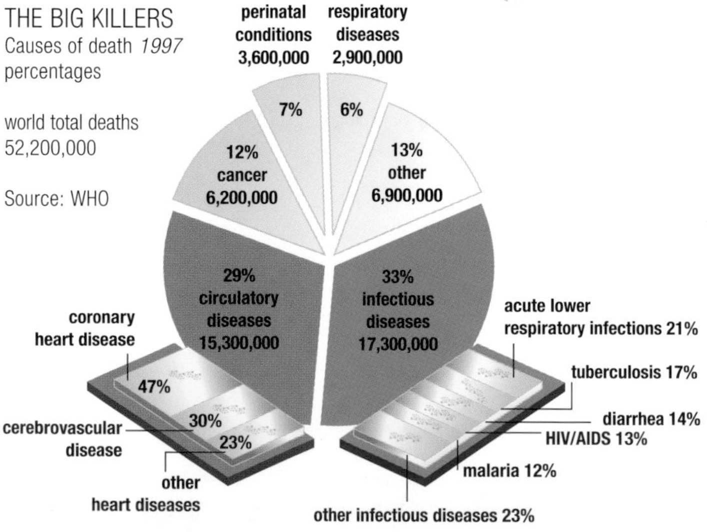

perinatal conditions 3,600,000 7%
respiratory diseases 2,900,000 6%
12% cancer 6,200,000
13% other 6,900,000
29% circulatory diseases 15,300,000
33% infectious diseases 17,300,000

coronary heart disease 47%
cerebrovascular disease 30%
other heart diseases 23%

acute lower respiratory infections 21%
tuberculosis 17%
diarrhea 14%
HIV/AIDS 13%
malaria 12%
other infectious diseases 23%

Health Risks

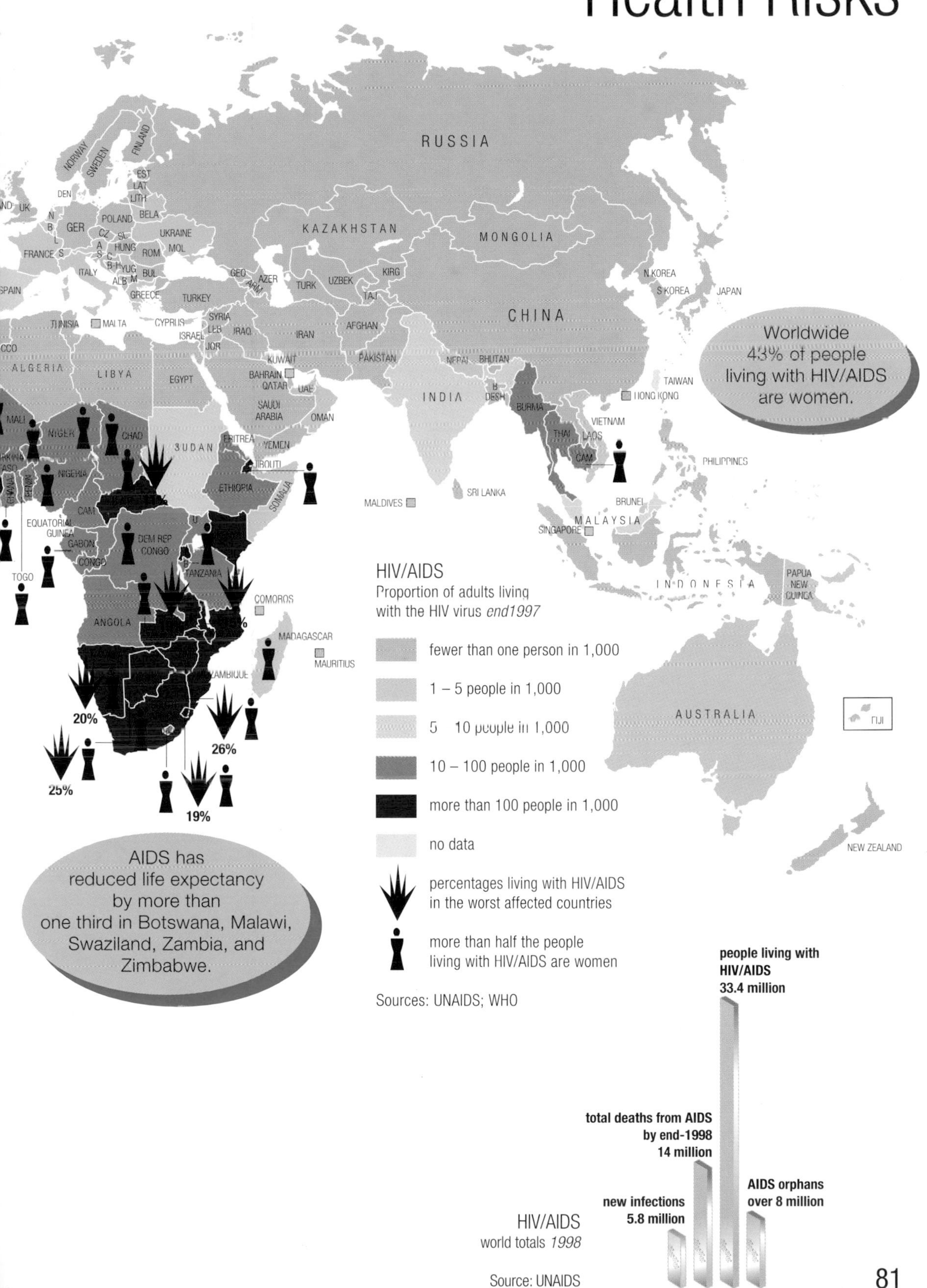
RUSSIA
KAZAKHSTAN
MONGOLIA
CHINA
INDIA
N.KOREA
S.KOREA
JAPAN
TAIWAN
HONG KONG
VIETNAM
LAOS
THAI
CAM
BURMA
B DESH
NEPAL
BHUTAN
PAKISTAN
AFGHAN
IRAN
IRAQ
SYRIA
LEB
ISRAEL
JOR
KUWAIT
BAHRAIN
QATAR
UAE
SAUDI ARABIA
OMAN
YEMEN
TURKEY
CYPRUS
GEO
AZER
ARM
TURK
UZBEK
KIRG
TAJ
NORWAY
SWEDEN
FINLAND
EST
LAT
LITH
DEN
UK
N
B
L
GER
POLAND
BELA
CZ
SL
A
HUNG
S
C
B-H
YUG
ALB
M
ROM
MOL
UKRAINE
BUL
GREECE
ITALY
FRANCE
SPAIN
TUNISIA
MALTA
ALGERIA
LIBYA
EGYPT
SUDAN
ERITREA
DJIBOUTI
ETHIOPIA
SOMALIA
MALI
NIGER
CHAD
NIGERIA
BENIN
GHANA
TOGO
CAM
EQUATORIAL GUINEA
GABON
CONGO
DEM REP CONGO
U
B
TANZANIA
ANGOLA
COMOROS
MADAGASCAR
MAURITIUS
20%
25%
26%
19%
PHILIPPINES
SRI LANKA
MALDIVES
BRUNEI
MALAYSIA
SINGAPORE
INDONESIA
PAPUA NEW GUINEA
AUSTRALIA
FIJI
NEW ZEALAND
Worldwide 43% of people living with HIV/AIDS are women.
AIDS has reduced life expectancy by more than one third in Botswana, Malawi, Swaziland, Zambia, and Zimbabwe.
HIV/AIDS
Proportion of adults living with the HIV virus *end1997*
fewer than one person in 1,000
1 – 5 people in 1,000
5 – 10 people in 1,000
10 – 100 people in 1,000
more than 100 people in 1,000
no data
percentages living with HIV/AIDS in the worst affected countries
more than half the people living with HIV/AIDS are women
Sources: UNAIDS; WHO
HIV/AIDS
world totals *1998*
new infections 5.8 million
total deaths from AIDS by end-1998 14 million
people living with HIV/AIDS 33.4 million
AIDS orphans over 8 million
Source: UNAIDS

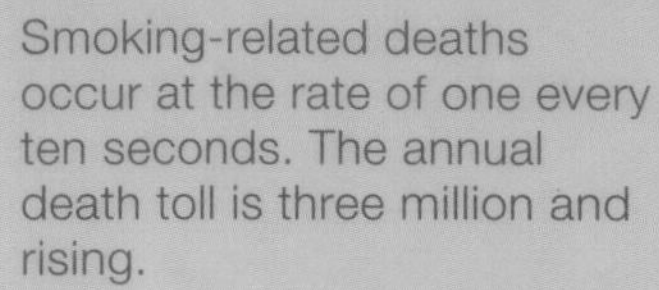

Smoking-related deaths occur at the rate of one every ten seconds. The annual death toll is three million and rising.

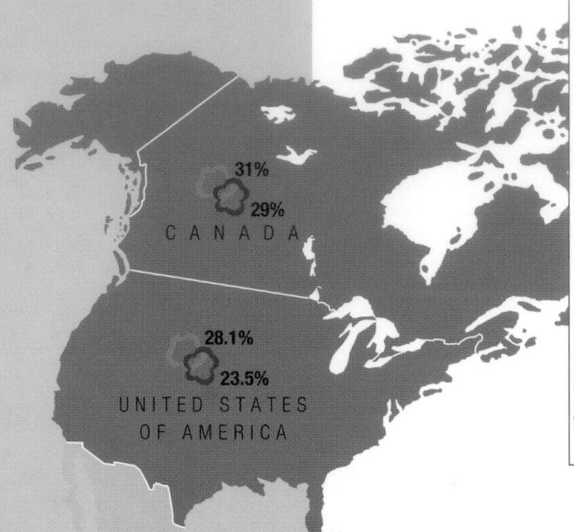

31%
29%
CANADA
28.1%
23.5%
UNITED STATES OF AMERICA
MEXICO
CUBA
JAMAICA
DOMINICAN REPUBLIC
HAITI
BELIZE
HONDURAS
GUATEMALA
EL SALVADOR
NICARAGUA
COSTA RICA
PANAMA
36%
11%
TRINIDAD & TOBAGO
VENEZUELA
GUYANA
SURINAME
FRENCH GUIANA
35.1%
19.1%
COLOMBIA
ECUADOR
PERU
39.9%
25.4%
BRAZIL
BOLIVIA
PARAGUAY
CHILE
37.9%
25.1%
URUGUAY
ARGENTINA
40%
23%
ICELAND
NORWAY
SWEDEN
FINLAND
22%
24%
ESTONIA
LATVIA
LITHUANIA
DENMARK
37%
37%
43%
26%
IRELAND
UK
28%
26%
NETH
BEL
GERMANY
36.8%
21.5%
POLAND
BELARUS
CZECH REPUBLIC
SLOVAK
UKRAINE
FRANCE
40%
27%
SWITZ
AUSTRIA
HUNGARY
ROMANIA
SLO
CROATIA
B-H
YUG
BULG
49%
17%
38%
26%
ITALY
ALB
M
GREECE
49.8%
7.9%
PORTUGAL
SPAIN
48%
25%
TUNISIA
MOROCCO
39.6%
9.1%
ALGERIA
LIBYA
45%
WESTERN SAHARA
MAURITANIA
MALI
NIGER
CHAD
SENEGAL
GAMBIA
GUINEA-BISSAU
GUINEA
SIERRA LEONE
LIBERIA
BURKINA FASO
CÔTE d'IVOIRE
GHANA
TOGO
BENIN
NIGERIA
24.4%
6.7%
CAMEROON
CAR
EQUATORIAL GUINEA
GABON
CONGO
DEM REP CONGO
ANGOLA
ZAMBIA
NAMIBIA
BOTSWANA
SOUTH AFRICA
52%
17%
0.70%
$5,262
USA
0.76%
$1,402
Netherlands
2%
$891
Brazil
0.68%
$620
China
23%
$473
Zimbabwe
3%
$389
Greece
4%
$229
Bulgaria
3%
$7
Uganda
64%
$214
Malawi
7%
$15
Albania
4%
$4
Burundi

Tobacco consumption per person is still higher in the richer countries (24 a day compared to a world average of 15 a day), but has declined by 10-15 percent since the late 1970s.

Tobacco is big business. The main market opportunities now lie in less developed countries, not least China where tobacco consumption has increased by almost 50 percent in the last 20 years, and where a fifth of the world's population smoke almost a third of its cigarettes. Tobacco companies have adapted their sales strategies to meet the opportunity, and smoking-related deaths are projected to rise to 10 million a year by the 2020s, with 70 percent of those deaths in the poorer countries.

TOBACCO EXPORTS

Export revenue from tobacco and as a proportion of total export revenue
1993 US $ million
selected countries

Source: WHO, 1996

Smoking

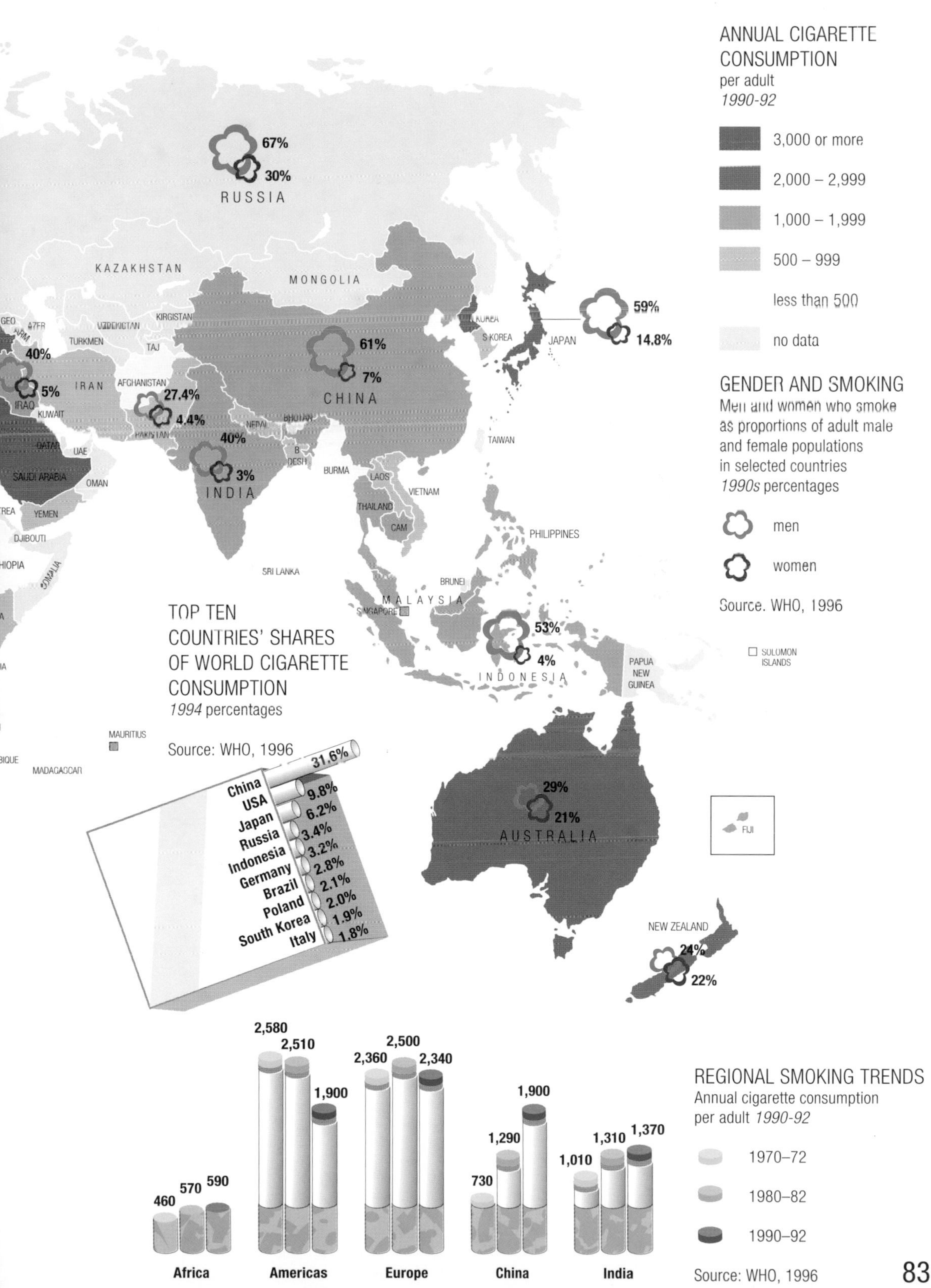

ANNUAL CIGARETTE CONSUMPTION
per adult
1990-92
3,000 or more
2,000 – 2,999
1,000 – 1,999
500 – 999
less than 500
no data
GENDER AND SMOKING
Men and women who smoke as proportions of adult male and female populations in selected countries
1990s percentages
men
women
Source: WHO, 1996
RUSSIA
67%
30%
KAZAKHSTAN
MONGOLIA
CHINA
61%
7%
JAPAN
59%
14.8%
S KOREA
TAIWAN
IRAN
IRAQ
40%
5%
KUWAIT
QATAR
UAE
SAUDI ARABIA
OMAN
YEMEN
DJIBOUTI
AFGHANISTAN
PAKISTAN
27.4%
4.4%
NEPAL
BHUTAN
INDIA
40%
3%
TURKMEN
KIRGISTAN
TAJ
B DESH
BURMA
LAOS
VIETNAM
THAILAND
CAM
PHILIPPINES
SRI LANKA
BRUNEI
MALAYSIA
SINGAPORE
INDONESIA
53%
4%
PAPUA NEW GUINEA
SOLOMON ISLANDS
MAURITIUS
MADAGASCAR
AUSTRALIA
29%
21%
FIJI
NEW ZEALAND
24%
22%
TOP TEN COUNTRIES' SHARES OF WORLD CIGARETTE CONSUMPTION
1994 percentages
Source: WHO, 1996
China 31.6%
USA 9.8%
Japan 6.2%
Russia 3.4%
Indonesia 3.2%
Germany 2.8%
Brazil 2.1%
Poland 2.0%
South Korea 1.9%
Italy 1.8%
REGIONAL SMOKING TRENDS
Annual cigarette consumption per adult 1990-92
1970–72
1980–82
1990–92
Source: WHO, 1996
Africa 460 570 590
Americas 2,580 2,510 1,900
Europe 2,360 2,500 2,340
China 730 1,290 1,900
India 1,010 1,310 1,370

This is the age of information and communication. The richest man in the world is not a merchant prince, a baron of industry, or an oil tycoon. He is an information magnate.

The amount of information that can be transmitted and the speed with which it can be sent have increased so fast that all the most extravagant adjectives have been used up.

The speed and reliability of communication are still increasing. Optical fibre technology is making possible a 400-fold increase in speed. New low-orbit satellites produce stronger signals and thus more reliable communications than their high-orbit predecessors.

In many poor countries, it may take a decade to install a telephone mainline. Cellphones promise a far cheaper and faster way of gaining access to the new communication system. Whether the theory of global coverage works in practice has yet to be seen.

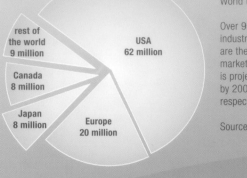

ON-LINE USERS *1998*

World total: 107 million

Over 90% of internet users are in industrial countries. China and India are the fastest growing internet markets, where the number of users is projected to increase 15-fold by 2000 to 4 million and 1.5 million respectively.

Source: Brown, *Vital Signs 1998-99*

ON-LINE HOSTS *1998*

A host computer can represent one or more internet users as part of a network.

Hosts per 1,000 people:
Most: Finland 877
Fewest: Africa, under 2

Sources: Network Wizards, 1998; Brown, *Vital Signs 1998-99*

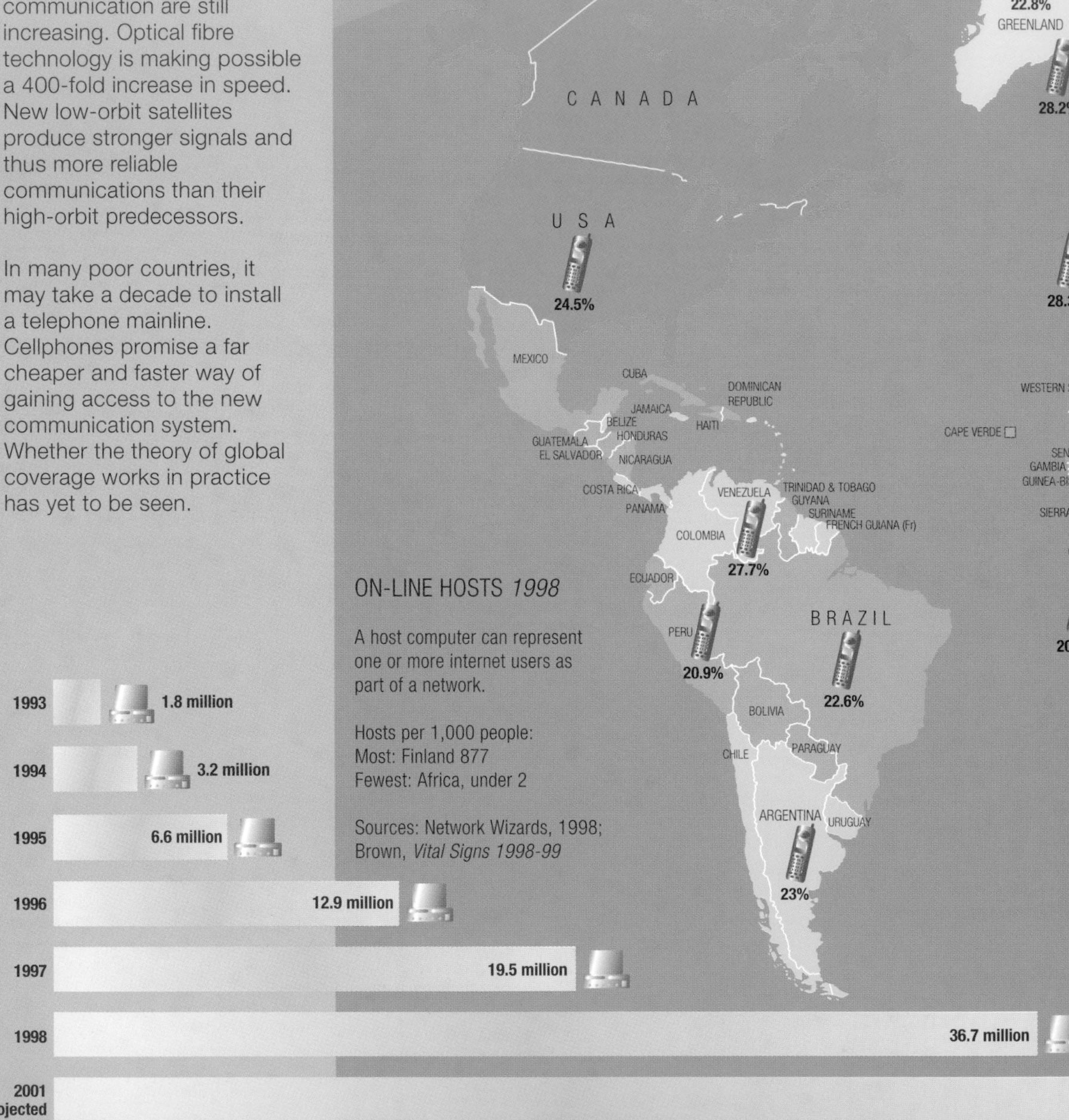

USA
62 million
Europe
20 million
Japan
8 million
Canada
8 million
rest of the world
9 million
CANADA
USA
24.5%
22.8%
GREENLAND
28.2%
26.2%
28.3%
MEXICO
CUBA
JAMAICA
BELIZE
HONDURAS
HAITI
DOMINICAN REPUBLIC
GUATEMALA
EL SALVADOR
NICARAGUA
COSTA RICA
PANAMA
VENEZUELA
TRINIDAD & TOBAGO
GUYANA
SURINAME
FRENCH GUIANA (Fr)
COLOMBIA
27.7%
ECUADOR
PERU
20.9%
BRAZIL
22.6%
BOLIVIA
CHILE
PARAGUAY
ARGENTINA
URUGUAY
23%
CAPE VERDE
WESTERN SAHARA
SENEGAL
GAMBIA
GUINEA-BISSAU
SIERRA LEONE
20.2%
1993
1.8 million
1994
3.2 million
1995
6.6 million
1996
12.9 million
1997
19.5 million
1998
36.7 million
2001 projected

Communications

LOW-ORBIT SATELLITES *1998*

The first low-orbit satellite system was launched in 1998 to provide universal mobile telephone reception for subscribers. Iridium's 66 satellites will be joined by other systems, including Globalstar and ICO by the turn of the century. By 2002, Teledesic, financed by a consortium including Bill Gates, will launch into orbit another 288 satellites.

Source: Pearson, 1998

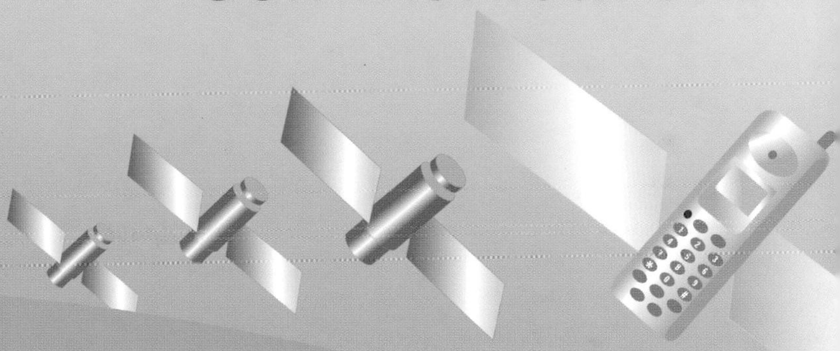

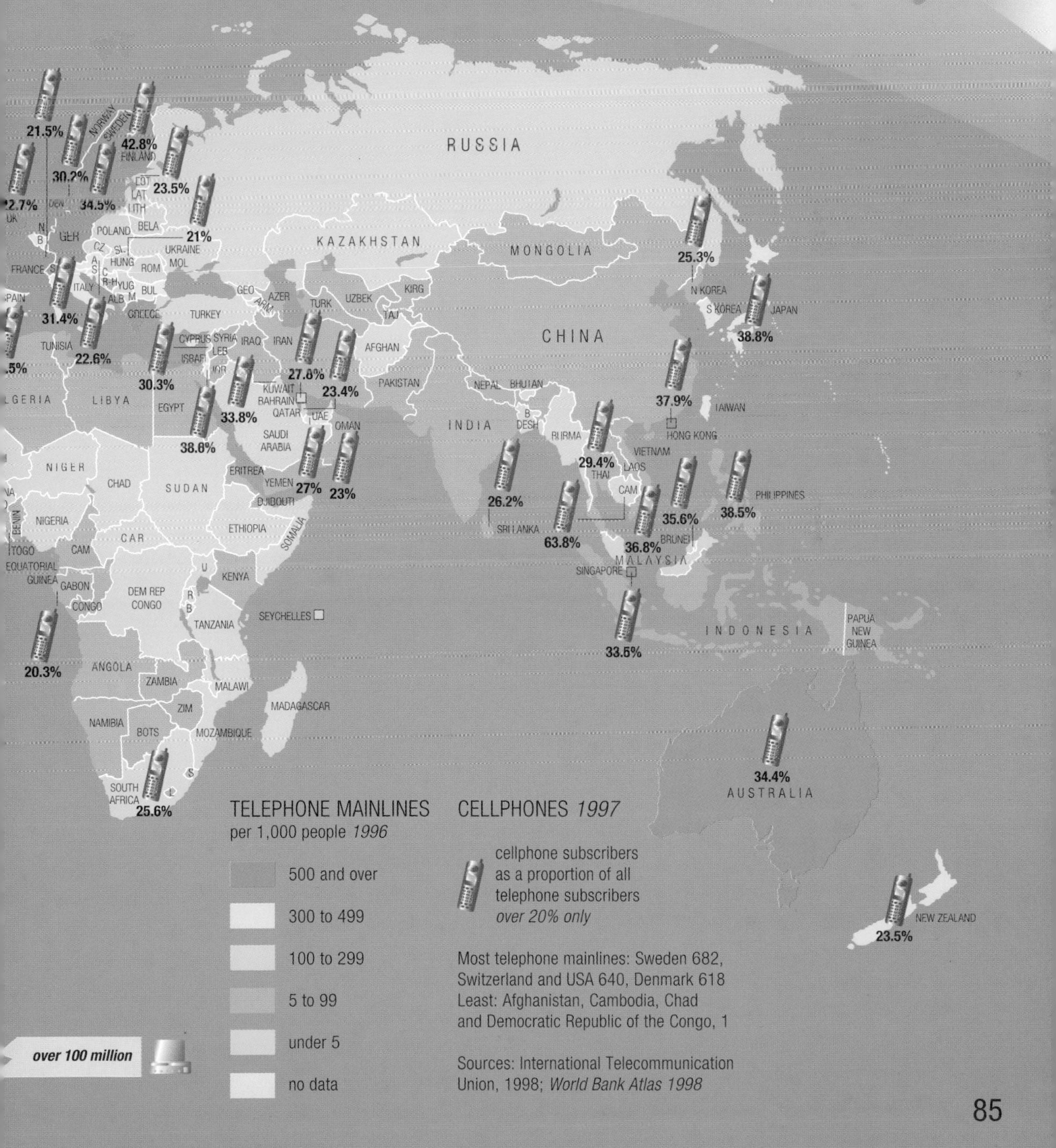

NEW ZEALAND
23.5%

TELEPHONE MAINLINES

per 1,000 people *1996*

- 500 and over
- 300 to 499
- 100 to 299
- 5 to 99
- under 5
- no data

over 100 million

CELLPHONES *1997*

cellphone subscribers as a proportion of all telephone subscribers *over 20% only*

Most telephone mainlines: Sweden 682, Switzerland and USA 640, Denmark 618
Least: Afghanistan, Cambodia, Chad and Democratic Republic of the Congo, 1

Sources: International Telecommunication Union, 1998; *World Bank Atlas 1998*

Many parts of the world have very limited access to television, while in rich countries televisions and TV channels proliferate.

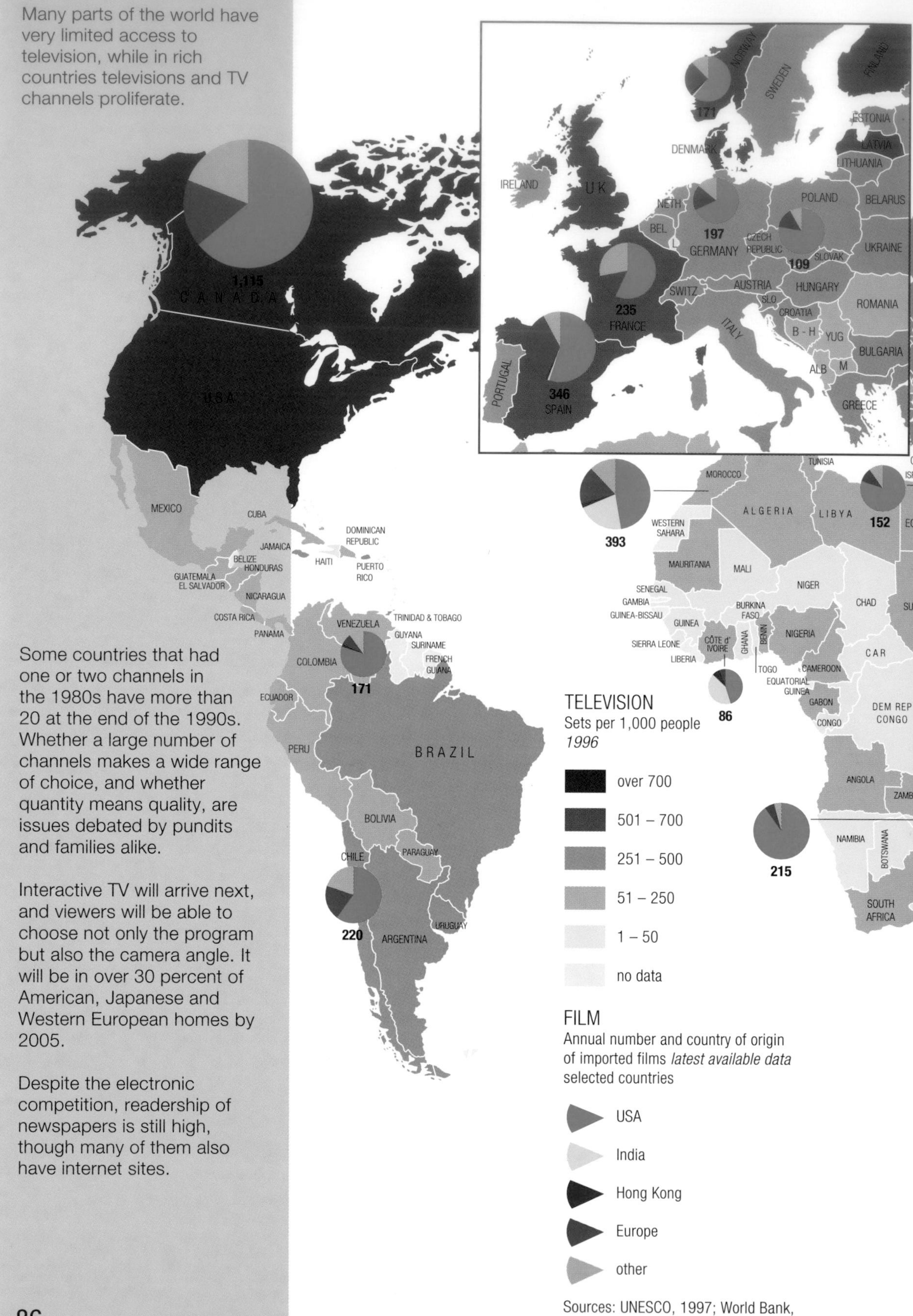

1,115
CANADA
USA
MEXICO
CUBA
JAMAICA
BELIZE
HONDURAS
GUATEMALA
EL SALVADOR
NICARAGUA
COSTA RICA
PANAMA
HAITI
DOMINICAN REPUBLIC
PUERTO RICO
TRINIDAD & TOBAGO
VENEZUELA
171
GUYANA
SURINAME
FRENCH GUIANA
COLOMBIA
ECUADOR
PERU
BRAZIL
BOLIVIA
PARAGUAY
CHILE
220
URUGUAY
ARGENTINA
IRELAND
UK
NORWAY
171
SWEDEN
FINLAND
ESTONIA
LATVIA
LITHUANIA
DENMARK
NETH
BEL
L
197
GERMANY
POLAND
BELARUS
CZECH REPUBLIC
109
SLOVAK
UKRAINE
235
FRANCE
SWITZ
AUSTRIA
HUNGARY
ROMANIA
SLO
CROATIA
B - H
YUG
BULGARIA
ITALY
ALB
M
GREECE
PORTUGAL
346
SPAIN
TUNISIA
MOROCCO
393
ALGERIA
LIBYA
152
EGYPT
WESTERN SAHARA
MAURITANIA
MALI
NIGER
CHAD
SENEGAL
GAMBIA
GUINEA-BISSAU
GUINEA
SIERRA LEONE
LIBERIA
BURKINA FASO
CÔTE d'IVOIRE
GHANA
TOGO
BENIN
NIGERIA
86
CAR
CAMEROON
EQUATORIAL GUINEA
GABON
CONGO
DEM REP CONGO
ANGOLA
ZAMBIA
NAMIBIA
BOTSWANA
215
SOUTH AFRICA
TELEVISION
Sets per 1,000 people
1996
over 700
501 – 700
251 – 500
51 – 250
1 – 50
no data
FILM
Annual number and country of origin of imported films *latest available data* selected countries
USA
India
Hong Kong
Europe
other
Sources: UNESCO, 1997; World Bank, *World Development Indicators,* 1998

Some countries that had one or two channels in the 1980s have more than 20 at the end of the 1990s. Whether a large number of channels makes a wide range of choice, and whether quantity means quality, are issues debated by pundits and families alike.

Interactive TV will arrive next, and viewers will be able to choose not only the program but also the camera angle. It will be in over 30 percent of American, Japanese and Western European homes by 2005.

Despite the electronic competition, readership of newspapers is still high, though many of them also have internet sites.

Media

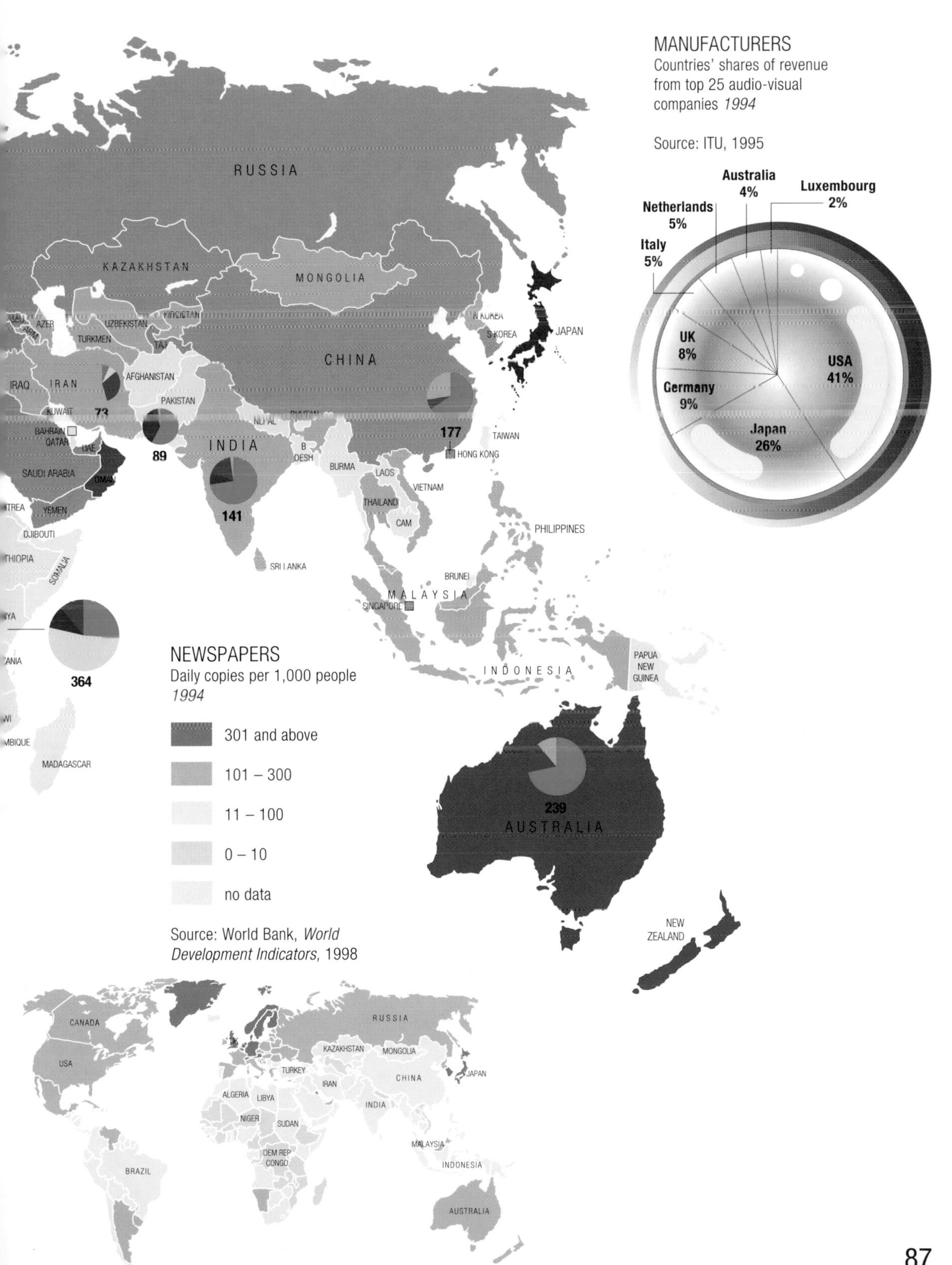
MANUFACTURERS
Countries' shares of revenue from top 25 audio-visual companies 1994
Source: ITU, 1995
Australia 4%
Luxembourg 2%
Netherlands 5%
Italy 5%
UK 8%
Germany 9%
Japan 26%
USA 41%
NEWSPAPERS
Daily copies per 1,000 people 1994
301 and above
101 – 300
11 – 100
0 – 10
no data
Source: World Bank, World Development Indicators, 1998
RUSSIA
KAZAKHSTAN
MONGOLIA
CHINA
JAPAN
S KOREA
AZER
UZBEKISTAN
TURKMEN
IRAQ
IRAN
AFGHANISTAN
PAKISTAN
KUWAIT
BAHRAIN
QATAR
UAE
SAUDI ARABIA
OMAN
YEMEN
DJIBOUTI
SOMALIA
INDIA
BURMA
LAOS
VIETNAM
THAILAND
CAM
TAIWAN
HONG KONG
PHILIPPINES
SRI LANKA
BRUNEI
MALAYSIA
SINGAPORE
INDONESIA
PAPUA NEW GUINEA
AUSTRALIA
NEW ZEALAND
MADAGASCAR
73
89
141
177
364
239
CANADA
USA
TURKEY
ALGERIA
LIBYA
NIGER
SUDAN
DEM REP CONGO
BRAZIL

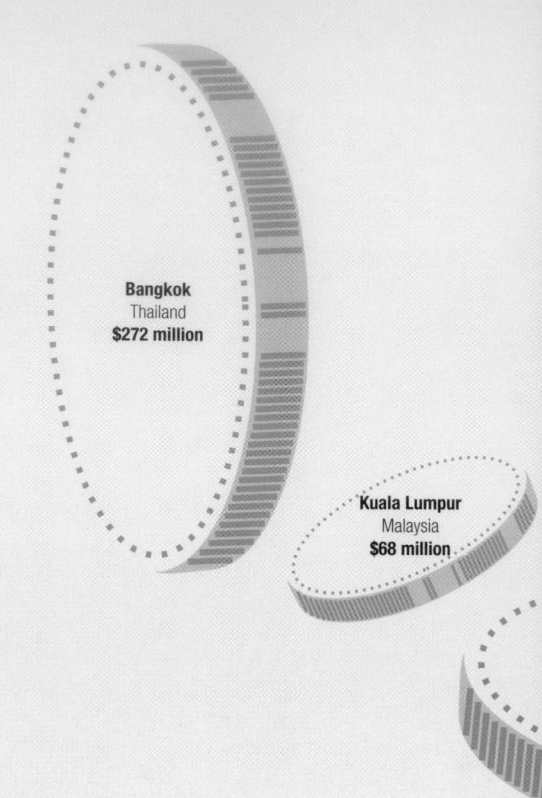
Bangkok
Thailand
$272 million
Kuala Lumpur
Malaysia
$68 million

Part Six **Sustaining the World**

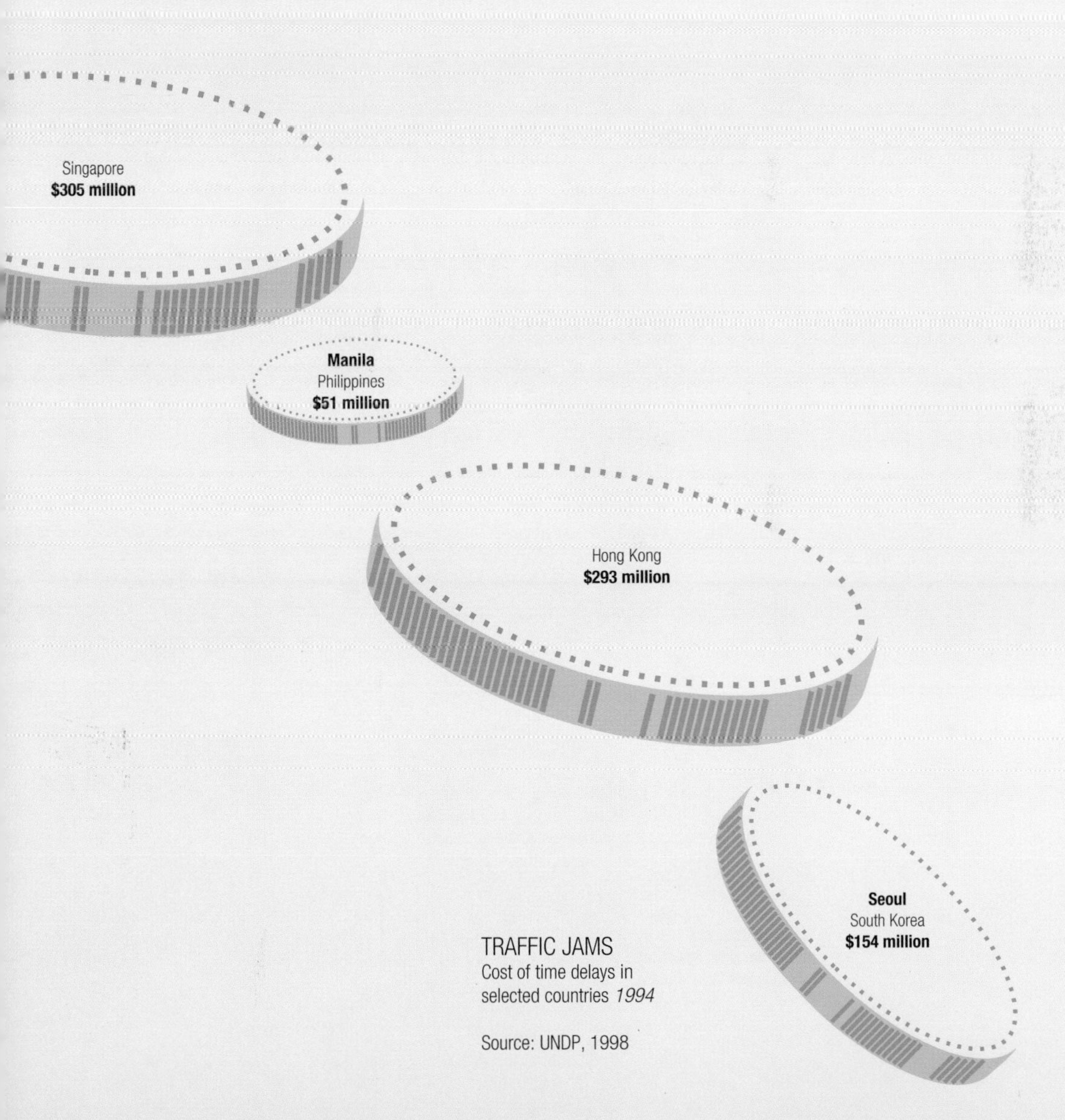

Singapore
$305 million
Manila
Philippines
$51 million
Hong Kong
$293 million
Seoul
South Korea
$154 million

TRAFFIC JAMS
Cost of time delays in selected countries *1994*

Source: UNDP, 1998

A steadily increasing percentage of the world's population lives in cities.

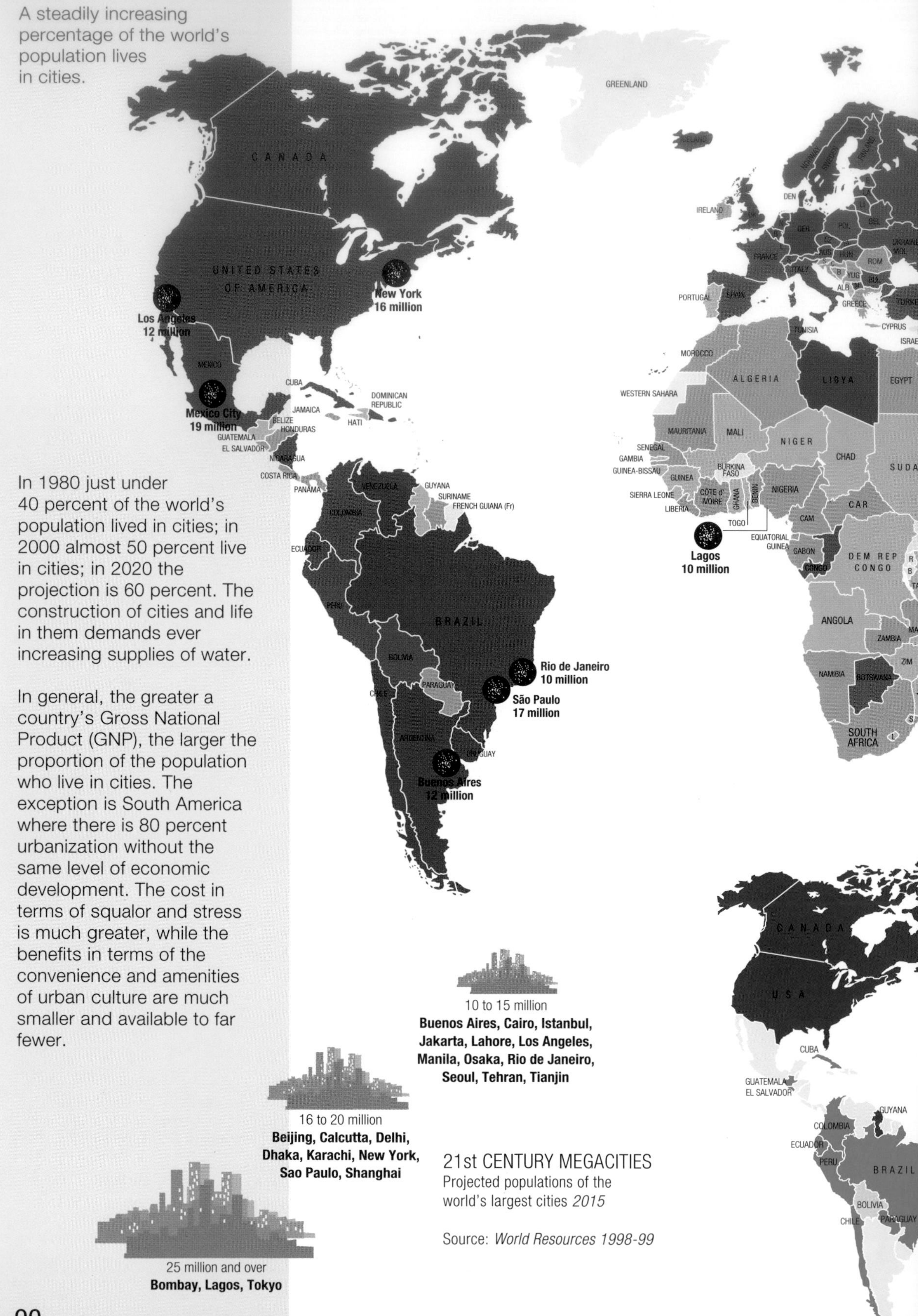
GREENLAND
CANADA
UNITED STATES OF AMERICA
New York
16 million
Los Angeles
12 million
MEXICO
Mexico City
19 million
CUBA
JAMAICA
DOMINICAN REPUBLIC
HAITI
BELIZE
HONDURAS
GUATEMALA
EL SALVADOR
NICARAGUA
COSTA RICA
PANAMA
VENEZUELA
GUYANA
SURINAME
FRENCH GUIANA (Fr)
COLOMBIA
ECUADOR
PERU
BRAZIL
BOLIVIA
PARAGUAY
CHILE
ARGENTINA
URUGUAY
Rio de Janeiro
10 million
São Paulo
17 million
Buenos Aires
12 million
IRELAND
UK
DEN
GER
POL
FRANCE
PORTUGAL
SPAIN
ITALY
GREECE
TURKEY
CYPRUS
ISRAEL
UKRAINE
ROM
BUL
MOROCCO
ALGERIA
TUNISIA
LIBYA
EGYPT
WESTERN SAHARA
MAURITANIA
MALI
NIGER
CHAD
SUDAN
SENEGAL
GAMBIA
GUINEA-BISSAU
GUINEA
SIERRA LEONE
LIBERIA
BURKINA FASO
CÔTE d' IVOIRE
GHANA
TOGO
BENIN
NIGERIA
CAM
CAR
EQUATORIAL GUINEA
GABON
CONGO
DEM REP CONGO
Lagos
10 million
ANGOLA
ZAMBIA
ZIM
NAMIBIA
BOTSWANA
SOUTH AFRICA
CANADA
USA
CUBA
GUATEMALA
EL SALVADOR
GUYANA
COLOMBIA
ECUADOR
PERU
BRAZIL
BOLIVIA
CHILE
PARAGUAY

In 1980 just under 40 percent of the world's population lived in cities; in 2000 almost 50 percent live in cities; in 2020 the projection is 60 percent. The construction of cities and life in them demands ever increasing supplies of water.

In general, the greater a country's Gross National Product (GNP), the larger the proportion of the population who live in cities. The exception is South America where there is 80 percent urbanization without the same level of economic development. The cost in terms of squalor and stress is much greater, while the benefits in terms of the convenience and amenities of urban culture are much smaller and available to far fewer.

10 to 15 million
Buenos Aires, Cairo, Istanbul, Jakarta, Lahore, Los Angeles, Manila, Osaka, Rio de Janeiro, Seoul, Tehran, Tianjin

16 to 20 million
Beijing, Calcutta, Delhi, Dhaka, Karachi, New York, Sao Paulo, Shanghai

25 million and over
Bombay, Lagos, Tokyo

21st CENTURY MEGACITIES
Projected populations of the world's largest cities *2015*

Source: *World Resources 1998-99*

Cities

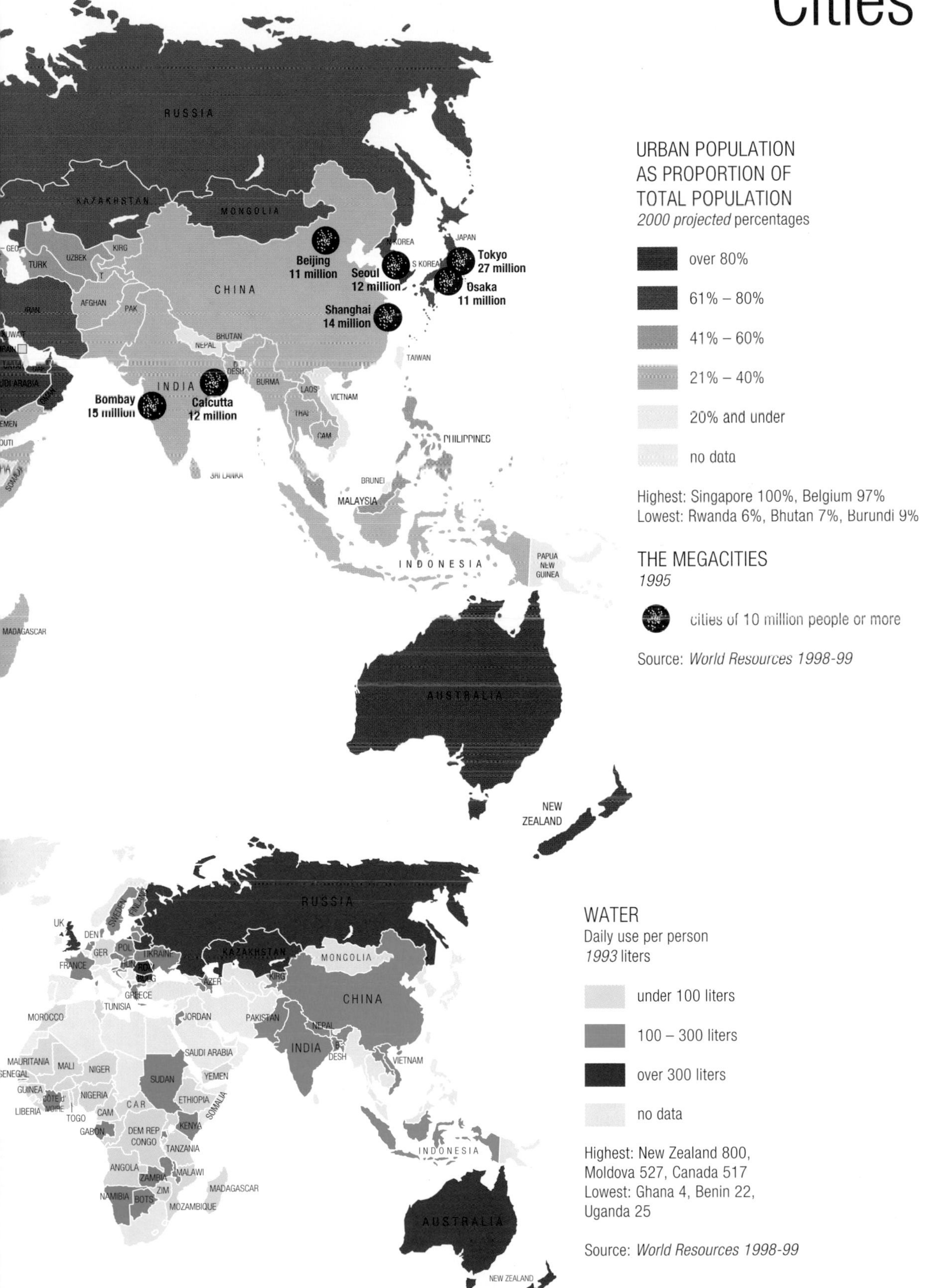
RUSSIA
KAZAKHSTAN
MONGOLIA
CHINA
INDIA
JAPAN
N KOREA
S KOREA
TURK
UZBEK
KIRG
AFGHAN
PAK
IRAN
NEPAL
BHUTAN
BURMA
LAOS
VIETNAM
THAI
CAM
TAIWAN
PHILIPPINES
SRI LANKA
BRUNEI
MALAYSIA
INDONESIA
PAPUA NEW GUINEA
AUSTRALIA
NEW ZEALAND
MADAGASCAR
Beijing 11 million
Seoul 12 million
Tokyo 27 million
Osaka 11 million
Shanghai 14 million
Bombay 15 million
Calcutta 12 million
UK
DEN
GER
POL
FRANCE
UKRAINE
GREECE
TUNISIA
MOROCCO
JORDAN
PAKISTAN
SAUDI ARABIA
YEMEN
MAURITANIA
MALI
NIGER
SENEGAL
GUINEA
NIGERIA
LIBERIA
TOGO
CAM
CAR
SUDAN
ETHIOPIA
SOMALIA
GABON
DEM REP CONGO
KENYA
TANZANIA
ANGOLA
ZAMBIA
MALAWI
NAMIBIA
BOTS
ZIM
MOZAMBIQUE
AZER
DESH

URBAN POPULATION AS PROPORTION OF TOTAL POPULATION
2000 projected percentages

- over 80%
- 61% – 80%
- 41% – 60%
- 21% – 40%
- 20% and under
- no data

Highest: Singapore 100%, Belgium 97%
Lowest: Rwanda 6%, Bhutan 7%, Burundi 9%

THE MEGACITIES
1995

- cities of 10 million people or more

Source: *World Resources 1998-99*

WATER
Daily use per person
1993 liters

- under 100 liters
- 100 – 300 liters
- over 300 liters
- no data

Highest: New Zealand 800, Moldova 527, Canada 517
Lowest: Ghana 4, Benin 22, Uganda 25

Source: *World Resources 1998-99*

There are 600 million passenger cars worldwide, more than twelve times the number in the late-1940s. It is likely that the car population will continue to grow faster than the human population at least until 2020.

Cars are a convenient, decentralized, affordable means of transport. But over 300,000 deaths and 8 million injuries a year are caused by traffic accidents, making the car a much more dangerous means of transport than trains and planes. Cars also cause more air pollution, emission of greenhouse gases (see **Global Warming**, pp.98-9) and noise than trains. The USA is the greatest gas guzzler. This is where the automobile revolution began and became the basis of the country's pre-eminent industrial strength for much of the twentieth century. Here, still, the love affair with cars involves more of the population than in any other country, although car ownership is not so far behind in a few other countries, and the USA's roads are by no means the world's most congested.

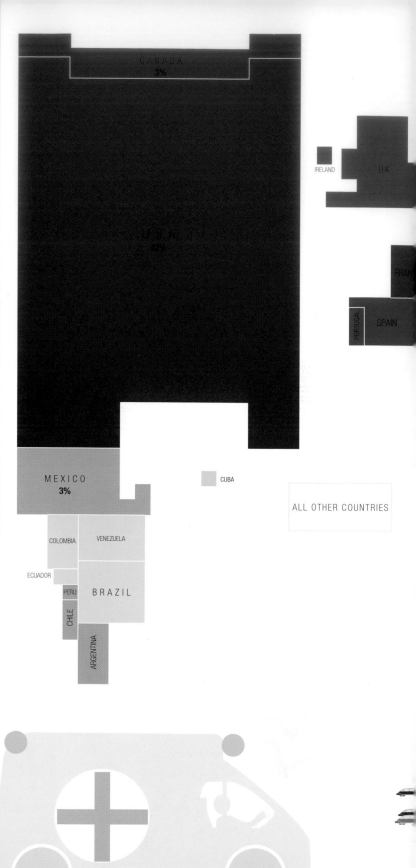

CANADA
3%
USA
IRELAND
UK
FRANCE
PORTUGAL
SPAIN
MEXICO
3%
CUBA
ALL OTHER COUNTRIES
COLOMBIA
VENEZUELA
ECUADOR
PERU
BRAZIL
CHILE
ARGENTINA

ROAD ACCIDENTS
People killed or injured per 1,000 vehicles *1996* selected countries

Source: World Bank, *World Development Indicators,* 1998

Guinea 147
Tanzania 104
Kenya 75
India 65
Algeria 44
Chile 33
USA 17
Japan 14
UK 14
Saudi Arabia 13
Germany 12
Spain 7
France 6

Traffic

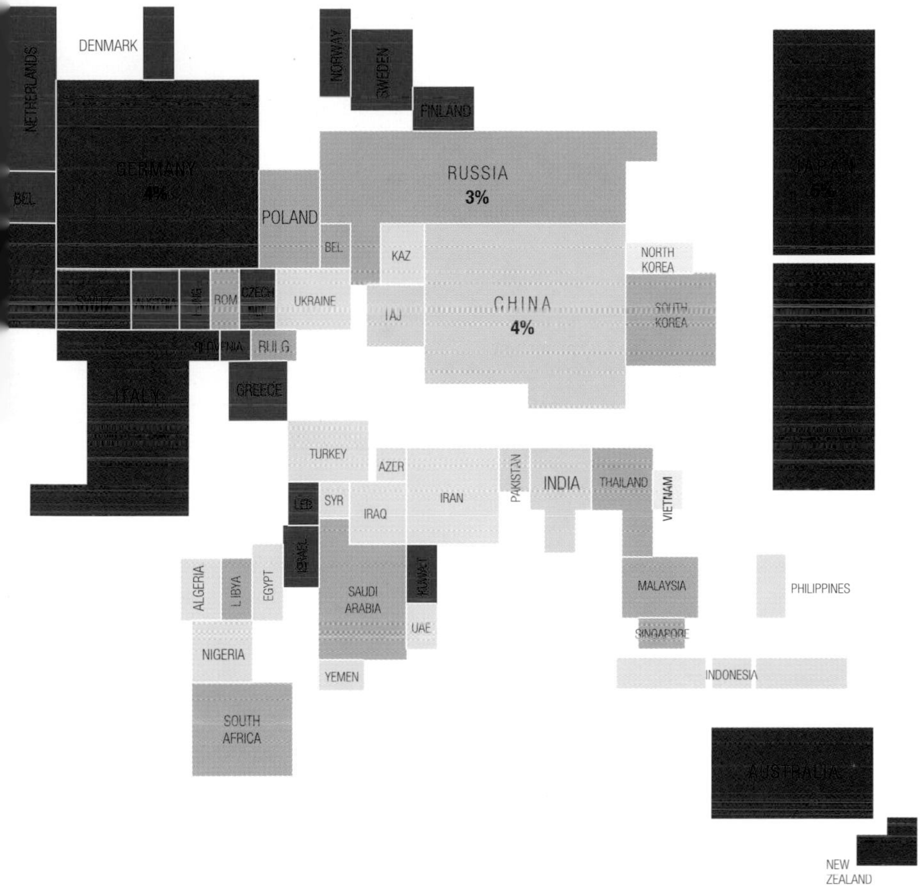

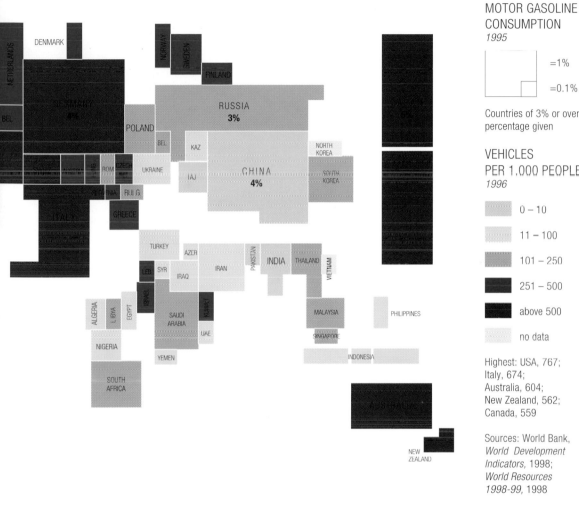

STATES' SHARES OF MOTOR GASOLINE CONSUMPTION
1995

=1%

=0.1%

Countries of 3% or over: percentage given

VEHICLES PER 1,000 PEOPLE
1996

0 – 10

11 – 100

101 – 250

251 – 500

above 500

no data

Highest: USA, 767; Italy, 674; Australia, 604; New Zealand, 562; Canada, 559

Sources: World Bank, *World Development Indicators,* 1998; *World Resources 1998-99,* 1998

TRAFFIC CONGESTION
Number of vehicles per kilometre of road *1996* selected countries

Source: World Bank, *World Development Indicators,* 1998

Hong Kong 276

Lebanon 205

Kuwait 156, Argentina 154

Italy 122

Israel 98

Puerto Rico 74

UK 63, Japan 60

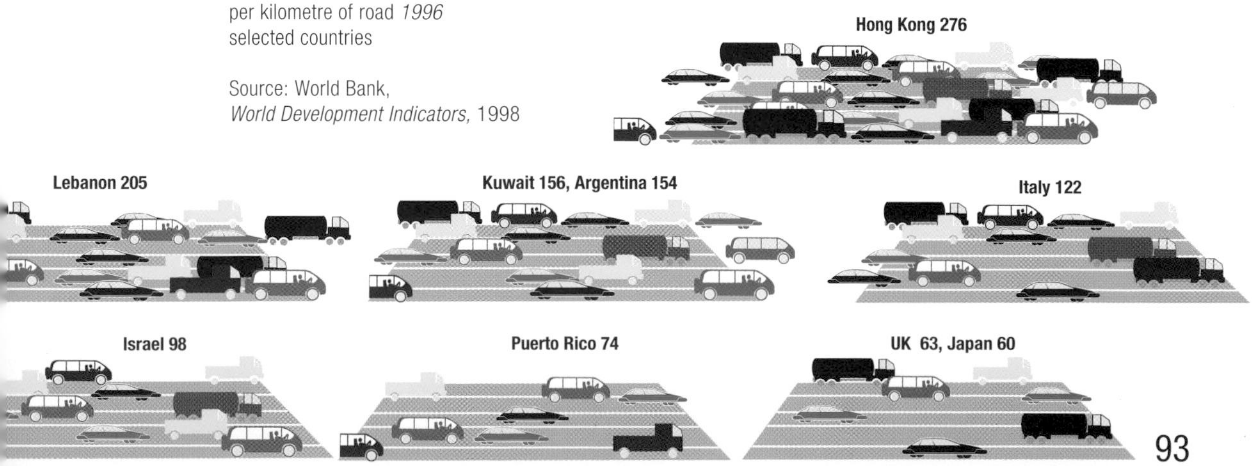

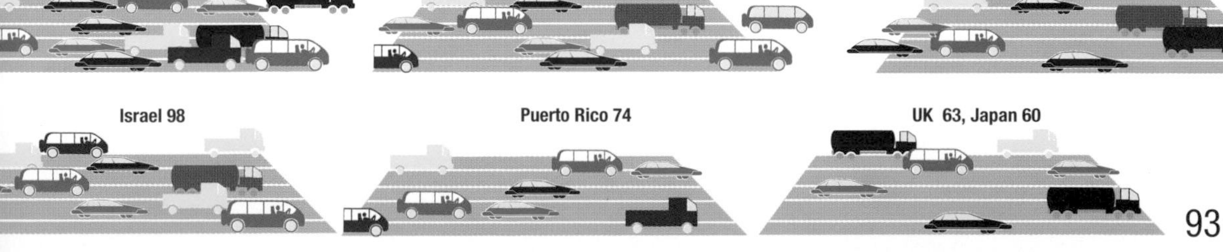

World food production continues to increase. Though malnutrition is severe in many parts of the world's poorest countries, famines have occurred in recent decades only as one of the effects of war.

Being able to import enough from one of the breadbasket countries can compensate for lack of self-sufficiency in food production. It is where deficiency in domestic food production is accompanied by low income per person that the problems of malnutrition arise. In the global perspective, the problem is not a shortage of food but the way it is distributed.

In richer countries the problems are different. There, eating disorders are a social-psychological problem, not a material lack.

Other problems, such as Bovine Spongiform Encephalitis (otherwise known as mad cow disease) arise from the techniques used in the food industry. Genetic modification of foods has been introduced and started to boom without public discussion of possible risks and necessary safeguards.

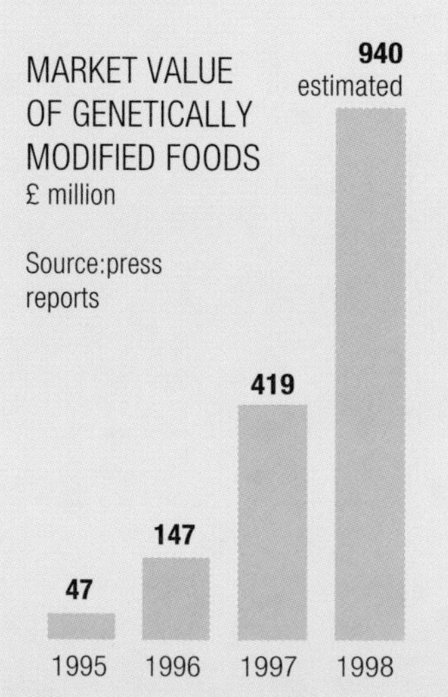
MARKET VALUE
OF GENETICALLY
MODIFIED FOODS
£ million
Source:press
reports
47
147
419
940
estimated
1995
1996
1997
1998

CANADA
USA
MEXICO
COLOMBIA
VENEZUELA
ECUADOR
BRAZIL
CHILE
ARGENTINA

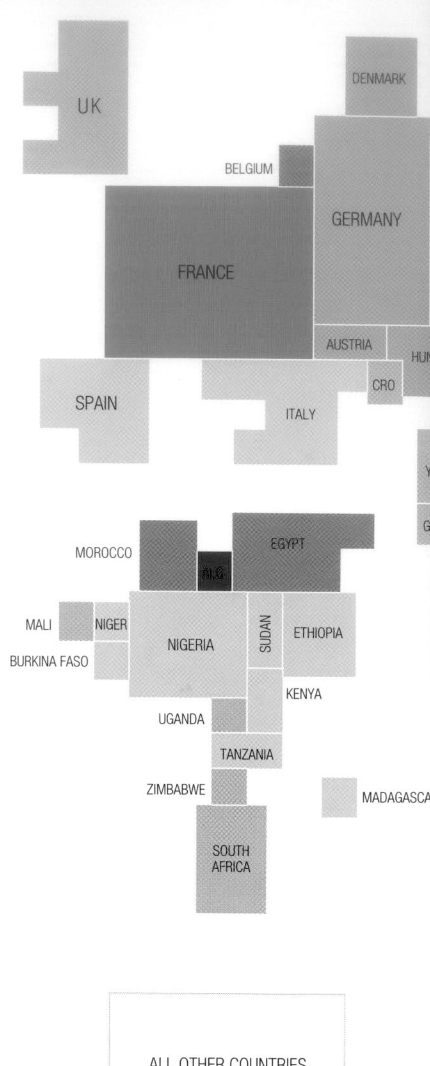
UK
DENMARK
BELGIUM
GERMANY
FRANCE
AUSTRIA
CRO
SPAIN
ITALY
MOROCCO
ALG
EGYPT
MALI
NIGER
NIGERIA
SUDAN
ETHIOPIA
BURKINA FASO
KENYA
UGANDA
TANZANIA
ZIMBABWE
MADAGASCAR
SOUTH AFRICA

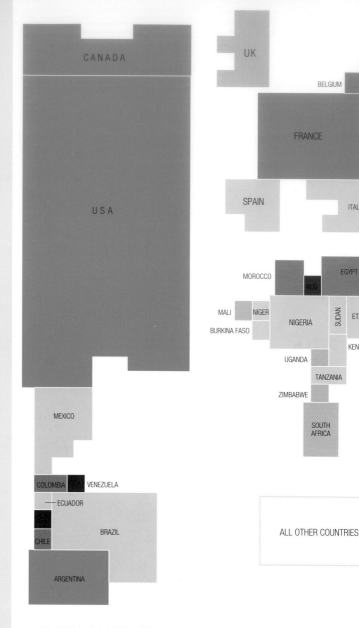

ALL OTHER COUNTRIES

GENETICALLY MODIFIED FOODS ON SALE IN THE USA

Products approved and engineered for insect or pesticide/insecticide resistance include:

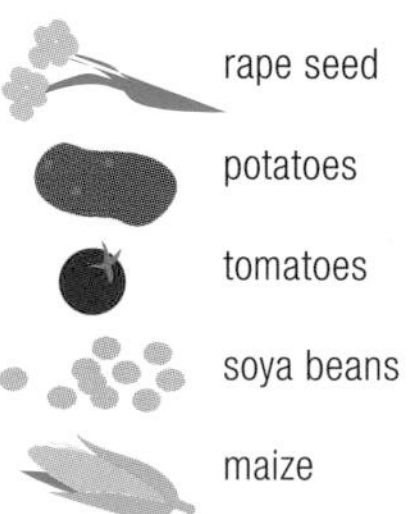
rape seed
potatoes
tomatoes
soya beans
maize

Source: press reports

TOP IMPORTERS OF CEREALS

Percentage of world total *1996*

Source: FAO, 1996

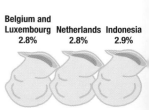

Belgium and Luxembourg 2.8%
Netherlands 2.8%
Indonesia 2.9%

SWEDEN
FINLAND

RUSSIA
BEL
UKRAINE
MOLDOVA
KAZAKHSTAN
UZB
TURKEY
AFGHANISTAN
IRAN
SYRIA
IRAQ
SAUDI ARABIA
PAKISTAN
CHINA
NORTH KOREA
JAPAN
NEPAL
BANGLADESH
BURMA
THAILAND
CAM
VIETNAM
PHILIPPINES
MALAYSIA
INDIA
INDONESIA
SRI LANKA
AUSTRALIA

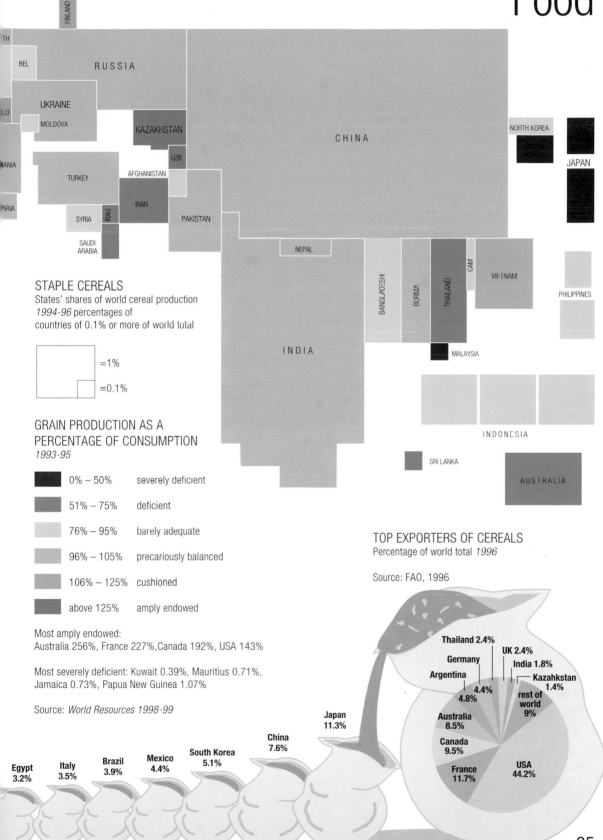

STAPLE CEREALS

States' shares of world cereal production *1994-96* percentages of countries of 0.1% or more of world total

=1%

=0.1%

GRAIN PRODUCTION AS A PERCENTAGE OF CONSUMPTION

1993-95

0% – 50%	severely deficient
51% – 75%	deficient
76% – 95%	barely adequate
96% – 105%	precariously balanced
106% – 125%	cushioned
above 125%	amply endowed

Most amply endowed:
Australia 256%, France 227%,Canada 192%, USA 143%

Most severely deficient: Kuwait 0.39%, Mauritius 0.71%, Jamaica 0.73%, Papua New Guinea 1.07%

Source: *World Resources 1998-99*

TOP EXPORTERS OF CEREALS

Percentage of world total *1996*

Source: FAO, 1996

Thailand 2.4%
UK 2.4%
Germany 4.4%
India 1.8%
Argentina 4.8%
Kazahkstan 1.4%
rest of world 9%
Australia 8.5%
Canada 9.5%
France 11.7%
USA 44.2%
Japan 11.3%
China 7.6%
South Korea 5.1%
Mexico 4.4%
Brazil 3.9%
Italy 3.5%
Egypt 3.2%

Energy is a commodity that is traded, on which fortunes are based, and whose security of supply is a key element of some countries' strategic policies.

Up to a point, the bigger and more advanced national economies consume more energy in total and per person. But only up to a point. As the economic center of gravity in the richer countries shifts from manufacturing industry to the service and information sectors, energy efficiency increases. The richer countries generally use less energy per unit of wealth produced than the developing countries. The growth in commercial energy consumption since 1980 has been faster in middle-income and low-income countries.

The source of most energy consumed is still non-renewable coal, oil, and gas. The environmental and health hazards of their profligate use have been ignored for most of the industrial age. In time, the non-renewable energy sources will run down and there will be a faster pace of change towards using renewables such as nuclear fusion, wind, tide and waves.

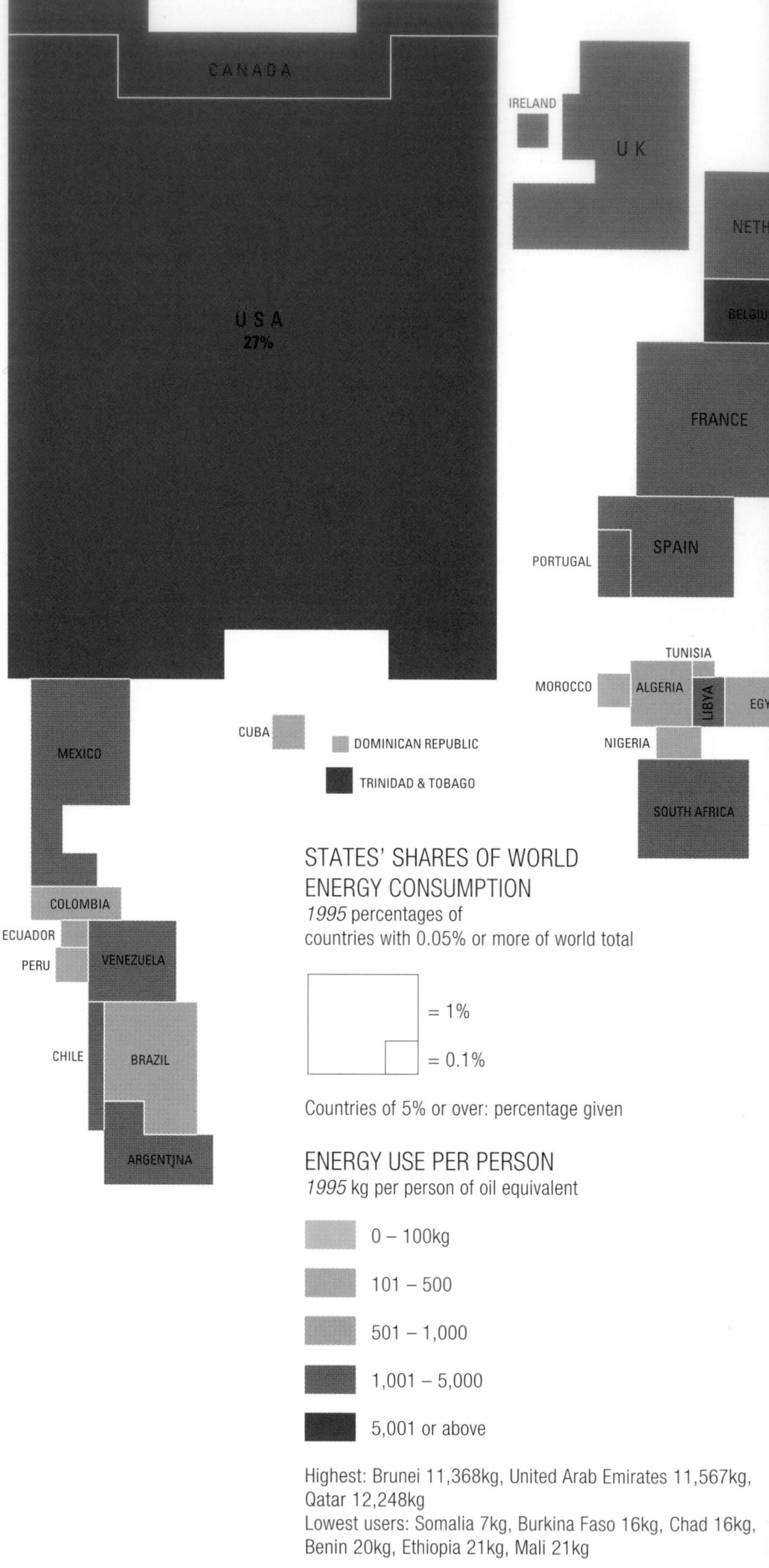
CANADA
USA
27%
IRELAND
UK
NETH
BELGIUM
FRANCE
PORTUGAL
SPAIN
TUNISIA
MOROCCO
ALGERIA
LIBYA
EGYP
NIGERIA
SOUTH AFRICA
MEXICO
CUBA
DOMINICAN REPUBLIC
TRINIDAD & TOBAGO
COLOMBIA
ECUADOR
PERU
VENEZUELA
CHILE
BRAZIL
ARGENTINA
= 1%
= 0.1%
0 – 100kg
101 – 500
501 – 1,000
1,001 – 5,000
5,001 or above

STATES' SHARES OF WORLD ENERGY CONSUMPTION
1995 percentages of countries with 0.05% or more of world total

Countries of 5% or over: percentage given

ENERGY USE PER PERSON
1995 kg per person of oil equivalent

Highest: Brunei 11,368kg, United Arab Emirates 11,567kg, Qatar 12,248kg
Lowest users: Somalia 7kg, Burkina Faso 16kg, Chad 16kg, Benin 20kg, Ethiopia 21kg, Mali 21kg

Sources: World Bank, *World Development Indicators,* 1998; *World Resources 1998-99*

Energy

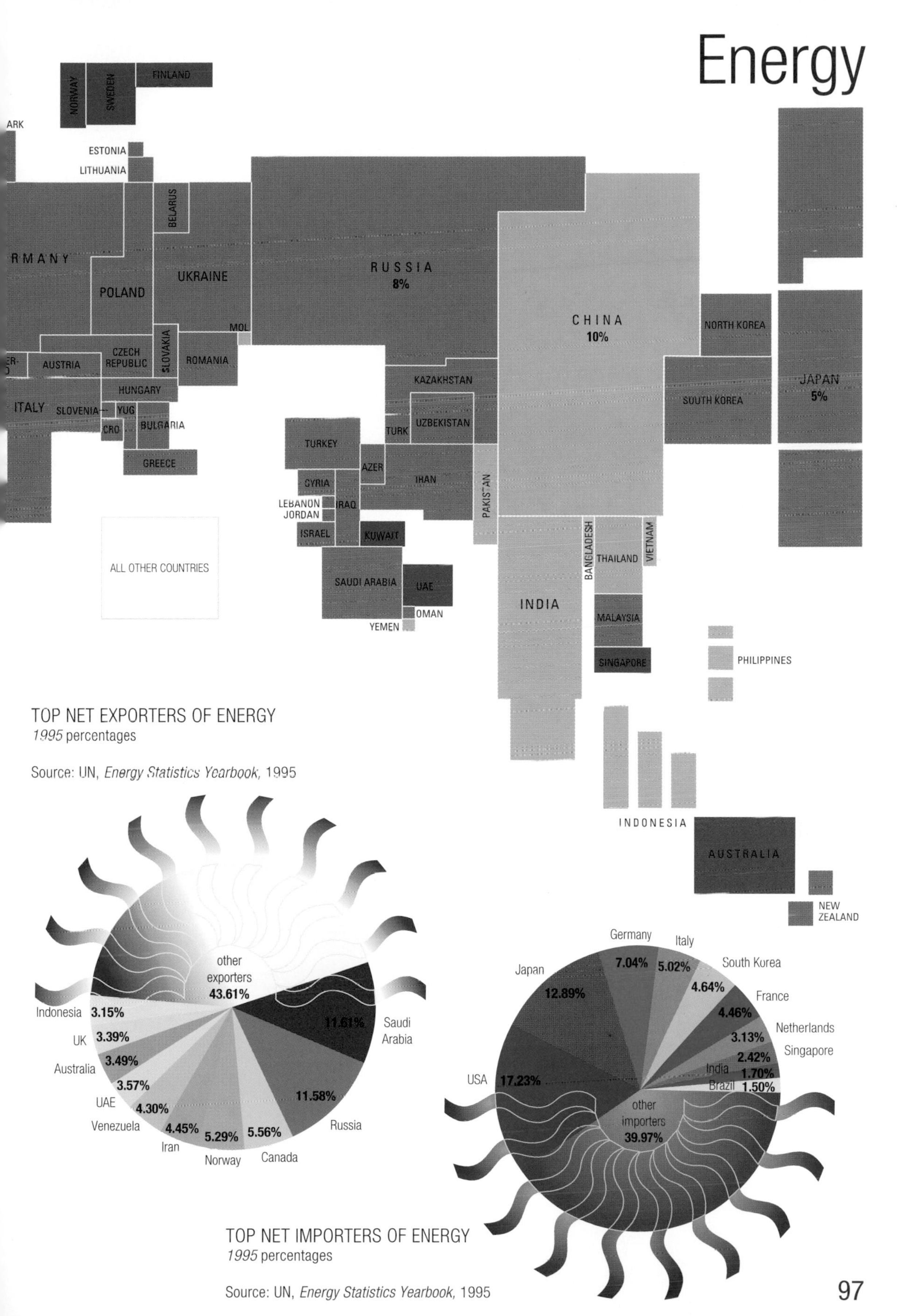
ARK
NORWAY
SWEDEN
FINLAND
ESTONIA
LITHUANIA
BELARUS
RMANY
POLAND
UKRAINE
RUSSIA
8%
CHINA
10%
NORTH KOREA
SOUTH KOREA
JAPAN
5%
MOL
CZECH REPUBLIC
SLOVAKIA
ROMANIA
AUSTRIA
HUNGARY
ITALY
SLOVENIA
YUG
CRO
BULGARIA
GREECE
KAZAKHSTAN
UZBEKISTAN
TURK
TURKEY
AZER
IRAN
SYRIA
LEBANON
JORDAN
IRAQ
ISRAEL
KUWAIT
PAKISTAN
SAUDI ARABIA
UAE
OMAN
YEMEN
ALL OTHER COUNTRIES
INDIA
BANGLADESH
THAILAND
VIETNAM
MALAYSIA
SINGAPORE
PHILIPPINES
INDONESIA
AUSTRALIA
NEW ZEALAND
other exporters 43.61%
Saudi Arabia 11.61%
Russia 11.58%
Canada 5.56%
Norway 5.29%
Iran 4.45%
Venezuela 4.30%
UAE 3.57%
Australia 3.49%
UK 3.39%
Indonesia 3.15%
Japan 12.89%
Germany 7.04%
Italy 5.02%
South Korea 4.64%
France 4.46%
Netherlands 3.13%
Singapore 2.42%
India 1.70%
Brazil 1.50%
USA 17.23%
other importers 39.97%

TOP NET EXPORTERS OF ENERGY
1995 percentages

Source: UN, *Energy Statistics Yearbook*, 1995

TOP NET IMPORTERS OF ENERGY
1995 percentages

Source: UN, *Energy Statistics Yearbook*, 1995

As energy use increases, so do greenhouse gases. The main greenhouse gas is carbon dioxide (CO_2). Its production is particularly associated with the use of fossil fuels and cement. Heavy logging means CO_2 is no longer so well absorbed by forests. Other important greenhouse gases include chlorofluorocarbons (CFCs), which are responsible for depleting the earth's protective layer of ozone.

Small changes in average world temperatures will cause large changes to human and animal habitats and living conditions. The most fearsome scenarios include ice caps melting, and the consequent flooding of low-lying coastal areas and small island states. These projections are hotly contested. International controls on emissions of greenhouse gases are technically feasible and have been agreed but implementation is slow.

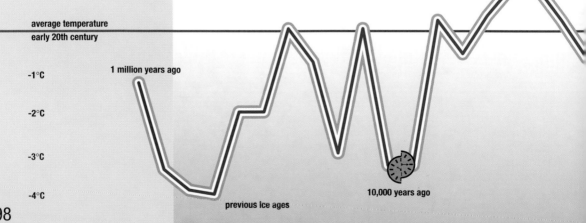

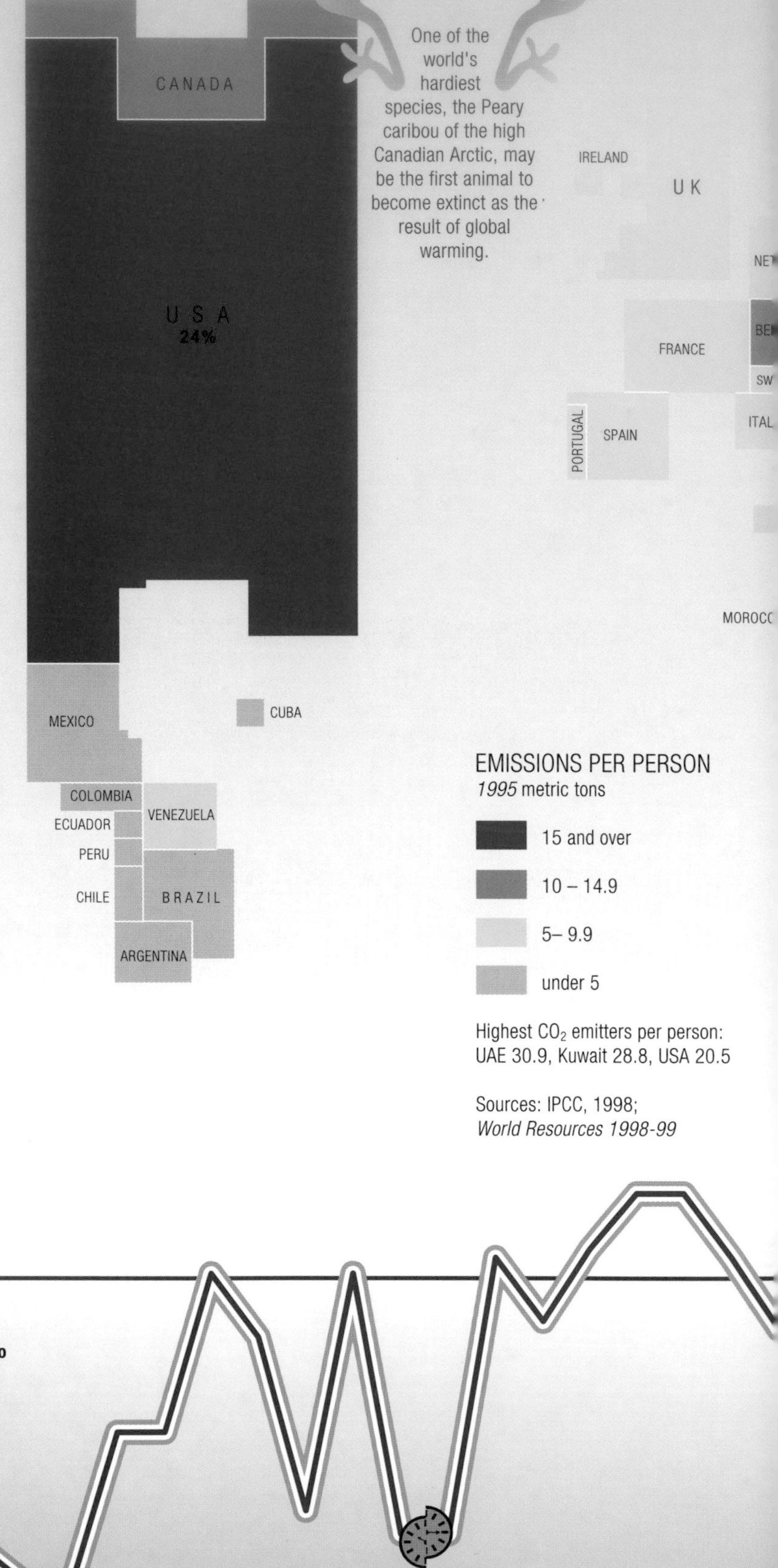
CANADA
USA
24%
MEXICO
CUBA
COLOMBIA
ECUADOR
VENEZUELA
PERU
CHILE
BRAZIL
ARGENTINA
IRELAND
UK
FRANCE
PORTUGAL
SPAIN
MOROCC
EMISSIONS PER PERSON
1995 metric tons
15 and over
10 – 14.9
5– 9.9
under 5
average temperature early 20th century
-1°C
-2°C
-3°C
-4°C
1 million years ago
previous Ice ages
10,000 years ago

One of the world's hardiest species, the Peary caribou of the high Canadian Arctic, may be the first animal to become extinct as the result of global warming.

Highest CO_2 emitters per person: UAE 30.9, Kuwait 28.8, USA 20.5

Sources: IPCC, 1998; *World Resources 1998-99*

Global Warming

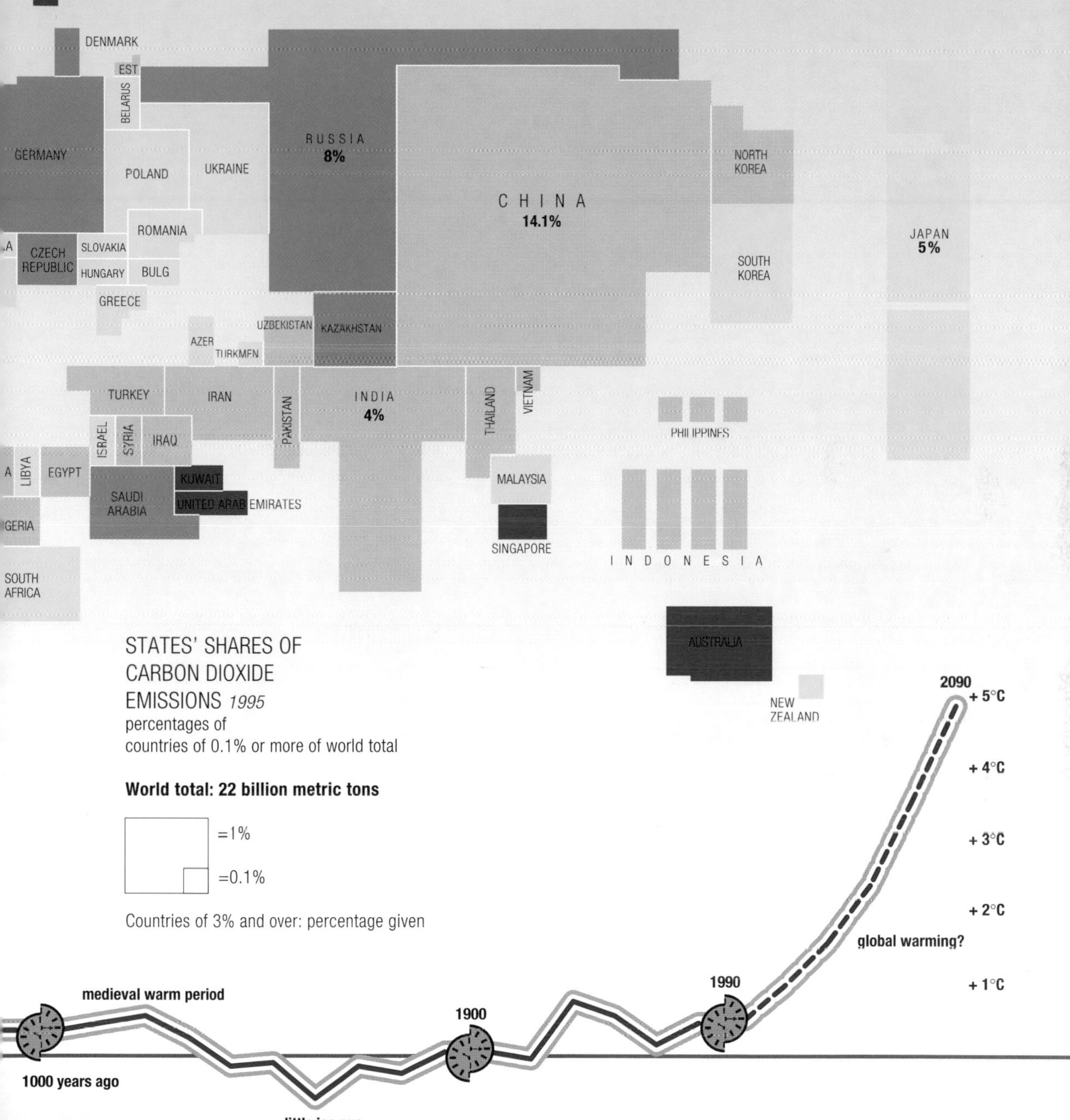
NORWAY
SWEDEN
FINLAND
DENMARK
EST
BELARUS
GERMANY
POLAND
UKRAINE
RUSSIA
8%
CHINA
14.1%
NORTH KOREA
SOUTH KOREA
JAPAN
5%
ROMANIA
CZECH REPUBLIC
SLOVAKIA
HUNGARY
BULG
GREECE
UZBEKISTAN
KAZAKHSTAN
AZER
TURKMEN
TURKEY
IRAN
PAKISTAN
INDIA
4%
THAILAND
VIETNAM
PHILIPPINES
ISRAEL
SYRIA
IRAQ
LIBYA
EGYPT
KUWAIT
SAUDI ARABIA
UNITED ARAB EMIRATES
MALAYSIA
SINGAPORE
INDONESIA
GERIA
SOUTH AFRICA
AUSTRALIA
NEW ZEALAND
=1%
=0.1%
2090
+ 5°C
+ 4°C
+ 3°C
+ 2°C
global warming?
+ 1°C
1990
medieval warm period
1900
1000 years ago
little ice age
change in timescale

STATES' SHARES OF CARBON DIOXIDE EMISSIONS *1995*
percentages of countries of 0.1% or more of world total

World total: 22 billion metric tons

Countries of 3% and over: percentage given

PAST AND FUTURE GLOBAL TEMPERATURES COMPARED WITH AVERAGE TEMPERATURE AT BEGINNING OF 20th CENTURY
degrees celsius

Source: IPCC.

Forests hold soil on the ground, regulate the supply of water to the surrounding region, and are part of the climate system.

Between 1960 and 1990, about 20 percent of the world's tropical forest was lost. The global average rate of loss of forests and wooded land is 2 percent a year; among the poorer countries of the world it is 8 percent a year. For these countries, in an unstable world trade system, hardwood remains a crucial way, often the only way, of earning hard currency (see **Debt**, pp.36–7).

In the 1990s worldwide awareness has grown about loss of forest cover, and the consequences for global warming and diminished biodiversity. In many countries this concern has led to a slower rate of deforestation, although some slowed only because there is not much forest left to cut down. In a few countries there is some net reforestation, but worldwide the loss continues.

DEFORESTATION

Annual rate *1990-95* percentages

- 3% or over
- 2% – 2.9%
- 1% – 1.9%
- under 1%
- no deforestation
- reforesting countries
- no data
- increasing deforestation since 1980-90

Highest rates of deforestation: Lebanon 7.8%; Jamaica 7.2%

Sources: *World Bank Atlas*, 1997 and 1998

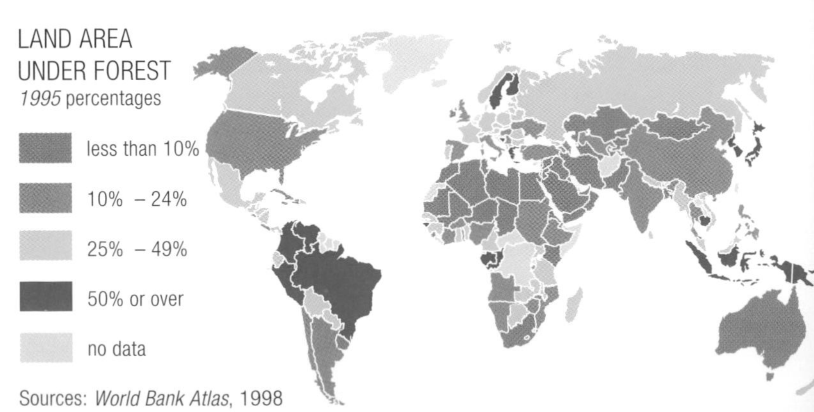
LAND AREA
UNDER FOREST
1995 percentages
less than 10%
10% – 24%
25% – 49%
50% or over
no data

Sources: *World Bank Atlas*, 1998

Forests

RUSSIA
NORWAY
SWEDEN
FINLAND
EST
LAT
LITH
DEN
UK
N
B
L
GER
POLAND
BELA
UKRAINE
MOL
CZ
SL
A
S
HUNG
ROM
FRANCE
S
C
B-H
YUG
M
ALB
BUL
ITALY
GREECE
GEO
AZER
ARM
TURKEY
SPAIN
MOROCCO
TUNISIA
ALGERIA
LIBYA
EGYPT
CYPRUS
SYRIA
LEB
ISRAEL
JOR
IRAQ
IRAN
KUWAIT
BAHRAIN
QATAR
UAE
SAUDI ARABIA
OMAN
YEMEN
KAZAKHSTAN
TURK
UZBEK
KIRG
TAJ
AFGHAN
PAKISTAN
MONGOLIA
CHINA
N KOREA
S KOREA
JAPAN
NEPAL
BHUTAN
INDIA
B DESH
TAIWAN
BURMA
LAOS
VIETNAM
THAI
CAM
PHILIPPINES
SRI LANKA
BRUNEI
MALAYSIA
SINGAPORE
INDONESIA
PAPUA NEW GUINEA
AUSTRALIA
NEW ZEALAND
MALI
NIGER
CHAD
SUDAN
ERITREA
DJIBOUTI
ETHIOPIA
SOMALIA
BURKINA FASO
GHANA
BENIN
TOGO
NIGERIA
CAR
CAM
EQUATORIAL GUINEA
GABON
CONGO
DEM REP CONGO
U
KENYA
R
B
TANZANIA
ANGOLA
ZAMBIA
MALAWI
ZIM
NAMIBIA
BOTS
MOZAMBIQUE
MADAGASCAR
MAURITIUS
S
SOUTH AFRICA
L
REFORESTATION
Annual rate *1990-95*
percentages
Source: *World Bank Atlas*, 1998
Armenia, Ireland, Uzbekistan
Greece
Kazakhstan
France
Belarus, Estonia
Latvia, Portugal
Lithuania, New Zealand
Hungary, UK
USA
Norway
Canada, Italy, Poland, Slovakia, Ukraine
2.7%
2.3%
1.9%
1.1%
1%
0.9%
0.6%
0.5%
0.3%
0.2%
0.1%

The number of biological species in the world is not known. Estimates range from 14 million to over 100 million. Millions of previously unknown species were found during the 1990s near ocean floors. The number of identified species is 1.7 million.

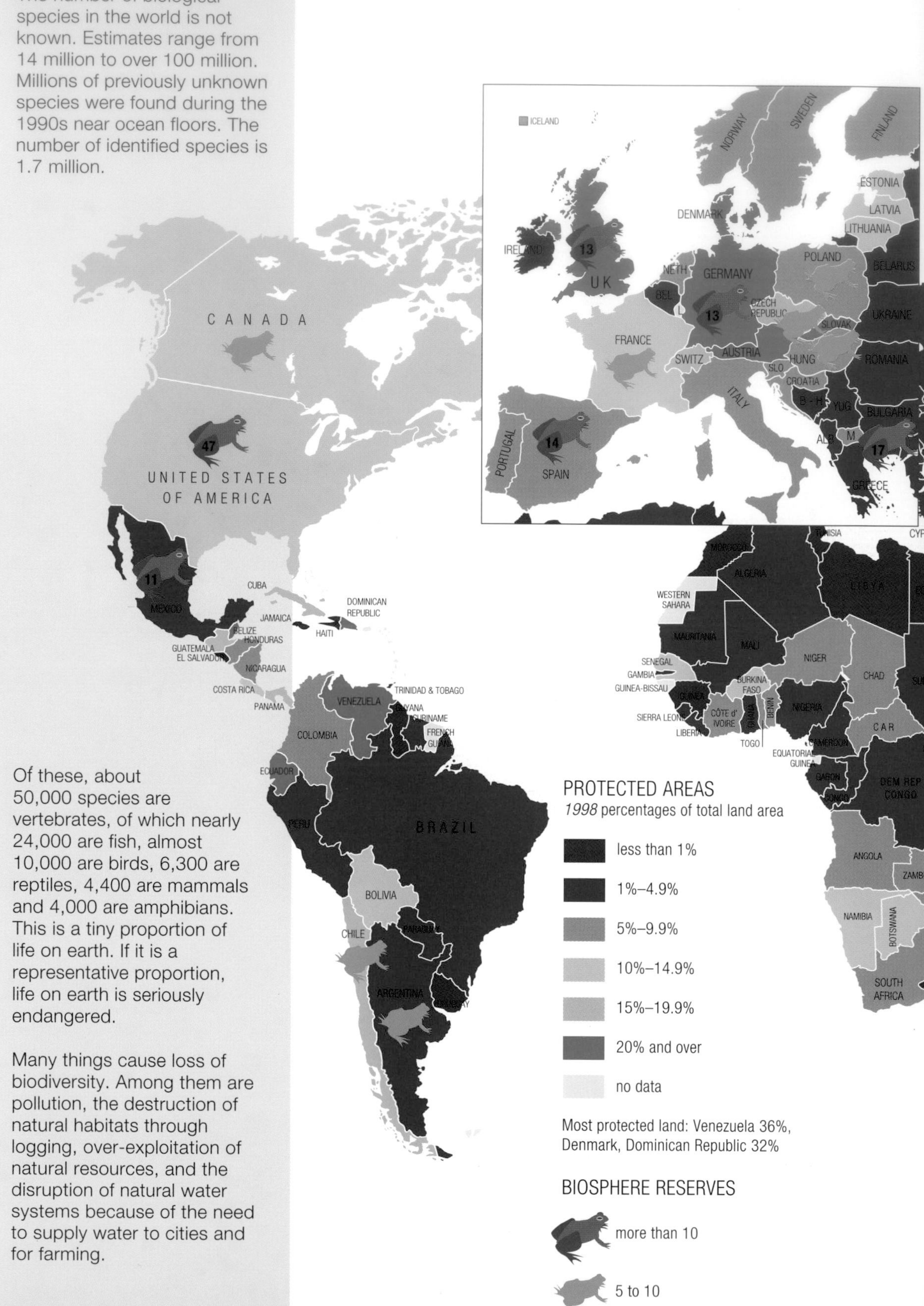
ICELAND
NORWAY
SWEDEN
FINLAND
ESTONIA
LATVIA
LITHUANIA
DENMARK
IRELAND
13
UK
NETH
GERMANY
POLAND
BELARUS
BEL
L
13
CZECH REPUBLIC
UKRAINE
SLOVAK
FRANCE
SWITZ
AUSTRIA
HUNG
ROMANIA
SLO
CROATIA
ITALY
B - H
YUG
BULGARIA
PORTUGAL
14
SPAIN
ALB
M
17
GREECE
CANADA
47
UNITED STATES OF AMERICA
11
MEXICO
CUBA
JAMAICA
HAITI
DOMINICAN REPUBLIC
BELIZE
HONDURAS
GUATEMALA
EL SALVADOR
NICARAGUA
COSTA RICA
PANAMA
TRINIDAD & TOBAGO
VENEZUELA
GUYANA
SURINAME
FRENCH GUIANA
COLOMBIA
ECUADOR
PERU
BRAZIL
BOLIVIA
CHILE
PARAGUAY
ARGENTINA
URUGUAY
TUNISIA
CYPRUS
MOROCCO
ALGERIA
LIBYA
WESTERN SAHARA
MAURITANIA
MALI
NIGER
CHAD
SENEGAL
GAMBIA
GUINEA-BISSAU
GUINEA
BURKINA FASO
SIERRA LEONE
LIBERIA
CÔTE d'IVOIRE
GHANA
TOGO
BENIN
NIGERIA
CAR
CAMEROON
EQUATORIAL GUINEA
GABON
CONGO
DEM REP CONGO
ANGOLA
ZAMBIA
NAMIBIA
BOTSWANA
SOUTH AFRICA
PROTECTED AREAS
1998 percentages of total land area
less than 1%
1%–4.9%
5%–9.9%
10%–14.9%
15%–19.9%
20% and over
no data
Most protected land: Venezuela 36%, Denmark, Dominican Republic 32%
BIOSPHERE RESERVES
more than 10
5 to 10
Source: World Resources, 1998-99

Of these, about 50,000 species are vertebrates, of which nearly 24,000 are fish, almost 10,000 are birds, 6,300 are reptiles, 4,400 are mammals and 4,000 are amphibians. This is a tiny proportion of life on earth. If it is a representative proportion, life on earth is seriously endangered.

Many things cause loss of biodiversity. Among them are pollution, the destruction of natural habitats through logging, over-exploitation of natural resources, and the disruption of natural water systems because of the need to supply water to cities and for farming.

Biodiversity

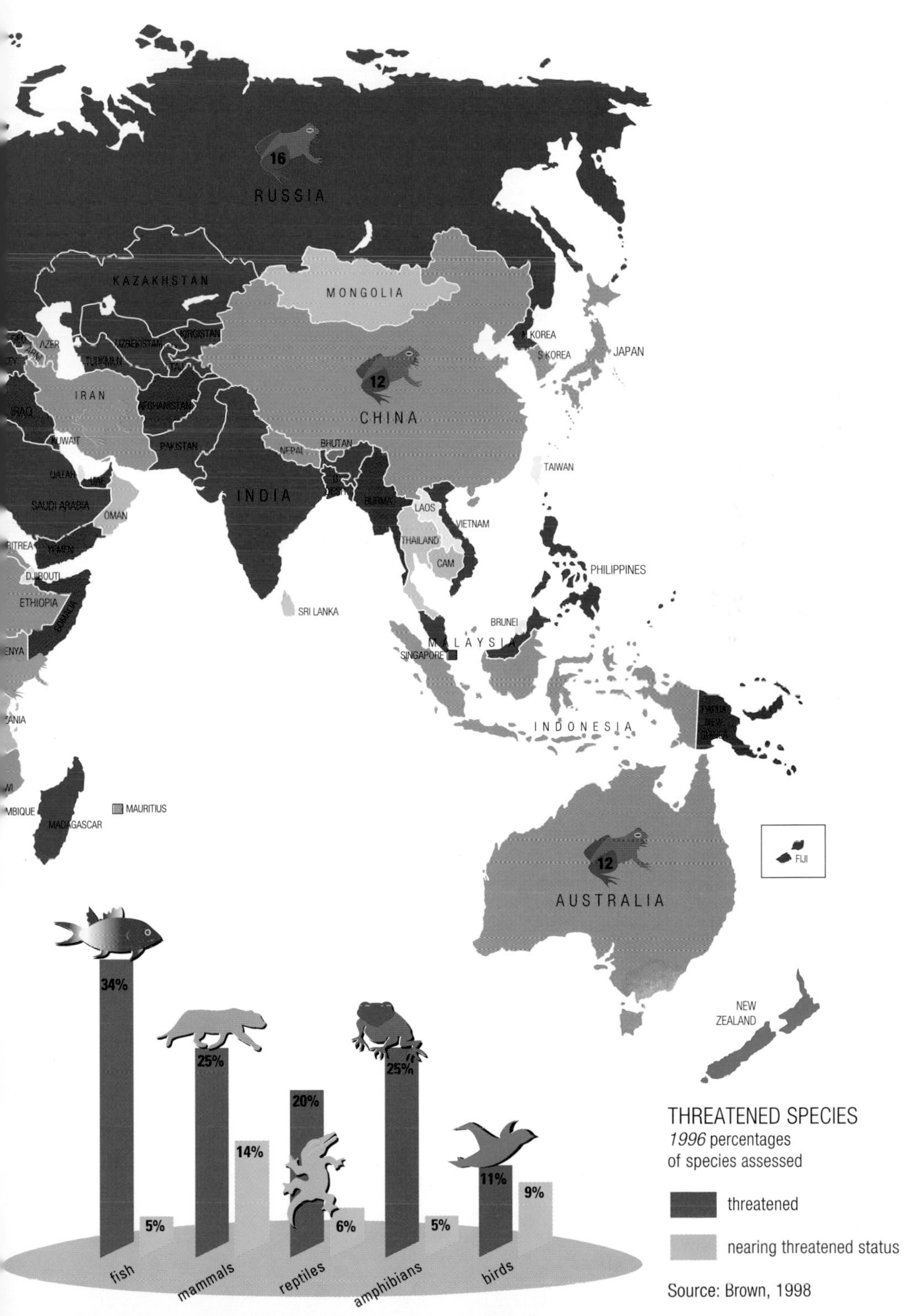
RUSSIA
16
KAZAKHSTAN
MONGOLIA
N KOREA
S KOREA
JAPAN
AZER
UZBEKISTAN
TURKMEN
KIRGISTAN
IRAN
IRAQ
AFGHANISTAN
12
CHINA
KUWAIT
PAKISTAN
NEPAL
BHUTAN
TAIWAN
QATAR
UAE
SAUDI ARABIA
OMAN
INDIA
BURMA
LAOS
VIETNAM
THAILAND
CAM
PHILIPPINES
ERITREA
YEMEN
DJIBOUTI
ETHIOPIA
SOMALIA
SRI LANKA
BRUNEI
MALAYSIA
SINGAPORE
KENYA
INDONESIA
PAPUA NEW GUINEA
MAURITIUS
MADAGASCAR
FIJI
12
AUSTRALIA
NEW ZEALAND
34%
5%
25%
14%
20%
6%
25%
5%
11%
9%
fish
mammals
reptiles
amphibians
birds
THREATENED SPECIES
1996 percentages
of species assessed
threatened
nearing threatened status

Source: Brown, 1998

Countries	1 Land area 1998 1,000 hectares	2 Population millions		3 Young and old people percentage of population 2000		4 Population density 1996 people per 1,000 hectares
		1998	2025	under 15 years	over 65 years	
Afghanistan	65,209	23.3	45.2	41.7	2.7	320
Albania	2,740	3.4	4.3	29.7	6	1,241
Algeria	238,174	30.1	47.3	36.6	3.8	121
Angola	124,670	12	25.5	47.4	2.8	90
Argentina	273,669	36.1	47.2	27.7	9.7	129
Armenia	2,820	3.6	4.2	24.5	8.7	1,290
Australia	768,230	18.4	23.9	21	11.9	24
Austria	8,273	8.2	8.3	17.1	14.4	980
Azerbaijan	8,660	7.7	9.7	29.5	6.9	877
Bahamas	1,390	0.3	0.4	27.0	5.4	–
Bahrain	68	0.6	0.9	30.8	3.0	–
Bangladesh	13,017	124	180	35.6	3.3	9,224
Barbados	43	–	–	–	–	–
Belarus	20,748	10.3	9.6	18.8	13.8	499
Belgium	3,282	10.2	10.3	17.4	16.4	3,221
Belize	2,280	0.2	0.4	39.7	4.1	96
Benin	11,062	5.9	12.3	46.5	2.8	503
Bhutan	4,700	1.9	3.6	43	3.2	386
Bolivia	108,438	8	13.1	39.6	4	70
Bosnia-Herzegovina	5,100	4	4.3	18.9	9.8	711
Botswana	56,673	1.5	2.6	41.9	2.4	26
Brazil	845,651	165.2	216.6	28.4	5.2	190
Brunei	580	0.3	0.5	32.9	3.5	–
Bulgaria	11,055	8.4	7.5	16.9	15.8	766
Burkina Faso	27,360	11.4	23.5	47	2.7	394
Burma	65,755	47.6	67.6	34	4.6	698
Burundi	2,568	6.6	12.3	45	2.7	2,423
Cambodia	17,652	10.8	17	40.4	3	582
Cameroon	46,540	14.3	28.5	43.5	3.6	291
Canada	922,097	30.2	36.4	19.3	12.6	32
Central African Rep.	62,298	3.5	6	41.6	4	54
Chad	125,920	6.9	12.6	43	3.6	52
Chile	74,880	14.8	19.5	28.5	7.2	193
China	929,100	1,255.1	1,480.4	24.9	6.7	1,321
Colombia	103,870	37.7	52.7	32.5	4.6	351
Comoros	220	0.1	1.3	47.9	2.7	–
Congo	34,150	2.8	5.7	45.7	3.3	206
Congo, Dem. Rep.	226,705	49.2	105.9	48	2.9	78
Costa Rica	5,106	3.6	5.6	33.1	5.1	685
Côte-d'Ivoire	31,800	14.6	24.4	43	3	441
Croatia	5,592	4.5	4.2	17.3	14.6	805
Cuba	10,982	11.1	11.8	21.2	9.6	1,003
Cyprus	930	0.8	1.0	24.7	11.3	–

Sources: Col 1: UN *World Resources 1998-99;* 1998; **Col 2:** UN *World Resources 1998-99;* 1998; **Col 3:** UN *World Resources 1998-99;* 1998; **Col 4:** UN *World Resources 1998-99;* 1998;

World Table

5 GNP per capita 1996 US $ per person	6 Women Working 1996 % of total labor force	7 Gender-related Development Index 1998 rank	8 Cars 1996 per 1,000 people	9 Telephone mainlines 1996 per 1,000 people	Countries
250a	35	–	–	1	Afghanistan
820	41	91	20	19	Albania
1,520	25	96	25	44	Algeria
270	46	145	19	5	Angola
8,380	31	48	127	174	Argentina
630	48	75	0	154	Armenia
20,090	43	9	485	519	Australia
28,110	41	15	458	466	Austria
480	44	100	36	85	Azerbaijan
11,940a	46	21	–	278	Bahamas
7,840a	19	60	–	241	Bahrain
260	42	140	0	3	Bangladesh
6,560	46	16	–	370	Barbados
2,070a	49	51	101	208	Belarus
26,440	40	14	424	465	Belgium
2,700	22	72	–	133	Belize
350	48	135	7	6	Benin
–	40	147	–	3	Bhutan
830	37	110	29	47	Bolivia
–	38	–	22	90	Bosnia Herzegovina
3,020a	46	85	15	48	Botswana
4,400	35	56	84	96	Brazil
–	34	36	–	263	Brunei
1,190	48	47	204	313	Bulgaria
230	47	161	4	3	Burkina Faso
220a	43	120	1	4	Burma
170	49	159	–	2	Burundi
300	53	129	5	1	Cambodia
610	38	124	7	5	Cameroon
19,020	45	1	440	602	Canada
310	47	142	0	3	Central African Rep.
160	44	152	2	1	Chad
4,860	32	46	71	156	Chile
750	45	93	3	45	China
2,140	38	41	20	118	Colombia
450	42	130	–	8	Comoros
670	43	117	14	8	Congo
130	44	132	17	1	Congo, Dem. Rep.
2,640	30	39	81	155	Costa Rica
660	33	141	20	9	Côte-d'Ivoire
3,800	44	61	175	309	Croatia
1,170a	38	69	2	32	Cuba
10,260a	38	30	–	485	Cyprus

Col 5: World Bank, *World Bank Atlas,* 1998, a: data for earlier year, or for part of the country only; **Col 6:** World Bank, *World Bank Atlas,* 1998; **Col 7:** UNDP, *Human Development Report,* 1998; **Col 8:** World Bank, *World Development Indicators,* 1998; **Col 9:** World Bank, *World Bank Atlas,* 1998.

Countries	1 Land area 1998 1,000 hectares	2 Population millions		3 Young and old people percentage of population 2000		4 Population density 1996 people per 1,000 hectares
		1998	2025	under 15 years	over 65 years	
Czech Republic	7,728	10.2	9.6	17.6	12.6	1,326
Denmark	4,243	5.3	5.3	18.6	14.7	1,234
Djibouti	2,320	0.7	1.0	42.3	3.4	–
Dominican Republic	4,838	8.2	11.1	33.1	4.5	1,646
Ecuador	27,684	12.1	17.8	33.8	4.7	423
Egypt	99,545	65.7	95.8	35	4.5	636
El Salvador	2,072	6	9.2	35.6	4.7	2,797
Equatorial Guinea	2,805	0.4	0.8	43.1	4	146
Eritrea	10,000	3.5	6.5	43.6	3.1	328
Estonia	4,227	1.4	1.3	17.6	13.9	348
Ethiopia	100,000	62.1	136.3	47.1	2.8	582
Fiji	1,827	0.8	1.1	31.3	4.5	436
Finland	30,459	5.2	5.3	18.4	14.6	168
France	55,010	58.7	60.4	18.3	16.2	1,060
Gabon	25,767	1.2	2.1	39.8	5.7	43
Gambia	1,000	1.2	2	41.2	3.1	1,141
Georgia	6,970	5.4	5.8	22	12.6	781
Germany	34,927	82.4	80.9	15.4	15.9	2,346
Ghana	22,754	18.9	36.3	43.4	3	784
Greece	12,890	10.5	10	15.3	17.8	814
Guatemala	10,843	11.6	21.7	42.9	3.7	1,008
Guinea	24,572	7.7	15.2	47	2.6	306
Guinea-Bissau	2,812	1.1	1.9	41.7	4.2	388
Guyana	19,685	0.9	1.1	29.9	4.2	43
Haiti	2,756	7.5	12.5	40	3.8	2,634
Honduras	11,189	6.1	10.7	41.6	3.4	520
Hong Kong	110	6.3	6.5	17.4	11.2	–
Hungary	9,234	9.9	8.7	17	14.5	1,088
Iceland	10,025	0.3	0.3	23.8	11.3	27
India	297,319	975.8	1,330.2	32.7	5	3,177
Indonesia	181,157	206.5	275.2	30.8	4.7	1,107
Iran	162,200	73	128.3	43.1	4.1	431
Iraq	43,737	21.8	41.6	41.4	3.1	471
Ireland	6,889	3.6	3.7	21.1	11.4	516
Israel	2,062	5.9	8	28.1	9.5	2,747
Italy	29,406	57.2	51.8	14.2	17.7	1,946
Jamaica	1,083	2.5	3.4	30.2	6.4	2,300
Japan	37,652	125.9	121.3	15.2	16.5	3,329
Jordan	8,893	6	11.9	43.3	2.9	628
Kazakhstan	267,073	16.9	20	27.5	7.1	63
Kenya	56,914	29	50.2	43.4	2.9	488
Kirgistan	19,180	4.5	5.9	35	6	233
Korea (North)	12,041	23.2	30	27.3	5.3	1,866

Sources: Col 1: UN *World Resources 1998-99;* 1998; **Col 2:** UN *World Resources 1998-99;* 1998; **Col 3:** UN *World Resources 1998-99;* 1998; **Col 4:** UN *World Resources 1998-99;* 1998;

World Table

5 GNP per capita 1996 US $ per person	6 Women Working 1996 % of total labor force	7 Gender-related Development Index 1998 rank	8 Cars 1996 per 1,000 people	9 Telephone mainlines 1996 per 1,000 people	Countries
4,740	47	25	325	273	Czech Republic
32,100	46	10	331	618	Denmark
780a	–	–	–	13	Djibouti
1,600	29	81	28	83	Dominican Republic
1,500	27	78	41	73	Ecuador
1,080	29	111	23	50	Egypt
1,700	35	103	29	56	El Salvador
530	35	126	–	9	Equatorial Guinea
2,860a	47	155	2	5	Eritrea
3,080	49	59	277	299	Estonia
100	41	158	1	3	Ethiopia
2,470	28	52	–	88	Fiji
23,240	48	5	379	549	Finland
26,270	44	7	437	564	France
3,950	44	112	22	32	Gabon
320a	45	154	8	19	Gambia
850	46	98	79	105	Georgia
28,870	42	17	500	538	Germany
360	51	121	5	4	Ghana
11,460	37	20	223	509	Greece
1,470	27	113	9	31	Guatemala
560	47	157	2	2	Guinea
250	40	153	7	7	Guinea Bissau
690	33	95	–	60	Guyana
310	43	144	4	8	Haiti
660	30	114	4	31	Honduras
24,290	37	33	55	547	Hong Kong
4,340	44	34	239	261	Hungary
26,580	44	4	–	573	Iceland
380	32	128	4	15	India
1,080	40	88	11	21	Indonesia
1,033a	25	92	29	95	Iran
14,710a	18	127	1	33	Iraq
17,110	33	27	272	395	Ireland
15,870	40	22	208	446	Israel
19,880	38	23	571	440	Italy
1,600	46	65	41	142	Jamaica
40,940	41	13	374	489	Japan
1,650	22	90	50	60	Jordan
1,350	47	73	61	118	Kazakhstan
320	46	122	10	8	Kenya
550	47	97	32	75	Kirgistan
970a	45	58	–	49	Korea (North)

Col 5: World Bank, *World Bank Atlas,* 1998, a: data for earlier year, or for part of the country only; **Col 6:** World Bank, *World Bank Atlas,* 1998; **Col 7:** UNDP, *Human Development Report,* 1998; **Col 8:** World Bank, *World Development Indicators,* 1998; **Col 9:** World Bank, *World Bank Atlas,* 1998.

Countries	1 Land area 1998	2 Population		3 Young and old people percentage of population 2000		4 Population density 1996
	1,000 hectares	1998 millions	2025	under 15 years	over 65 years	people per 1,000 hectare
Korea (South)	9,873	46.1	52.5	21.4	6.7	4,590
Kuwait	1,782	1.8	2.9	33.2	2	947
Laos	23,080	5.4	10.2	45.4	3	218
Latvia	6,205	2.4	2.1	18.2	14.4	404
Lebanon	1,023	3.2	4.4	32.9	5.8	3,015
Lesotho	3,035	2.2	4	41	4.1	685
Liberia	9,632	2.7	6.6	43.7	3.6	233
Libya	175,954	6	12.9	44.7	2.9	32
Lithuania	6,480	3.7	3.5	19.5	13.5	575
Luxembourg	260	0.4	0.5	18.5	14.5	–
Macedonia	2,543	2.2	2.5	22.3	9.4	855
Madagascar	58,154	16.3	34.5	45.8	2.6	264
Malawi	9,408	10.4	20.4	46.4	2.7	1,046
Malaysia	32,855	21.4	31.6	35.3	4.1	626
Mali	122,019	11.8	24.6	47.2	2.5	91
Malta	32	–	–	–	–	–
Marshall Islands	–	–	–	–	–	–
Mauritania	102,522	2.5	4.4	41.5	3.3	23
Mauritius	203	1.2	1.5	26.6	6	5,562
Mexico	190,869	95.8	130.2	33.1	4.7	486
Moldova	3,297	4.5	4.9	23.4	9.8	1,348
Mongolia	156,650	2.6	4	36.4	3.8	16
Morocco	44,630	28	39.9	33.8	4.3	605
Mozambique	78,409	18.7	35.4	44.7	3.2	227
Namibia	82,329	1.7	3	41.6	3.8	19
Nepal	14,300	23.1	40.6	42	3.5	1,540
Netherlands	3,392	15.7	16.1	18.2	13.6	4,592
New Zealand	26,799	3.7	4.9	23	11.3	134
Nicaragua	12,140	4.5	7.6	40.8	3.2	349
Niger	126,670	10.1	22.4	48.6	2.4	75
Nigeria	91,077	121.8	238.4	45	2.9	1,263
Norway	30,683	4.4	4.7	19.8	15	142
Oman	21,246	2.5	6.5	47.7	2.3	108
Pakistan	77,088	147.8	268.9	41.8	3.2	1,816
Panama	7,443	2.8	3.8	31.3	5.5	360
Papua New Guinea	45,286	4.6	7.5	38.7	3	97
Paraguay	39,730	5.2	9.4	39.5	3.5	125
Peru	128,000	24.8	35.5	33.4	4.8	187
Philippines	29,817	72.2	105.2	36.7	3.6	2,324
Poland	30,442	38.7	40	19.8	11.8	1,268
Portugal	9,150	9.8	9.4	16.7	15.7	1,072
Qatar	1100	0.6	0.8	27.1	2.2	–
Romania	23,034	22.6	21.1	18.5	13.2	984

Sources: Col 1: UN *World Resources 1998-99;* 1998; **Col 2:** UN *World Resources 1998-99;* 1998; **Col 3:** UN *World Resources 1998-99;* 1998; **Col 4:** UN *World Resources 1998 99;* 1998;

World Table

5 **GNP per capita 1996** US $ per person	6 **Women Working 1996** % of total labor force	7 **Gender-related Development Index 1998** rank	8 **Cars 1996** per 1,000 people	9 **Telephone mainlines 1996** per 1,000 people	**Countries**
10,610	41	37	151	430	Korea (South)
17,390a	29	50	338	232	Kuwait
400	47	125	3	6	Laos
2,300	50	71	153	298	Latvia
2,970	28	68	298	149	Lebanon
660	37	123	6	9	Lesotho
490a	39	–	–	2	Liberia
5,540a	21	79	87	59	Libya
2,280	48	62	212	268	Lithuania
45,360	37	32	–	593	Luxembourg
990	41	64	139	170	Macedonia
250	45	139	5	3	Madagascar
180	49	150	3	4	Malawi
4,370	37	45	131	183	Malaysia
240	46	160	3	2	Mali
7,910a	27	44	–	484	Malta
1,890	–	–	–	0	Marshall Islands
470	44	138	8	4	Mauritania
3,710	32	54	63	162	Mauritius
3,670	31	49	92	95	Mexico
590	49	101	39	140	Moldova
360	46	84	12	39	Mongolia
1,290	35	116	40	45	Morocco
80	48	156	0	3	Mozambique
2,250	41	99	40	54	Namibia
210	40	148	–	5	Nepal
25,940	40	12	363	543	Netherlands
15,720	44	8	461	499	New Zealand
380	36	115	16	26	Nicaragua
200	44	162	4	2	Niger
240	36	133	7	4	Nigeria
34,510	46	2	379	555	Norway
4,820a	15	104	97	86	Oman
480	27	131	5	18	Pakistan
3,080	34	42	76	122	Panama
1,150	42	119	7	11	Papua New Guinea
1,850	29	89	14	36	Paraguay
2,420	29	80	58	60	Peru
1,160	37	82	9	25	Philippines
3,230	46	35	209	169	Poland
10,160	43	28	277	375	Portugal
11,600a	13	67	–	239	Qatar
31,600	44	57	107	140	Romania

Col 5: World Bank, *World Bank Atlas,* 1998, a: data for earlier year, or for part of the country only; **Col 6:** World Bank, *World Bank Atlas,* 1998; **Col 7:** UNDP, *Human Development Report,* 1998; **Col 8:** World Bank, *World Development Indicators,* 1998; **Col 9:** World Bank, *World Bank Atlas,* 1998.

Countries	1 **Land area 1998** 1,000 hectares	2 **Population** millions		3 **Young and old people** percentage of population **2000**		4 **Population density 199** people per 1,000 hectare
		1998	**2025**	**under 15 years**	**over 65 years**	
Russia	1,688,850	147.2	131.4	18	12.7	88
Rwanda	2,467	6.5	13	44.7	2.4	2,188
Saudi Arabia	214,969	20.2	42.4	40.7	2.9	88
Senegal	19,253	9	16.9	43.6	3	443
Seychelles	46	–	–	–	–	–
Sierra Leone	7,162	4.6	8.2	43.9	3	600
Singapore	61	3.5	4.2	22.6	7.1	55,475
Slovakia	4,808	5.4	5.5	20	11.1	1,112
Slovenia	2,012	1.9	1.7	15.7	14.2	956
Solomon Islands	2,799	0.4	0.8	43	2.9	140
Somalia	62,734	10.7	23.7	48	2.6	157
South Africa	122,104	44.3	71.6	36.2	4.5	347
Spain	49,944	39.8	37.5	15	16.5	794
Sri Lanka	6,463	18.5	23.9	26.2	6.6	2,801
Sudan	237,600	28.5	46.9	38.7	3.2	115
Suriname	15,600	0.4	0.6	32.3	5.5	28
Swaziland	1,720	0.9	1.7	41.7	2.7	512
Sweden	41,162	8.9	9.5	19.1	16.7	214
Switzerland	3,955	7.3	7.6	17.2	14.7	1,827
Syria	18,378	15.3	26.3	40.8	3.1	793
Taiwan	3,600	–	–	–	–	–
Tajikistan	14,060	6.1	9.7	39.5	4.6	422
Tanzania	88,359	32.2	62.4	45.1	2.6	349
Thailand	51,089	59.6	69.1	25.2	5.8	1,149
Togo	5,439	4.4	8.8	45.6	3.1	772
Trinidad & Tobago	513	1.3	1.7	26.1	6.5	2,528
Tunisia	15,536	9.5	13.5	32.2	4.9	589
Turkey	76,963	63.8	85.8	28.3	5.9	803
Turkmenistan	46,993	4.3	6.5	37.4	4.2	88
Uganda	19,965	21.3	45	49.1	2.2	1,015
Ukraine	57,935	51.2	46	17.8	14.3	891
United Arab Emirates	8,360	2.4	3.3	28.1	2.5	270
United Kingdom	24,160	58.2	59.5	18.9	15.8	2,407
United States	915,912	273.8	332.5	21.4	12.4	294
Uruguay	17,481	3.2	3.7	23.9	12.7	183
Uzbekistan	41,424	24.1	36.5	37.5	4.6	560
Venezuela	88,205	23.2	34.8	34	4.4	253
Vietnam	32,549	77.9	110.1	34.3	5.2	2,310
Western Sahara	26,600	–	–	–	–	–
Yemen	52,797	16.9	39.6	48.3	2.3	297
Yugoslavia	10,200	10.4	10.7	19.8	13.3	1,009
Zambia	74,339	8.7	16.1	46.3	2.3	111
Zimbabwe	38,685	11.9	19.3	43.6	2.7	296

Sources: Col 1: UN *World Resources 1998-99;* 1998; **Col 2:** UN *World Resources 1998-99;* 1998; **Col 3:** UN *World Resources 1998-99;* 1998; **Col 4:** UN *World Resource 1998-99;* 1998;

World Table

5 GNP per capita 1996 US $ per person	6 Women Working 1996 % of total labor force	7 Gender-related Development Index 1998 rank	8 Cars 1996 per 1,000 people	9 Telephone mainlines 1996 per 1,000 people	Countries
2,410	49	53	92	175	Russia
190	49	–	2	3	Rwanda
7,040a	14	102	90	106	Saudi Arabia
570	43	149	10	11	Senegal
6,850	–	–	–	200	Seychelles
200	36	163	4	4	Sierra Leone
30,550	38	29	120	513	Singapore
3,410	48	26	198	232	Slovakia
9,240	46	24	365	333	Slovenia
900	46	109	–	18	Solomon Islands
110a	43	–	–	2	Somalia
3,520	37	74	106	100	South Africa
14,350	36	19	376	392	Spain
740	35	70	6	14	Sri Lanka
310a	29	151	10	4	Sudan
1,000	32	63	–	132	Suriname
1,210	37	105	–	22	Swaziland
25,710	48	3	414	682	Sweden
44,350	40	18	462	640	Switzerland
1,160	26	94	10	82	Syria
–	–	–	–	–	Taiwan
340	44	106	0	42	Tajikistan
170	49	137	1	3	Tanzania
2,960	46	40	28	70	Thailand
300	40	136	19	6	Togo
3,970	37	38	94	166	Trinidad & Tobago
1,930	31	76	29	64	Tunisia
2,830	36	55	55	224	Turkey
940	45	87	–	74	Turkmenistan
300	48	146	2	2	Uganda
1,200	49	83	93	181	Ukraine
17,400a	14	66	79	302	United Arab Emirates
19,600	43	11	359	528	United Kingdom
28,020	46	6	521	640	United States
5,760	41	31	151	209	Uruguay
1,010	46	86	–	76	Uzbekistan
3,020	33	43	68	117	Venezuela
290	49	108	–	16	Vietnam
–	–	–	–	–	Western Sahara
380	29	143	15	13	Yemen
–	42	–	150	197	Yugoslavia
360	45	134	17	9	Zambia
610	44	118	29	15	Zimbabwe

Col 5: World Bank, *World Bank Atlas,* 1998, a: data for earlier year, or for part of the country only; **Col 6:** World Bank, *World Bank Atlas,* 1998; **Col 7:** UNDP, *Human Development Report,* 1998; **Col 8:** World Bank, *World Development Indicators,* 1998; **Col 9:** World Bank, *World Bank Atlas,* 1998.

Commentary on the maps

Population

Population census data vary in reliability. In some countries, the process of counting is not a great deal better than guesswork. In some others, the occasions of gathering the data are few and far between, meaning that a world population estimate at the end of the 1990s is using some data from the end of the 1970s. In most countries there are marginal groups who are not properly counted, either because they will not fully reveal their existence to the counters, or because the counters simply do not notice their existence. In some countries, such people who fall outside the system may amount to millions. Despite all the reservations about the data, there has been a clear pattern of fast population growth during the twentieth century, and slowing towards its end.

The main reason for population growth has nothing to do with rising birth rates. Rather, it has been a product of falling death rates. This itself is a result of improved living conditions, including vastly improved systems of sanitation and water supply, together with better nutrition and more widespread access to competent health care. Where population growth rates have declined, that is the result of falling birth rates, because people are having fewer children either as a result of government policy or their own choice. There is some speculation that new epidemics could reduce population growth and even population size in the future. The widespread use of antibiotics, for example, which extends to using antibiotic additives in feeding farm animals, is leading to the evolution of antibiotic-resistant bacteria. The apparent victory in battles against various infectious diseases may be only temporary.

Population is highly-concentrated in a small number of countries. Almost two-thirds of the world's population live in just ten countries: China, the largest population, followed by India, USA, Indonesia, Brazil, Russia, Pakistan, Bangladesh, Japan, and Nigeria.

Life Expectancy

Increases in life expectancy in the twentieth century are part of the story of increased population due to falling death rates. Both reflect essentially the same kinds of social change. Somewhat paradoxically, increased life expectancy is also part of the same story as the slowing of population growth during the 1990s, because both are produced by advanced economic development. The most dramatic improvement in average life expectancy in the twentieth century was in Japan, from 45 years in 1900 to 80 in the mid-1990s.

Average life expectancy is to a considerable degree a reflection of what happens early in life rather than later on. In countries where life expectancy is low, one central reason is that it is has not been possible to conquer mortal, communicable diseases that especially strike at children under five years old. Average life expectancy is one of the basic indicators used by the United Nations' Development Report in constructing its Human Development Index, the annual statistical expression of the human face of economic development. Life expectancy reveals a great deal about societies, albeit in simple and general terms. In particular, average life expectancy speaks volumes about the average level of access to clean water, a reasonable sufficiency of food, and adequate health services.

It is important to note, however, the importance of the term "average." The poor have shorter lives even when they live in rich countries, and the fact that the best medical facilities in the world are available in the USA does not mean these are equally available to everybody. Thus social differences that, literally, are a matter of life and death are smoothed out in the statistics of how long people live on average. These statistics also say nothing about the quality of people's lives.

Nutrition

The quality of consumption is of great importance, but before that the basic issue is quantity, and the basic requirement is sufficiency. The world as a whole produces more than enough food to feed its six billion people. Africa is the only major world region in which not enough food is produced to meet demand, but the surplus from other regions is in principle enough to meet the shortfall. Yet over 20 percent of the world's population live in absolute poverty and over 10 percent suffer from not just shortages of food but from chronic malnutrition. The problem is not the production of food but its distribution (see also **Food**, pp.94-5).

Those who are most at risk of being malnourished are children, for whom proper nutrition is especially important. The sharp end of the problem of inadequate food distribution lies in the countries picked out on this map by the symbols showing where more than 20 percent of children under five years old are underweight. The social and human problems revealed by these statistics include vulnerability to respiratory, diarrheal and parasitic diseases, all of which are major factors in malnutrition among children.

At the other end of the scales of wealth and weight, a super-abundance of calories is as much of a problem as a shortage of them. The rich world has too much to eat. Obesity is a major health issue, leading to problems such as heart disease, high blood pressure, impaired lung functioning, and arthritis.

The richer the country, the more fat there is in its national diet. In the 1990s, the people of northern Europe were eating considerably fewer vegetables and much more meat than in the 1940s. The proportion of animal fat in the national diet in countries where the average GNP per person (see **National Income,** pp.38-9) is lower than $1,200 is about six percent. In countries where the GNP per person is $12,000 or higher, the average fat content in the national diet is pushing 30 percent.

The Quality of Life

Everybody knows that being rich does not necessarily make you happy. It is true for countries as well as people, and comparisons of national economic wealth (see **National Income**, pp.38-9) tell only part of the story of economic and social development. The most important attempt to fill out the statistics of development by including people is the Human Development Index (HDI), published each year since 1990 by the United Nations' Development Programme. It combines statistics for annual economic output, average life expectancy, the rate of adult literacy, and a complex measure of the availability of education called the enrollment ratio. This last is the number of students enrolled in education as a percentage of the people of that age in the country. All these statistics are reformulated as indices, which are then multiplied together to produce a Human Development Index for each country.

While the HDI can tell us more about development than can economic statistics alone, it still provides an incomplete picture. All the usual reservations about how national statistics present the average and iron out the differences between the extremes are as relevant to the HDI as they are to the statistics used to compose it, such as those on the economy and longevity. Differences between social classes, between men and women, and between the regions of a country are inevitably neglected. The statisticians who produce the HDI are as aware of this as anybody else. They have produced a Gender-related Development Index (see **Gender Equality**, pp.72-3; also **Women Working**, pp.44-5). They also provide statistics on variations between regions and between classes (see **Inequality**, pp.22-3) within a country's national HDI. In this map, the overall picture is presented, without differentiation by gender, class or any other factor.

The big picture is that development in the rich countries is better for people than it is in the poor countries. One way of finding some nuance within this is to compare a country's ranking in the HDI with its economic position. This reflects something about the choices that have been made about how to use available resources, and choices about distribution. So a country that stood, for example, 100th in economic wealth but 50th in the global Human Development Index is a country doing particularly well for its people, distributing available resources for the good of the largest number. And a country that was 100th richest, but stood 150th is a country whose government is doing particularly badly for the people. The symbols on the map highlight those countries where the disparity between economic rank (based on a league table of real GDP per person) and HDI rank is higher or lower by at least 15 points.

Another reservation about the HDI is that it emphasizes education. That choice by the compilers of the HDI certainly can be justified (see **Literacy**, pp.70-1), but it is worth mentioning in order to show how statistical information reflects decisions about what information is deemed important (as well as what information it is feasible to collect and compare). Two of the four components of the HDI (literacy and the enrollment ratio) are about education. It could have been possible to choose others, though whether the picture that would then emerge would be very different is another matter. The statistics chosen for the HDI provide broad indicators of how well people can expect to fare in different countries; they can be thought of as symptomatic of the underlying situation. Looking at different symptoms might not change much.

Finland is one of the few rich countries that does significantly better in the HDI than its economic position, and thus it is a country where resources are used for the good of the largest number. Finland also ranks high on the suicide index. Suicide statistics may be especially unreliable: many suicides are disguised by medical authorities after the fact, in order to ease the pain of relatives, and sometimes for reasons of respectability. With that reservation mind, it is nonetheless significant that the northern hemisphere countries, in which suicide is most prevalent, are ones that have gone through major upheavals in the 1990s with the end of state socialism in central and eastern Europe. In those countries, to different degrees in each place, safe jobs were lost and the value of savings was wiped out, while in all of them people had to get to grips with a new and destabilizing reality.

Inequality

Societies composed of equals with nobody being better or worse off than anybody else have been envisaged but never created. The question is not whether there is inequality, but how much there is, and whether a case can be made that the degree of inequality that exists is actually beneficial. For example, the chance to earn a particularly large income may be an incentive to some to commit themselves to working particularly hard. This may produce more wealth, which is also enjoyed by those who have chosen to work less hard. There are few countries where it is possible to justify inequality in such noble terms. The most that can be said is that human society has not yet found a way to be stable without inequalities. It can also be said that human society has not really looked very hard for the possibility to organize itself that way; despite the rhetoric, the leaders of the former Soviet Union and its allies never tried to eliminate inequality, and nor did China's leaders even in the country's most revolutionary period.

There are many ways of measuring inequalities. Some of them are captured on this map, such as the contrast between the splendid wealth of the hyper-rich and the condition of the 86 percent of Zambia's population living below its national poverty line (see also **National Income**, pp. 38-9). Differences of income within countries, even poor ones, are as great as the differences between them.

Age

As a result of falling birth rates and increased life expectancy, the older population in most countries is growing faster than the population as a whole. This is an unprecedented social phenomenon. By 2025, the world population of people over 60 years old is expected to be about the same size as the total population of China in 1999. Increased longevity indicates major achievements in nutrition, social conditions, and the availability of health care, and falling birth rates are also associated with advanced economic and social development (see **Population**, pp.14-15, and **Life Expectancy**, pp.16-17). For these reasons, the largest proportions of older people are in the populations of richer countries. These countries face the most immediate challenges of dealing with the increased average age of the population. But populations are also ageing in many developing countries, according to the US Bureau of Census, and they have fewer resources with which to address the new challenges.

The challenges that arise are in public policies. One big issue is the costs of health care for those who have retired from paid employment, and of providing safe accommodation that suits older people's physical abilities. As the population as a whole ages, the need to produce the wealth to meet these costs (among others) falls on the shoulders of a proportionately smaller group of economically-active people.

This raises the related issue of the proper age of retirement. Lowering the age at which people can stop working for a living has been a great achievement and remains a goal for many countries. But if we retire at the age of 60 or 65, and then live for another 20 years with full intellectual faculties, but without being economically productive, it begins to make sense to allow more years of economic activity. Of course, whether the prospect of a longer working life is a nightmare or a delight, has everything to do with what kind of working life has been possible.

The statistics of economically-active people over 60 years old hide as many things as most statistics do. There is a great deal of activity by older people that is economically relevant but statistically invisible, such as working for voluntary organizations, or looking after grandchildren. And the high proportion of over-60s who work for a living in some countries in Africa does not reflect an ageing population (see **Life Expectancy,** pp.16-17) so much as the fact that economic hardship and relatively low life expectancy combine to deny people those years of restful retirement.

World Markets

The world economy is characterized by ever-rising levels of production in the long term, and fluctuation in the short term. The only certainties about the good times is that they will not last, but they will come back.

Coming out of recession in the early 1990s, the world economy entered a relatively prolonged period of growth. Lying behind this were the new technologies of information and communication, the emergence of new markets and investment possibilities in the former Soviet Union, China and some of the developing countries, and the integration of world financial markets. Currency crises and economic slowdown in east Asia in 1997 and 1998 brought the good times to an end. The knock-on effects were suffered most seriously in Russia and Brazil, but the European Union felt the blow too. In the USA, the stock markets continued to climb to unprecedently high levels, but worries grew that they were over-valued. As a century of unprecedented market expansion and economic growth came to an end, the central feature of millennial economic worries was that international investors' decisions might not be sufficiently far-sighted. Looking for quick returns on capital is economically productive during the boom phase of the economic cycle, and economically destructive once the downturn starts. But there was no reason to doubt the ability of the trade and economic system to adapt, to send the weakest to the wall, and thus to flourish again for a while.

Worldwide, at the end of 1998, more than 60 percent of the reserves held by central banks and of the bonds issued by them were denominated in US dollars, as was almost 75 percent of world trade. Then a new international currency arrived, the Euro. The 11 governments who launched it (Austria, Belgium, Finland, France, Germany, Ireland, Italy, Luxembourg, Netherlands, Portugal, Spain) have a combined population larger than the USA's and a combined economic output only the merest fraction below the USA's. If, as expected, the founder members of Euroland are joined by others, including the UK, in the first few years of the twenty first century, the Euro will be a major alternative to the US dollar. Whether this develops into rivalry, and if so how the rivalry is handled, will do much to shape world market conditions through the first decade of the twenty first century. The sharper the rivalry, the less stable market conditions will be, and the greater the chances of economic fortunes suddenly surging and then plummeting.

Trade and Industry

The concentration of wealth and power over economic and commercial affairs into the three zones of North America, Western Europe, and East Asia is intensifying. Already marked in 1980, when the three zones of economic power accounted for 70 percent of the world's exports in 1980, it had become an overwhelming 85 percent by the mid-1990s. Elsewhere, Africa's share of the world total fell from small to insignificant. Latin America lost ground, except for Mexico. The Middle East's share was cut by almost half, and the share of the former Soviet bloc countries of Eastern and Central Europe fell by somewhat more.

In Asia, Japan's output and exports boomed and then fell, and other east Asian countries became major economic forces. This was the region of the fastest economic growth in the 1980s and first half of the 1990s, and the area of sharpest economic blows in the closing years of the century.

Tourism

Tourism is one of the world's largest industries and it is getting bigger. Compared to the 1995 level, current projections expect the number of international journeys (including business travel as well as holidays) to double by the year 2020. Countries in east Asia, and especially China, are thought likely to figure high among the most popular destinations of the near future, as increased leisure time makes it possible for the well-off to take multiple holidays abroad each year.

We like to think that real life stops when it comes to holidays. Whether the dream is romance or relaxation, vacations are a safe place in which to project many different kinds of hopes. But real life does not stop. Romance may be there, but so too is the possibility of sexually-transmitted diseases. Among many factors involved in the international transmission of HIV/AIDS infections, one is the adoption of less watchful and careful patterns of behavior when travelling abroad. And the semi-fantasy life lived out by holiday-makers all too often clashes with the real life that continues to be lived by the inhabitants of the areas they go to visit. The ill-temper and irritation that these clashes can generate among tourists and locals alike is widespread. In many places the feelings of resentment come to be politicized and the presence of large numbers of international tourists is regarded as a symbol of invasion and cultural imperialism. For some groups, killing tourists is the logical next step in the argument.

Investment

Investment is risk, a bet on the future. Yesterday's corporate pioneer created today's cautious conglomerate. It is no surprise that, while some individual investors may go for long odds and big winnings, the biggest investments are made as safely as possible. This leads to a cautious, conservative pattern of behavior quite at odds with the image of the bold entrepreneur. Where there has been profit, it is safe to assume that there will be profit, until events prove otherwise. Thus capital investment follows previously successful capital investment. This leads to capital concentrating in what are seen to be the most productive regions of the world, and simultaneously reinforces concentrations of capital into vast enterprises.

With this, the great transnational corporations have shown an increasing ability to shape not just the policies of individual governments but, much more importantly, the global economic framework. Thanks largely to their influence, the world economy is becoming more and more globally integrated. This means that it is easier than ever before to move productive investment from one place to another, to find the best-regulated and lowest-paid workforces and the governments that offer the most favorable rates of taxation. At the same time, it is easier than ever before to attract labor to the places where it is most needed (see **Working Abroad**, pp.48-9). Meanwhile, international financial transactions take place around the clock.

Until the 1990s, western investors were relatively cautious about investing in China. As successes were registered and the profits started to flow, what had first been a cautious trickle became a flood. Inward investment into China increased by almost 1,000 percent during the course of the 1990s.

Debt

In the 1970s, banks in the rich countries were lending money on ever-increasing scales to governments in the developing world. These loans looked like the safest possible bets. Countries, it was often said, could not go bust. So governments of developing countries were encouraged to borrow for anything and everything, including a large number of extravagant prestige projects (ranging from national monuments and sports' stadia to overly-elaborate government buildings) as well as serious attempts to accelerate the pace of economic development.

In the early 1980s, several governments faced difficulty keeping up with their debt payments and were seeking new loans to repay old debts. Many of them faced problems of their own making, because the investment choices they had made were unwise. Some of them could be forgiven for their lack of judgement because they were encouraged into it by the lending banks. But many governments faced problems over which they had no control, because their loans were denominated in US dollars, and repayments became more expensive when the value of the dollar rose on the international exchanges. Equally difficult for them was the fact that the interest rates for many loans were variable and linked to interest rates in the lending bank's home country or in the USA. When interest rates rose, repayments became, even more expensive. And since high interest rates in the USA pushed up the value of the dollar, borrowers in developing countries were twice hit.

In some rich countries, panic struck. It dawned on the banks that countries could go bust after all, and that governments might default on their debts and simply not pay them back. Nightmare economic scenarios became fashionable, showing how a default by a major developing country could lead to more defaults, to the collapse of several banks in rich countries because they were over-extended on their loans, to a run on global bank capital, to a collapse of the rich world's banking system, and to economic chaos.

In response, the governments of the rich countries handed over much of the responsibility for running the international debt system to the World Bank and the International Monetary Fund (IMF). Heavy diplomatic and economic pressure on potential defaulters helped to keep the damage to a minimum. Some western banks did see decreased profits, but the nightmare scenarios never materialized. The World Bank and the IMF repackaged the debt of developing countries, linking a new schedule of repayments to harsh economic conditions that cut public spending, increased unemployment, reduced wages and opened the domestic market to unrestricted imports. Developing countries limped through two destructive decades, the 1980s and 1990s, struggling to export enough to earn the hard currency needed simply to pay the interest on their debts.

Debt pessimism has long been banished from the rich countries. In the international debt system, interest repayments from South to North exceed flows of aid from North to South. For the rich North, it is a comfortable system. Many countries have paid their creditors far more than they originally borrowed. In many cases, the original loans only helped a small elite who managed to protect the money they made out of the big development projects, often salting their wealth away in international bank accounts.

National Income

The most basic and crude measure of economic prosperity is national income, which is also an extremely revealing measure. The disparities of wealth on an international scale revealed by this map and on **Inequality** (pp. 22-3) are the basis of a reality of inequality and injustice that is repeated within countries.

Much of the economic data on which this map is ultimately based are suspect, because the data-gathering systems of many countries are not up to the task they are set, and because much relevant activity is excluded from the calculations for a variety of reasons. Nevertheless the broad picture remains a good representation of comparative wealth.

One element of the map reveals the kind of whimsy that often enters international comparisons. Comparisons of personal purchasing power are one of the most informative ways of comparing what national wealth means per person in the population. The exercise involves an act of imagination, to suppose that people from different countries call in at the same supermarket to buy the same goods, each using their average annual income. In such an event, an average inhabitant of Western Europe could afford to buy over 60 times as much as an average inhabitant of sub-Saharan Africa in the same period of time. But, of course, the measure, like all such comparisons, is false. With such disparities of income, they would not be shopping in the same stores and they would certainly not buy the same things. The truth is that some of the global disparities are so large that they defeat any serious attempt at comparison.

Jobs

In both the long-term development of the world economy and its short-term fluctuations, labor power is a key strategic resource. The abstractions that are necessary to understand the workings of the economy on a global level too easily divert attention away from the human realities shaped by economic influences. But the core of economic activity throughout history has been working people, and the evolving patterns of economic development are in large part a story of people changing their ways of working, either because they choose to or because they have no choice and simply have to.

Within the short-term cycles of growth and slump in the world economy (see **World Markets**, pp.28-9), it is ordinary working people who lose their security and incomes when market logic dictates that the companies in which they work must close. And in the long-term evolution of economic history, it would be impossible to develop heavy industry if it were not possible to get people to leave the land and move to cities. And it would be equally impossible to make the economic shift towards greater dependence on service industries if it were not possible to get workers out of heavy industry and into light manufacture and fast food.

The work habits and discipline that are required to work in traditional agriculture are neither more nor less demanding than the habits and discipline required to work in heavy industry or service industry; they are simply different. Along the way, there are many casualties (see **Unemployment**, pp.46-7), though some get back to the employment frontlines relatively quickly, and for many there is a need and a possibility of major relocation (see **Working Abroad**, pp.48-9).

Hidden from most statistics, there is a large and unknown number of children who work for pay. In several countries, there is still no legal minimum age of employment, although in very many countries there are legal restrictions on the type of work children are allowed to do. But the key problem is not the legal standards that exist, but whether they are respected. It is hard to imagine the economic justification – let alone the moral justification – for employing children who are less than six years old, but the practice still exists.

Women Working

About 36 percent of the world's paid labor force is female. In most countries, the percentage is between 25 and 50 percent. The two countries where more than 50 percent of the paid workers women, and the 11 where fewer than 50 percent are women, are extremes. The proportion of the workforce that is female has been rising steadily since the1970s and is expected to carry on increasing until at least 2010. Women are also taking senior administrative and management roles in growing numbers.

Despite this progress, the rightness of women working remains a matter of controversy. In countries where women's economic contribution is as vital as men's, there is every now and again a call for women to restrict themselves to the roles of wife and mother. In some countries, husbands have the legal right to restrict or even prohibit their wives' participation in the paid workforce. In progressive Norway, with a high percentage of women in active political life (see **Gender Equality**, pp.72-3) and, as this map shows, very good provision for maternity leave, one of the hottest political debates of the late-1990s is government's decision to pay direct cash support to women who will agree to stay home to look after their children instead of taking advantage of widely-available childcare facilities.

Reluctance to allow women into the paid labor force has fed into reluctance to value their work equally with men's, in financial terms as well as other ways. In all countries, the general pattern is a wage differential in favour of men. In some countries, the differential is gross. One consequence of globalization will probably be to keep reducing these differentials and to gain steadily more acceptance of women's equal role and rights in the workplace. Whether men will therefore take on an equal role in the home will continue to be a major issue, both for individuals and on a social scale, for many years to come.

In the Nordic countries, with the most advanced policies on maternity leave, men can share parental leave, enabling a couple to break down the traditional gender division of labor and men to get closer to their babies and toddlers. Moreover, parental leave may be taken at different times over a period. The high Swedish allocation, for example, is available over a period of eight years. The Norwegian allocation can be used with a mixture of 100 percent time off for a short period and a mere reduction in working hours for the rest of the time. These flexible arrangements require the agreement of the employer but are financed by the government as a basic social right.

Unemployment

A radical philosopher and his fellow-thinkers used to refer to the unemployed as the reserve army of labor. Just as any army needed its reserves to call on in time of need, so a bit of unemployment helped the functioning of capitalism, whether you praised it or, like Karl Marx, believed and hoped that history would soon bury it. It has, however, become clear in the late twentieth century that there are two sides to the coin of unemployment.

During the long period of economic growth from 1952 to 1973, many governments in the developed world claimed that their economic policies aimed at full employment. Though the rhetoric often masked a quiet realization that Marx was right about the need for a reserve labor force, unemployment levels were low for a prolonged period. During the late 1970s and early 1980s, in almost all developed countries, any pretensions to the target of full employment were dropped. Economic adjustment was too deep and too painful and throwing too many people out of work for the fiction to be tenable any longer. Now it is increasingly openly realised that the smooth functioning of our economic system requires the kind of labor discipline and flexibility that is best obtained by having a large pool of unemployed people. They not only provide replacements for workers who will not fulfil their companies' needs, they also function as an encouragement to those in work to keep up the pace of their work.

The other side of the coin is the social instability that results from large numbers of people having no hope and little experience of work. A sense of detachment from society often results from long-term unemployment. For some people, this may lead to a conscious decision to cease participating in mainstream economic life. For others, it leads to a disorientation that can produce personally and socially destructive behavior patterns including alcoholism and violence. The pattern in many of the richer countries is towards a major social and economic gulf between those who are in work and the long-term unemployed.

Unemployment statistics are massaged almost everywhere to make the problems look less bad than they are. In some countries, only those who are actively seeking work are officially regarded as unemployed. People who want work but are hampered by physical disabilities may also be excluded from the unemployment statistics. Women who have lost their jobs are often omitted from the official figures. And, in many countries, unemployment statistics suffer from the lack of data-gathering capacity that also affects other statistics.

Working Abroad

It is no small decision to move to another country, where skin color, language and ways of life are likely to be different. Even when others have made the move already, so that there are communities capable of easing the newcomer into the new society, both the decision and the adjustment are difficult. They are made no easier by the array of forces, either exploitative or hostile or both, that less affluent migrant workers must confront. It is hardly surprising that data on migrant workers is patchy, both as to their numbers and as to the earnings that they manage to send home.

Leaving home to find work abroad often means breaking up the family. The personal upheaval that entails often leads to both the man, who leaves, and the woman, who stays, entering unsafe sexual relationships. In some regions, labor migration has been identified as one of the major factors in the transmission of HIV/AIDS.

The data on labor migration are inconsistent and incomplete. There are no statistics on labor migration either in or out of a majority of countries. Some countries provide statistics on either foreigners working there or nationals working abroad. A small handful of countries provide statistics on labor migration in both directions. Of those countries that provide statistics, some report the figures for non-nationals as proportions of the working population, while others give figures for foreign-born workers (some of whom have presumably become citizens of the country where they live and work) as proportions of the whole population.

Political Systems

The end of the Cold War in 1989 and the dissolution of the Soviet Union in 1991 brought in a new era of hegemony for western-style democracy. Democratic states outlasted non-democratic states in the Cold War itself. There was a great body of evidence to support the claim that there have been no wars between established democracies (states in which fair competitive elections have led to a peaceful handover of power from one head of government to his or her rival). The evidence was also that the world had been getting steadily more democratic since the mid-1970s (Jaggers and Gurr, 1995), with a spurt to new democratic heights beginning in 1989.

Despite the apparent superiority and evident attractions of western-style electoral democracy, some reservations arise. The USA is a diligent promoter of democratic constitutions, yet its own levels of democratic participation in presidential and federal elections are disturbingly low by world standards. Political democracy engages people because it speaks to their dreams and hopes. Yet the widespread disillusion caused by broken election promises is capable of leading to support for the most socially regressive and politically aggressive leaders and programs. Though democratic systems do have the capacity to absorb conflict and ensure it is pursued without open violence, it is not easy to introduce democracy into a country held back by dictatorship and worn down by war. Western approaches to peacebuilding in war-torn countries have relied too much on a quick democratic fix, usually achieved through a flawed election, full of the kind of irregularities that would not be tolerated in mature European democracies. In other words, democracy is a superior system, but it is not an easy system.

Attempting to catch the nuances of different political systems and situations on a single map necessarily leads to loss of many important differences. The case of Iran is illustrative.

In the previous edition of this atlas, Iran was shown as a theocratic state, because its constitution gives the highest powers to religious authorities. For this edition, it seemed more appropriate to list it as a country in transition to a multi-party democratic system, because of the results of recent elections. Yet it is a close call between the two, and depends in part on the view that the social forces in Iran that are pushing towards some kind of multi-party arrangement will in the end be stronger than the forces of religious and social conservatism pushing in the other direction. Likewise Indonesia, at the time of preparing the atlas, is a country that equally well could be listed as one-party, transitional or chaotic. The decision to list it under the last heading reflects a view that decades of centralized, corrupt, and cruel government have left multiple lines of division and conflict that will haunt Indonesian governments for years to come, be they democratic or not.

Military Spending

To understand why it is possible for the USA to bomb both Iraq and Yugoslavia and still have forces in reserve, look no further than at the unchallenged scale of its military spending. When one country is responsible for one-third of world military spending, it has a pre-eminent position indeed. And much of the rest of the world's spending on armed forces is carried out by the USA's allies. Even so, the USA, like most of the major military powers, has reduced its military spending since the Cold War ended. At the end of the 1990s, after a decade of cuts, there are the first signs that this downward trend is reversing.

It is in many ways both complex and fruitless to attempt to compare national military spending in the former Soviet Union with what has happened in the countries that emerged from its dissolution. However, rough comparisons indicate that the downward trend in military spending in eastern Europe is even more marked than it has been in the West.

Comparing military spending by different countries is a complex exercise, because the laws of supply and demand are different in the civilian and military sectors, and the free movement of labor, goods and services that is regarded as healthy and normal in one sector is regarded as treachery and espionage in the other. This means that the comparative scale of spending in different countries cannot be measured simply by reference to the ordinary international rates of currency exchange. Military and civilian rates of wage and price inflation are also different, which can lead to changes in levels of military spending being disguised from international view. Since the US dollar is routinely used as the expression of comparable value, fluctuations in the value of the dollar also have an important effect on the calculations.

Armed Forces

The end of the Cold War led to cuts in both military spending and total armed forces. In the first half of the 1990s, the size of the world's armed forces fell by about 15 percent. There was a further reduction by five percent in the second half of the decade. But it was not only the end of that long military confrontation that made it possible to reduce the size of armed forces.

It is not only the number of military personnel that measures military strength, but the equipment they use and their capacity to use it. The technological substitution that removes jobs in the civilian labor market and produces more for less – thanks to robotics and computerization – has its parallel in the military world. The most important technological advances in the last two decades have not been to increase the power of weaponry, but to improve the accuracy with which it can be targeted, and the speed with which information can be gathered from the battlefield, processed, and fed into tactical decision-making. These developments both permit the best-armed states to reduce their forces and to some extent necessitate personnel cuts, because the technology is so expensive.

In the search for people of the right motivation and skills to take part in the military, it seems likely that two slow shifts will continue. One is away from conscription as the means of recruiting for the armed forces. The other is towards including women, and including them in combat as well as support roles. For a long time, in almost every country in the world, views about the social roles of men and women have awarded the warrior role to the former. This has been explained by reference to various assumptions about men and women, ranging from women's lesser muscle power to their more peaceful instincts. The former argument is hard to sustain when most military tasks require deftness and stamina rather than brute strength, and the latter argument has been tested in practice by the USA, which sets the world's military fashions. There appears to be no shortage of US women willing and able to take on the warrior role.

War

War is open armed conflict between two or more parties over a political issue involving control of government and/or territory. A war figures in the lists used to compile this map if there is continuity between the clashes between the two sides, if there is central organization on both sides, and if it causes more than 25 deaths in any given year, in the context of a conflict that in total has caused several hundred deaths. The low casualty threshold is required so as not to lose sight of armed conflicts that go quiet for long periods, only to explode nastily into action when international observers, pundits, and politicians have stopped watching.

The fact that most wars during the 1990s were within countries, even if with international intervention and interference, leads to numerous problems in the data. Simply knowing when a war has started and when it has finished is very difficult when the war has been localized in a remote region of a country that has limited information systems. But the more serious data problems concern war deaths. Government armed forces generally have good information about how many military personnel they have. Insurgent forces, though irregular, are also centrally organized and tend to have a reasonably good idea of how many fighters they have. Both sides in a civil war can therefore generally work out their casualty rates and keep a close eye on them. However, it is probable that some 75 percent of deaths in contemporary wars are civilians (some put the proportion of civilian casualties even higher, at over 90 percent). Since there is no agency whose task it is to count the civilian dead of wars as they die, there is no hard information about the numbers. Instead there is a range of estimates that are usually highly politicized.

After the International Campaign to Ban Landmines received the Nobel Peace Prize in 1997, it was quietly acknowledged that estimates of how many landmines lay in the ground were little better than guesswork and were highly exaggerated. Since the damage done by even anti-personnel landmines is not exaggerated, and since a field cannot be used for farming nor a path for walking down if there is a danger that even one landmine is there, the uncertainties in the data are insignificant. Anti-personnel landmines have much less military utility than the military often claimed for them, and they cause grievous physical and social damage to civilians. Achieving the 1997 treaty to ban them was a major humanitarian achievement. Among the countries that have not accepted the treaty are China and the USA.

Peacekeeping

The United Nations' first peace operation was to deploy an observer mission in 1948 to supervise the truce between the newly-founded state of Israel and the neighbouring Arab states. Over 50 years later, the observer mission is still there. The first peacekeeping force as such (and the third UN peace operation) was established in 1956 to monitor the ceasefire that ended the Suez War between Egypt on one side and Britain, France, and Israel on the other.

In the next three decades, UN peacekeeping forces in their distinctive blue helmets were repeatedly deployed to monitor and observe compliance with ceasefire agreements and military withdrawals. They developed a distinctive theory of operations. Although military personnel made up the core of peacekeeping forces, the approach was distinctly non-martial. The only weapons carried were small arms, which could only be used as a last resort, when the lives of UN soldiers were in danger. Successful peacekeeping relied on co-operation with both parties, both of which had come to the point of wanting an agreement to end hostilities, but either of which might not be quite able to fulfil the agreement. UN forces, in other words, were there to help the conflict parties fulfill their best intentions; coercion was not part of the UN role.

As the Cold War wound towards its close in the late 1980s, there were growing ambitions for what the UN could achieve in the new world political situation. The upshot was a concept of peace operations presented by then UN Secretary-General Boutros Boutros-Ghali in 1992 and adopted by the United Nations. It included peacekeeping in the traditional mode, and added preventive deployment, peacebuilding and peace enforcement. The last concept is approximately the same as going to war, but doing so with a UN mandate. When NATO started to bomb Yugoslavia in March 1999, it did so without the approval of the UN Security Council. Apart from that crucial political distinction, the tactics of the operation that unfolded in the following months were completely compatible with the concept of peace enforcement.

The map refers to activities during 1998. Had it included 1999, it would not have included the bombing of Yugoslavia. Nor does it include the operations to enforce the no-fly zones in northern and southern Iraq, nor missile and bombing raids against Iraq to try to force it to accept UN inspections of its military production facilities. These exercises in old-fashioned power politics have nothing to do with peacekeeping.

Non-UN peacekeeping forces included on the map are: an international force in Egypt to monitor the demilitarization of the Sinai; Russian forces in Georgia, where they are keeping peace in the breakaway regions of Abkhazia and South Ossetia; Russian forces in Moldova, where they maintain peaceful relations over the secession of the Trans-Dniestr Republic; international West African forces in Sierra Leone and Liberia; the international force known as the Stabilization Force (or S-FOR, for short) in Bosnia-Hercegovina; and international forces (largely Russian) in Tajikistan. The inclusion of the latter force as peacekeepers would have been rather questionable in 1993 when they were first deployed, but their role has evolved over the years.

Refugees

A refugee is a person who has crossed an international border in fleeing from danger. The refugee's belief that the danger exists must be well-founded. If it is, then the refugee is protected under international law. A refugee who does not cross an international border is described as an Internally Displaced Person (IDP), and is not protected by international law. Nor is somebody who crosses an international border, but does not get properly registered in a host country; such a person is described as somebody living in refugee-like circumstances. The data in this cartogram include all three categories.

Data on refugees are, like data on war deaths, notoriously unreliable. IDPs and people who are living in refugee-like situations are essentially unknown quantities. Yet the statistical information on those refugees who have crossed international borders is no better: the numbers are routinely negotiated because the host government in a country neighboring the source of the refugees is receiving financial assistance to look after them. Payment is made per refugee. Host governments may not want high numbers of refugees, but high refugee numbers increase the inflow of money. Registered refugees are negotiated realities.

In the cartogram, a million people in refugee-like circumstances from the former Soviet Union are omitted because the data source could not trace them to their country of origin. However, they have been included in the small map on where refugees find refuge. The same condition of partial statistical inclusion pertains for Kurds in refugee-like conditions in Syria; the data do not exist to identify how many are from which of the neighbouring countries with large Kurdish populations. The map reflects the situation in 1997, and therefore excludes the large movements of Kosovar refugees and IDPs in 1998 (over 200,000) and 1999 (presumed over a million).

Human Rights

Reporting the human rights' abuses that are known in any particular country is not necessarily the same as reporting the human rights situation. The worse the human rights situation, the less possible it is to report all or even most abuses.

The categories of abuse that are reported in this map are the extremes. The most common kinds of extra-judicial execution are the targeted assassination of political opponents, the murder of prisoners of war, and the systematic elimination of people regarded as socially undesirable, such as criminals for whom the police and justice system have no resources, and street children with no home or family. Only actions that are openly or otherwise endorsed by the state or a powerful faction within it are included. Non-governmental activities, such as physical violence by drug cartels, insurgent armies and privately-organized vigilante groups, have been excluded, even though they do often constitute an abuse of human rights as systematic as anything the state can manage.

Each category of abuse in the main map implies that the next one down is also perpetrated; for example, a state that sanctions extra-judicial executions also can be expected to use torture, arbitrary arrest, and random official violence.

Ethnicity

Ethnic diversity is often seen as a problem. The ethnic cleansers in the Balkans seek to eliminate it. Observers of the Balkan wars of the 1990s often see it as the source of violence. Regarded sanely, however, ethnic diversity would simply be one of many kinds of diversity which make people both various and interesting. Ethnic diversity should be celebrated; those societies that have most successfully absorbed ethically-diverse populations are the ones that have most openly celebrated difference.

Of all the factual quicksand in this atlas, ethnic data may be the worst, the most likely to suck author and readers alike into furious arguments about fine points of definition and distinction. In this map, minorities are defined in terms of ethnic identity, language, race or nation, but not religion. Religion often enters into the cultural and social differences that define one ethnic group as distinct from another; where it does not (for example, between Catholic and Protestant English), there is no reason to regard it as an ethnic category by itself.

The counting of minority populations for this map has not been restricted to citizens or those born in the country in question. Migrant workers, immigrants, and foreign residents are all included, where they are ethnically different from the host population. To identify countries in which there is more than one official language, it is defined as the language or languages of government, as defined by the government itself. In addition, countries whose so-called national languages are different from the stated official language are also included, as are countries where there is clear, even if pragmatic rather than formal, official acceptance of the use of an alternative language.

However tight the conventions for counting minorities, what we count and how we count is highly dependent on the political situation.

In South Africa, there are more minorities now than there were during the era of apartheid. Then, black was one category; with the end of apartheid, that one category has been broken down into several. The difference does not lie in who people are, but in the political meaning of their identity. This highlights an important point about the politics of identity – that it is at all times arbitrary. Brazil, which is shown on the map as a country of great ethnic diversity, could equally well be regarded as a great deal more homogenous. Like the British or US nationalities, Brazilian nationality has been constructed over time out of many groups with many different identities.

Literacy

Through the ages, many societies have functioned well without widespread literacy. But in modern societies literacy is a necessary working tool of social life and economic activity.

Reading and writing are not innate. They have to be learned, and for greatest ease of use in adult life they have to be learned when young. Properly learned, they allow members of modern societies to carry out daily essential tasks, to absorb information and explanations about the world we inhabit, to enter a world of imagination, beauty and adventure, and to carry out personal communication about a similarly broad range of matters. It is therefore entirely appropriate that literacy and access to education are two of the four indicators used in the Human Development Index (see **The Quality of Life**, pp.20-1). However, for all its many advantages, literacy is not the same as wisdom.

While literacy is most appreciated and used by adults, acquiring it is the task of youths and children. High levels of functional illiteracy in adults are evidence, therefore, of a country's incapacity to provide some of the basics for people under the age of 15. Sometimes, this incapacity is the result of more or less conscious decisions, or at least of open prejudice, for in most countries more women than men are illiterate.

Gender Equality

The Gender-related Development Index (GDI) has been worked out by the United Nations' Development Programme in the context of its annually reported Human Development Index (see **The Quality of Life**, pp. 20-1). It is based on the same four indicators: income per person, life expectancy, adult literacy, and the education enrollment ratio (see notes to **The Quality of Life,** p.115-16). These indicators are then divided by gender. For example, Italy's adult literacy rate of 98.1 percent is made up of rates of 97.6 percent for women and 98.6 percent for men. To take another example, women's share of earned income in the USA is 40.3 percent (thus, 59.7 percent is men's) while in Norway it is 42.4 percent (and men's share is 57.6 percent).

As in the Human Development Index (HDI), the richer countries are bound to come out high in the GDI, because of the sheer weight of resources they have, and because of their widespread access to education and long life expectancies. As with the HDI, therefore, it is revealing to look at nuances within the big picture. Where the GDI gives a country a significantly lower ranking than the HDI, that is the sign of a significant inequality for women. Thus, for example, while the map shows that women in the USA are significantly better off than women in Brazil, they face the same scale of gender inequalities.

In 1979 the United Nations adopted a Convention on the Elimination of All Forms of Discrimination Against Women. By the end of 1998, 163 governments had ratified the Convention. Not all of them pursue the implementation of the Convention's provisions with equal fervor. Among the 30 governments that had not ratified the Convention were seven African states, a minority of Arab states, 13 other Asian and Pacific states, the European statelets of the Holy See (the Vatican), Monaco and San Marino, and the USA.

Religion

The world's two largest religions are Christianity (about 1.9 billion believers) and Islam (just over 1 billion). Approximately 80 percent of the world's population claim some religious allegiance. What this means in practice varies between religions, countries and individuals. In Western Europe, for example, far more people profess Christianity than practice it, to judge from low attendance at weekly services. The same range of different meanings is evident when it comes to the connection of Church and State. The British monarch for example is also head of the country's state-established church. But in practical terms, the UK is one of the most secular countries in Europe, itself the world's most secular continent.

Worldwide, there is a growing acceptance of the model of the secular state that guarantees religious tolerance. This acceptance is the product of a complex combination of factors, including the growth of individualism and personal choice, and the declining significance of public religious rituals. Yet in some countries the resistance to the evolution of religious tolerance is intense and it remains inconceivable that the heads of state and government could not be members of the main national faith. Even in countries that regard themselves as secular and tolerant of religious difference, formal links between political parties and religious affiliation are common, as in the Christian Democratic parties of Western Europe.

Sexual Freedom

There has been a long history of persecution of male and female homosexuals, and in most countries the persecution and isolation continue. Some countries do not use laws so much as social pressure to secure conformity with the preferred norm of sexual behavior.

Legislating sexuality should be approached with care. Important issues of personal freedom from sexual abuse are involved in some legislation, such as laws against paedophilia. But other laws merely express a desire to eliminate what is different but not in fact threatening or dangerous behavior. The futility of having such laws should be evident, if only because homosexuality has survived all the legislation against it. Where the futility of such laws is recognized, the statute books often remain unchanged simply because legislators are too embarrassed to discuss repealing them.

In the complex mix of pressures to conform and perform, some people conclude they have the wrong gender. Though it is conventional to view gender difference as a polarity of male and female, it is scientifically and physiologically more accurate to view it as a spectrum. There are famous cases of men who have lived as women and women who have lived as men, including being married, for many years. Gender reassignment today is carried out with the aid of a surgeon. States that truly respect individual freedom of choice re-issue all personal documents with the newly-adopted gender incorporated into them. Other states place a variety of restrictions on the reissuing of personal documentation and on some rights, such as legal marriage.

Reproductive Rights

There are two classic views about the controversy on the right to abortion, summarized in the US shorthand that makes one group pro-life (anti-abortion) and the other group pro-choice (not pro-abortion, but pro- the right to abortion). The first view is that the argument is about the sanctity of life; the second view is that the argument is about women's autonomy.

There is also a third view, which argues that in addition to the paradigm clash between sanctity of life and women's autonomy, the issue is also how far it is possible to control behavior by legislation. The legal situation rarely describes the reality. Where abortion is legal it is not necessarily straightforwardly or quickly available. When abortion is illegal, back-street abortionists thrive, charging high fees for dangerous and often unsuccessful procedures. The region of the world that is most restrictive in abortion rights is Latin America (except Cuba); this region also has one of the highest abortion rates in the world.

Data on access to and use of contraceptives are only systematically available for women in long-term relationships, primarily marriage. But the use of contraceptives by people not in long-term relationships is of equal social and personal importance. Although some teenagers deliberately and knowingly choose to get pregnant, high rates of teenage pregnancy show that the onset of sexual self-awareness has not been accompanied by all the necessary elements of sexual knowledge. This is often the result of deficient education both at home and in schools.

Health Risks

Acquired Immune Deficiency Syndrome (AIDS) is easy to prevent, hard to catch and, so far, impossible to cure. The most effective treatments currently involve expensive cocktails of drugs. These help some people delay the onset of the conditions associated with full-blown AIDS, but at heavy cost in terms of side effects, vulnerability to other illnesses, and dependence on the treatment. With these pharmaceutical combinations, treatment cannot be interrupted; if it is, resuming it is pointless since it no longer works.

Figures for HIV/AIDS infections (HIV is the virus that leads to AIDS) keep changing as the epidemic spreads and information improves. That the news about AIDS has continually worsened suggests that many countries where the figures are relatively low may simply be cases of under-reporting. For individuals, there are many reasons why people are reluctant to confront the fact that they have been infected. It is also possible to carry the virus for years without showing symptoms. Some governments are still reluctant to admit that the incidence of AIDS is as high as it really is. For all these reasons, it seems likely that the epidemic is far from its peak. Initial reports on the 1998 World Health Organization figures (the map shows 1997 data) confirm this, for AIDS has reportedly overtaken tuberculosis in the ranking of the world's most deadly infectious diseases.

Nonetheless, tuberculosis affects about a third of the world's population, and an estimated 50 million people have developed strains of the disease that are resistant to treatment by currently known and used drugs.

A lifestyle disease is one that results from the style of life, rather than being caught by infection or contact. As the term has come to be used, it refers particularly to health problems that are the result of diet, smoking, and high stress living. Lifestyle diseases include cancer, diabetes, and heart disease. In the affluent parts of Europe and North America, neuro-psychiatric conditions, ranging from depression through dependence on alcohol or narcotics to dementia and panic disorders, are as serious a cause of health problems as heart disease and cancer.

Smoking

It takes about five and a half minutes to smoke a cigarette. That is also the average time by which a heavy smoker's life is shortened per cigarette smoked. The good news is that two-thirds of smokers die from causes other than tobacco, and that, of the third who do die from tobacco, half die beyond middle age.

In rich countries, where smoking is slowly declining, approximately equal numbers of men and women smoke. In poorer countries, where smoking is on the increase, about half the men but only five percent of the women smoke, suggesting the market opportunities yet to be exploited.

Perhaps the oddest of all the statistics about this oddest of all bad habits is a US opinion poll in the early 1990s reporting that among the nearly 90 percent of people annoyed by cigarette smoke are about a third of smokers.

Communications

Globalization (see **Investment**, pp.34-5) would have been impossible without the revolution in technologies of communication and information in the last 40 years of the twentieth century. It is not just the pace of scientific invention and technological innovation that is striking, but the speed with which new technologies have been absorbed by economies and societies. For big business, video-conferencing is already old hat. Satellite TV hook-ups are the next step. In daily life, mobile telephones are commonplace. In less than a generation, the internet has evolved from being a super-sophisticated way of linking military computers, to being a daily reality for large numbers of ordinary people.

The poorer countries are inevitably slower to receive and absorb the new technologies, but they may be able to hurdle over a stage in the process. Email, for example, has proven to be more reliable than communicating by fax, partly because the transmission times are shorter, partly because the transmission process stores the message if it does not get through at the first attempt. In most poor countries, getting a conventional telephone is much slower than getting hold of a mobile phone, and if you can afford one the chances are you can afford the other. Relatively speaking, communication nets for mobile phones will be introduced more quickly in poor countries than they were in the richer countries. Now that the technology is established, business travellers want to be able to stay in touch with their homebase wherever they are.

Media

The USA is the major source of the world's entertainment output for film and television. Since the end of World War Two, the beginning of the modern media age, US government representatives involved in trade talks have never failed to press for an open door for American movies and TV shows. The stories and images purveyed by the US entertainment industry appear so attractive that most governments that tried to resist this pressure would be extremely unpopular at home.

The power of the media to exert direct influence on people, politics, and events remains hard to pin down. Politicians are becoming adept in sophisticated techniques of media management. A new political breed of spin doctor has emerged, their work openly acknowledged on all sides, as they massage information to produce stories of maximum partisan advantage. Between spinners and reporters, there is a subtle and complex relationship in which it is never quite clear who has the upperhand, though it is quite certain that it is not the voters.

Cities

Balancing the costs and gains of urban life is a major challenge for economic development. In Europe (where 75 percent of the population live in urban areas) and North America (77 percent), the major shift of population from the land to the cities began with the shift of employment from agriculture to industry (see **Jobs**, pp.42-3). Other regions have steadily followed suit and the process of urbanization is almost universal and still accelerating.

However, some earlier projections of the size of mega-cities are now thought to have been somewhat exaggerated. Improved communications and transport make the vision of numerous urban conglomerations of 30 or 40 million people as unlikely as it is unpleasant. The economic advantages of very large cities have declined and the most economically dynamic areas of Western Europe and North America now appear to be smaller cities. This also appears to be true in China.

Traffic

A large part of the economic history of the twentieth century is bound up in the car, in the techniques that were invented to make it run, produce it in large numbers, and sell it. Though assembly-line production was not invented for the car, it was the first consumer product for which it was used on a really large scale. In that and other ways, there were enormous spin offs from the early production of large numbers of cars.

The development of the oil industry is equally a part of the automobile story. It creates the link between domestic use of cars and the major questions of grand strategy and security in the Middle East, which have themselves been a crucial part of the international history of the second half of the twentieth century.

For reasons of energy consumption and congestion, it hardly seems possible that car production can continue to increase. Currently, just over 50 percent of the passenger miles travelled on land consist of journeys in cars. One projection suggests that the half century to the year 2050 will see that proportion cut to 35 percent. Yet that same projection suggests that the total number of passenger miles travelled by car will increase fivefold.

Food

Of the many wrongs in the world for which there is no excuse, malnutrition is foremost among them. There is no doubt that the task of producing enough food is serious and demanding. China, for example, has the challenge of feeding 20 percent of the world's population while only having about 7 percent of the world's arable land.

There is equally no doubt that technology has risen to the challenge and that more than enough food is available to feed the world. There remain concerns about the long-term damage done to farmland by the use of intensive farming techniques, including the heavy use of fertilizers, pesticides and insecticides. There are also reasons for concern about the extensive use of water for agricultural irrigation in the name of achieving self-sufficiency in food supply. Israel's triumph in turning desert into fertile farmland, for example, has been achieved at the expense of irretrievable damage to the natural water supply from underground aquifers. Often food imports would be an economically and environmentally more sensible way of proceeding.

Food technology continues to advance. During the 1990s, the UK experienced the negative effects of badly-regulated food production. Revelations that the factory farming of poultry was leading to widespread salmonella in eggs and chickens, were followed by the well-publicized scare over Bovine Spongiform Encephalitis (BSE) or "mad cow disease." The outbreak of BSE in the UK's beef and diary herds was the result of modern feeding systems to make cows bigger and beefier by radically changing their diets to include animal offal. Included in the offal were diseased sheep brains, and thus came BSE.

It may be because of this experience that the UK was one of the few countries to enter a serious debate about the safety of introducing genetically modified (GM) foods. Unfortunately, if not untypically, the debate began only after the commercial exploitation of GM foods was well-established.

Energy

Everything that runs, runs on energy. Everything that runs and is made by people, runs on energy that is provided by activities that themselves consume energy. The more that is produced, the more energy is consumed, and much of the energy comes from sources that are non-renewable. It is a recipe for global disaster, yet if asked to select one long-term problem about which it is possible to have confidence, the world's energy supply would be the one to choose.

There are two reasons for confidence about the energy future. The first is precisely that energy is a basic requirement for economic activity. It is unthinkable that profit oriented-enterprise will neglect energy.

The second reason for confidence is that there are many alternative techniques of energy production available. Nodding ducks can garner energy from the waves; barrages can get it from tides; windmills can take it from the air; solar panels from the sun. For large-scale energy production in the future, many experts believe that fusion will be cheaper, cleaner and easier than fission (which provides nuclear power, along with the side-products of plutonium and radioactive waste).

Global Warming

Since the rising trend in average world temperatures was spotted in the1980s, and the term "global warming" was coined, there has been no shortage of controversy about whether the phenomenon is real. As the graph across this map shows, in the past there have been fluctuations in average temperatures that are as great and greater than those the world has experienced over the past two decades. Temperatures that are rising now might come back down of their own accord in a decade or so, it is argued.

The argument is not just about the evidence, but also its explanation. Where previous fluctuations in world average temperatures occurred for whatever natural reason, the current rising trend fairly conclusively seems to be the result of industrial activity, population increase and increasing urbanization (see **Cities,** pp.90-1), and deforestation (see **Forests**, pp.100-01). These factors were not present in previous periods of temperature increase. While the long-term meaning is not clear, it is unsafe to assume that what is happening today is no different from what has happened before. Commonsense suggests that the internationally-agreed greenhouse gas restrictions should be implemented sooner rather than later. When it comes to the natural environment, too many business leaders and cautious politicians seem to believe it is not worth checking whether something is safe until it proves to be unsafe – a view they would not apply to crossing a road.

Forests

Trees let the world breathe. If they continue to be cut down our children are going to live in a suffocating world. The problem is that it takes very little knowledge or skill to cut trees down but a great deal of care and foresight to let them grow again. Nature could do the job perfectly well by itself, of course, but nature is not left alone to get on with it.

The concern about deforestation links the themes on the maps of **Global Warming** (pp.98-9) and **Biodiversity** (pp.102-03). Forests are the home and source of much more than wood. Though forests are often cut down to make way for farmland, the loss of trees can destroy farmland, especially on hills and uplands. The loss of trees also means the loss of all kinds of animal life. We already know enough about the biodiversity threatened by forest destruction to realize that we have no comprehensive understanding of how much has already been lost.

Despite increasing awareness of the dangers of deforestation, it continues and in some countries it has even accelerated in the 1990s. If the trend is to be reversed, alternative economic activities will have to be generated so that poor farmers no longer need to slash and burn their way through forests, and so that hard-pressed governments can find other ways of earning badly-needed foreign currency.

Biodiversity

The fact that 20 percent of bird species are in danger of extinction means that birds as a whole are relatively safe. Among mammals and fish, 40 percent of species are in danger.

One writer on "green economics" coined the term "the hidden elbow." It was a play on words on the concept invented by the great eighteenth century economist Adam Smith, that the workings of a market economy are regulated by a "hidden hand." The hidden hand makes the system run smoothly, however clumsy, uncertain and poorly-directed are the individual activities within it.

By contrast, the concept of the hidden elbow suggests that a great deal of environmental damage happens by accident and mischance, out of ignorance and clumsiness. The loss of biodiversity epitomizes the operations of the hidden elbow. In view of what is known about the loss of biodiversity, it must be concluded that species have been destroyed before humans have even noticed their existence. There is little reason to believe that the loss of biodiversity will soon be stopped, although some high-profile species may be saved from extinction due to the pressure of an increasingly-concerned public.

Select Bibliography

Amnesty International, *Amnesty International Report*, London: Amnesty, 1997, 1998 editions

Amnesty International, *The Death Penalty: List of Abolishionist and Retentionist Countries as of 31 March 1998, revised 22 January 1999*, London: Amnesty, 1999

Amnesty International UK, *Breaking the Silence: Human Rights Violations Based on Sexual Orientation*, London: Amnesty, 1997

Amnesty International section française, *Briser le Silence: Violations des driots de l'Home liées à l'orientation sexuelle*, Paris: Amnesty, 1998

Banks, Arthur C. and Thomas C. Mullen, *Political Handbook of the World 1998*, New York: McGraw-Hill, 1998

Barrett, David B., *World Christian Encyclopedia*, Nairobi: Oxford University Press, 1982

Brown, Lester R., Michael Renner and Christopher Flavin, *Vital Signs: Environmental Trends that are Shaping our Future*, London: Earthscan, 1998

The Encyclopedia Britannica, Chicago: Encyclopedia Britannica, 1997

Food and Agriculture Organisation, *FAO Yearbook: Trade*, Vol. 50, Rome: FAO, 1996

Hendriks, Aart, Rob Tielman, and Evert van der Veen, eds., *The Third Pink Book: A Global View of Lesbian and Gay Oppression*, Buffalo, NY: Prometheus Books, 1993

International Committee of the Red Cross, *Landmines and Blinding Weapons* (press documentation) Geneva: International Committee of the Red Cross,1995

International Institute for Strategic Studies, *The Military Balance 1998/99*, London: IISS, 1998

International Labour Office, *Migrants, Refugeees and International Co-operation*, Geneva: ILO, 1994

International Labour Office, *Yearbook of Labour Statistics 1998*, Geneva: ILO, 1998

International Panel on Climate Change, viewed 22 Dec 1998, at www.ipcc.html

International Telecommunications Union, *Cellular Subscribers*, Geneva: ITU 1998

International Telecommunication Union, *World Telecommunication Development Report*, Geneva: ITU, 1995

Jacobs, Michael, *The Green Economy*, London: Pluto Press, 1991

Jaggers, Keith and Ted Robert Gurr, Tracking Democracy's Third Wave with the Polity III Data, *Journal of Peace Research*, 32 (4) November 1995: 469-82

Keesing's Record of World Events, Harlow, Essex: Longmans, serial

Kidron, Michael. and Ronald Segal, *The State of the World Atlas*, fifth edition, London and New York: Penguin, 1995

Mackay, Judith, *The State of Health Atlas*, London and New York, Simon and Schuster, 1993

National Council for Civil Liberties, *Integrating Transsexual and Transgendered People: Amicus Brief for Sheffield and Horsham v UK*, NCCL: London, 1997

Network Wizards, viewed Nov 10 1998, at www.nw.com/zone/WWW/top.html

O'Brien, Joanne and Martin Palmer, *The State of Religion Atlas*, London and New York, Simon and Schuster, 1993

Pearson, Ian, ed., *The Macmillan Atlas of the Future*, New York: Macmillan USA, 1998

Population Action International, *Contraceptive Choice: Worldwide Access to Family Planning*, Washington DC: PAI, 1997

Population Action International, *Reproductive Risk: A Worldwide Assessment of Women's Sexual and Mental Health*, Washington DC: PAI, 1995

Population Action International, *World Contraceptive Use*, New York: UN, 1998

Seager, Joni, *The State of Women in the World Atlas*, second edition, London and New York: Penguin, 1997

Smith, Dan, *The State of War and Peace Atlas*, third edition, London and New York, Penguin, 1997

The Statesman's Yearbook, ed. Barry Turner, New York: St Martin's Press and London: Macmillan, 1996-97, 1997-98, 1998-99

United Nations, *The Blue Helmets: A Review of United Nations Peace-keeping*, 3rd edition New York: United Nations, 1996

United Nations, *Energy Statistics Yearbook*, New York: Oxford University Press, 1997

United Nations Population Division, *World Contraceptive Use*, New York: UN, 1998

United Nations, *World Investment Report: Transnational Corporations, Market Structure and Competitive Policy*, New York: UN, 1998

UNAIDS, *Joint United Nations Programme on HIV/AIDS, AIDS Epidemic Update: Dec. 1998*, New York: UNAIDS and Geneva: WHO, 1998

UNCTAD, *Handbook of International Trade and Development Statistics*, New York: UN, 1995

UNDP, *Human Development Report 1998*, New York: Oxford University Press, 1998

UNESCO, *UNESCO 1997 Statistical Yearbook,* Paris: UNESCO, 1997

UNESCO, *World Education Report 1998: Teachers and Teaching in a Changing World*, Paris: UNESCO, 1998

UNICEF, *The Progress of Nations*, New York: Oxford University Press, 1997 and 1998

UNICEF, *The State of the World's Children*, 1998, New York: Oxford University Press, 1998

Uppsala University, see Wallenstein and Sollenberg

US Bureau of the Census, *Global Aging into the 21st Century*, Washington, DC: US Bureau of the Census, 1996

US Bureau of the Census, International Data Base, International Programs Center, Washington D.C, 1998

US Committee for Refugees, *World Refugee Survey*, New York, UN, 1998

Wallensteen, Peter and Margareta Sollenberg, Armed Conflict and Regional Conflict Complexes, 1989-97, *Journal Of Peace Research*, 35 (5), Sept. 1998: 621-34

World Bank, *The World Bank Atlas 1998*, Washington DC: World Bank, 1998

World Bank, *World Development Indicators*, Washington DC: World Bank, 1998

World Bank, *World Development Report*, Washington DC: World Bank, 1998

World Health Organization, *Tobacco Alert*, Geneva: WHO, 1996

World Health Organization, *Unsafe Abortion*, Geneva: WHO, 1995

World Health Organization, *World Health Report 1998*, Geneva: WHO, 1998

World Resources Institute, *World Resources: A Guide to the Global Environment 1998-99* , New York: Oxford University Press, 1998

World Tourism Organization, *Tourism 2020 Vision: A New Forecast*, Madrid: WTO, 1998

World Trade Organization, *Annual Report*, Geneva: WTO, 1997 and 1998

Index